Sexual thought is now an integral component of our intellectual history. Accordingly, the most important modern sexual theorists deserve as much attention from intellectual historians as the great philosophers, theologians, and social thinkers of the twentieth century.

Ellis, Kinsey, and Masters and Johnson are—after Freud—the most influential sexual thinkers of this century. They are the intellectuals most responsible for the way we have come to conceive of our sexuality. Paul Robinson has examined their writings in order to identify the assumptions, biases, tensions, and modes of reasoning that characterize their work. This method emphasizes their role as theoreticians—as men and women who not only have contributed a significant body of facts about human sexuality, but have fashioned distinctive ways of thinking about the human sexual experience as well.

0376

Ph.D. from Harvard. Since 1967 he has taught European intellectual history at Stanford University. He is the author of *The Freudian Left* and *Social Thought in America and Europe*, and is now at work on a study of opera and history.

The Modernization of Sex

BOOKS BY PAUL ROBINSON

The Freudian Left

Social Thought in America and Europe
(editor, with David M. Kennedy)

The Modernization of Sex

Paul Robinson

THE MODERNIZATION OF SEX

Havelock Ellis,
Alfred Kinsey,
William Masters
and Virginia Johnson

HARPER & ROW, PUBLISHERS

New York / Evanston / San Francisco / London

To my mother

Beryl Robinson Gore

Excerpts from William Masters and Virginia Johnson, *Human Sexual Response* (Boston: Little, Brown, 1966) and *Human Sexual Inadequacy* (Boston: Little, Brown, 1970), are reprinted by permission of the publisher.

FIRST EDITION

Library of Congress Cataloging in Publication Data
Robinson, Paul A., date.
  The modernization of sex.
  Includes index.
  1. Ellis, Havelock, 1859–1939. 2. Kinsey, Alfred Charles, 1894–1956. 3. Masters, William H. 4. Johnson, Virginia E. 5. Sexologists. I. Title.
HQ18.3.R6   301.41′792′2   75–24500
ISBN 0–06–013583–2

76 77 78 79 10 9 8 7 6 5 4 3 2 1

Contents

Preface

Sex has always been a great issue, as important to the human experience as making a living, or conquering nature, or maintaining social order. But it has not always been the subject of serious thought. In fact, throughout most of European and American history sexual "thinking" has amounted to little more than an assortment of popular prejudices, sometimes codified by medical authorities or exploited by pornographers, but rarely achieving the coherence and dignity that one associates with the word "thought." The only significant exception is the work of the Marquis de Sade, whose intellectual isolation is reflected in the extreme character of his ideas.

In the twentieth century, however, thinking about sex has become explicit and systematic, giving rise to a new intellectual type, the sexologist. Indeed, it is the fundamental assumption of this book that sexual thought is now an integral component of our intellectual history, and, accordingly, that the most important modern sexual theorists deserve as much attention from intellectual historians as the great philosophers, theologians, and social thinkers of the age.

Only one modern sexual theorist has in fact attracted such intellectual attention: Sigmund Freud. Freud, however, is so much more than a sexual theorist that he would figure prominently in modern intellectual history even if he had never written a word about sex. Conversely, had he written only about sex, he would probably be as neglected by intellectual historians as the figures I examine in this book.

Havelock Ellis, Alfred Kinsey, and William Masters and Virginia Johnson are, after Freud, the most influential sexual thinkers of the century. Along with him they are the intellectuals most responsible for the way we have come to conceive of our sexuality. In the three intellectual portraits that follow, I have examined their writings very much as one might those of a major philosopher or political theorist. That is, I have been concerned to identify the assumptions, the biases, the tensions, and the modes of reasoning that characterize their work, as well as the important similarities and differences in their respective treatments of particular sexual issues. This approach represents intellectual history of the purest variety. It ignores biographical and practical considerations in order to focus exclusively on ideas themselves. It is an unusual, and perhaps even a reckless, approach to take when treating anything so emotionally charged as human sexuality. But I have risked it in order to emphasize the role of my protagonists as theoreticians—that is, as men and women who not only have contributed a significant body of facts about human sexuality but have fashioned distinctive ways of thinking about the human sexual experience as well.

I wish to thank the John Simon Guggenheim Foundation and Stanford University for supporting my research at various points in the book's evolution. The first chapter appeared as an article in the Winter 1973 issue of *Salmagundi*.

Parts of the manuscript were read by Carl Degler, Martin Duberman, David Lynch, and Scott Massey, each of whom made criticisms and suggestions for which I am most grateful. I also benefited on many occasions from the wise and knowledgeable counsel of William Abrahams. I owe my profoundest thanks to my brother, James Robinson, who is a master of the fine points of English usage, and to my colleague Peter Stansky, without whom the argument of this book would have been both less forcible and less judicious than is now the case. Each read the entire manuscript with great care, and both provided exactly the right blend of criticism and encouragement. Finally, I want to express my appreciation to Hugh Van Dusen and Cynthia Merman of Harper & Row. One could not have asked for more ideal editorial support.

Stanford University

1/Havelock Ellis

The word "modern" seems in the process of assuming a specific historical meaning. In the cultural and intellectual realms, at least, it now often carries the connotation of "pertaining to the twentieth century," or perhaps even "pertaining to the first half of the twentieth century," with the further implication that the years from 1890 to 1910 mark an important watershed in Western man's mental history. "Modern" most obviously bears this historical meaning in the case of the visual and musical arts, where the phrases "modern art" and "modern music" refer unambiguously to twentieth-century developments. A similar terminology is emerging among literary critics, who have adopted the substantive "modernism" (once the label for a theological deviation within Roman Catholicism) to designate the central literary tendency of the first half of the century, reserving the adjective "contemporary" for more recent trends. Science too recognizes the turn of the century as a period of basic theoretical reorientation, particularly in physics, and over a decade ago, in *Consciousness and Society*, H. Stuart Hughes documented an equally thoroughgoing revolution in early-twentieth-century social thought.

It should come as little surprise, then, to find that the years from 1890 to 1910 also saw a major transformation in sexual theory. Of course, we have long been aware that the "modern" way of thinking about sex emerged somewhere toward the beginning of the century, and we speak vaguely of the "sexual revolution." But the theorists of sexual modernism have never received the serious attention that is regularly lavished on their counterparts in science, social thought, and the arts. In fact, most of the pioneer modernists are now largely forgotten—witness the unfamiliarity of such names as Edward Carpenter, Albert Moll, Auguste Forel, Iwan Bloch, and Magnus Hirschfeld. The only survivor of the revolution would appear to be Sigmund Freud, whom we now think of as the virtual author of sexual modernism. Yet Freud's sexual doctrines were so highly individual, so much a part of his larger psychological system, that they offer an unreliable guide to the basic assumptions of the modern sexual tradition.

Those assumptions can be fairly simply stated. As has been generally recognized, sexual modernism represented a reaction against Victorianism—a term I use here as shorthand for the dominant sexual tradition of the nineteenth century. Victorianism, of course, was not monolithic. It never achieved quite the authority on the Continent that it enjoyed in England and America, and in Europe as a whole (though apparently not in America) it was on the wane throughout the last half of the century.[1] Still, I think it legitimate to speak of a more or less unified nineteenth-century style in sexual theory. Certainly the earliest modernists were quite self-conscious about their departure from what they conceived to be nineteenth-century sexual orthodoxy.

Against the Victorians, the modernists held that sexual experience was neither a threat to moral character nor a drain on vital energies. On the contrary, they considered it an entirely worthwhile, though often precarious, human activity, whose proper management was essential to individual and social well-being. Put bluntly—and I can think of no other way of putting it—the

---

1. For evidence on the historical course of Victorianism in Europe and America, see Gordon Rattray Taylor, *The Angel-Makers* (London, 1958) and Nathan G. Hale, Jr., *Freud and the Americans* (New York, 1971).

modernists were sexual enthusiasts. At the same time they sought to broaden the range of legitimate sexual behavior—to investigate and to apologize for those apparently deviant forms of sexuality that the Victorians, with their exclusive commitment to adult, genital, heterosexual intercourse, had been reluctant even to recognize. The modernists also rejected the nineteenth-century conception of female sexuality. Where the Victorians had all but denied woman a sexual existence, the modernists argued her sexual parity with the male, even at the risk of transforming her into an exclusively sexual being. Finally, the modernists entertained serious doubts about the traditional institutional contexts of human sexuality—marriage and the family—thereby raising to the level of explicit debate what seems to me the most vexing problem of human sexual psychology: the paradoxical need for both companionship and variety in erotic life.

The central figure in the emergence of this modern sexual ethos was not Freud, important though he may have been, but rather Henry Havelock Ellis. I would even go so far as to state that Havelock Ellis stands in the same relation to modern sexual theory as Max Weber to modern sociology, or Albert Einstein to modern physics. Although Freud formulated individual sexual doctrines that were to prove more influential, and while he is in every way the larger figure in our intellectual history, it was nonetheless Ellis who made the more extensive and, above all, the more representative contribution to sexual modernism. His great work, the *Studies in the Psychology of Sex*, the first six volumes of which were published between 1897 and 1910, established the basic moral categories for nearly all subsequent sexual theorizing, including even the recent work of William Masters and Virginia Johnson. It is precisely this moral and, as it were, categorical quality of Ellis's thought that I have stressed in my analysis of his sexual writings. Without ignoring his empirical contributions to our knowledge of human sexuality, I have been concerned primarily with his effort to establish a distinctly modern way of thinking about sexual matters.[2]

2. There are several biographies of Ellis, the most recent by Arthur Calder-Marshall (*The Sage of Sex* [New York, 1959]). Calder-Marshall is primarily interested in the drama of Ellis's private life, and the book attempts no systematic analysis of his thought.

I

Sexual Inversion, the first volume of the *Studies* to appear, serves as an admirable introduction to Ellis's modernist convictions. Although cast in the form of a scientific treatise, the book was in essence an apology for homosexuality—a classic example of Ellis's lifelong effort to broaden the spectrum of acceptable sexual behavior. The choice of language, the analogies, the case histories, and the explicit theoretical structure of the book all served to create an impression of homosexuality as an innocuous departure from the sexual norm, and one not without its advantages for society. Thus while the book may not have been a completely satisfying analytic treatment of the subject, its moral stance was magnificently consistent.

The opening chapter of *Sexual Inversion,* though seemingly devoid of theoretical interest, found Ellis indulging in two characteristically modern techniques of sexual persuasion: the argument from animal behavior (used so effectively a half-century later by Alfred Kinsey) and the argument from cultural relativism. Ellis simply noted that homosexuality had been observed among several animal species, particularly among birds, and that it existed in nearly all known human societies. He also suggested that homosexual behavior was regarded with "considerable indifference" by most non-Western peoples, and that even within Europe the lower classes showed little repugnance to it—observations transparently intended to cast doubt on the notion that homosexuality was "unnatural."[3]

At the expressly theoretical level Ellis made three principal contentions in *Sexual Inversion.* Undoubtedly the most important of these was his insistence on the congenital nature of inversion. Homosexuals, he argued, were born to their particular sexual orientation, and apparent cases of acquired inversion revealed, under careful scrutiny, merely the retarded emergence of an innate disposition. In support of this claim, Ellis cited the frequent occurrence of homosexuality within the same family, as well as the tendency of many inverts to manifest their sexual

3. *Sexual Inversion,* third (revised and enlarged) edition (1915), in *Studies in the Psychology of Sex* (New York, 1936), Volume I, Part Four, pp. 4–24.

preferences very early in life, "without previous attraction to the opposite sex."[4]

Ellis's congenital theory of inversion had been anticipated by several nineteenth-century thinkers, notably the German jurist Karl Heinrich Ulrichs. However, when *Sexual Inversion* first appeared in 1897, orthodox sexual opinion still maintained that many, perhaps even most, homosexuals developed their perversion as a result of some sexual excess, usually masturbation. The concept of acquired inversion was authoritatively defended by Richard von Krafft-Ebing, himself a transitional figure between Victorian and modern styles of sexual theorizing, and the most influential sexual psychologist of the last quarter of the nineteenth century. Krafft-Ebing's masterpiece, *Psychopathia Sexualis,* allowed the existence of both congenital and acquired inversion, and as the book passed through its many editions ever more emphasis was placed on the congenital variety. But even in the final version of 1902, Krafft-Ebing continued to insist on the reality of acquired homosexuality, and he pointed to masturbation as a major factor in its etiology.[5]

By arguing that homosexuality was invariably congenital, Ellis intended to undermine any suggestion that inversion might be considered a vice, a form of behavior willfully indulged out of either boredom or sheer perversity. Moral censure and legal prohibition were thus out of the question. At the same time, the congenital theory also set Ellis at odds with the Freudians, and with the generally antisomatic tendencies of much early-twentieth-century psychology. With Freud the notion of acquired inversion obtained a new lease on life, now no longer in the overtly moralistic form preferred by nineteenth-century thinkers, but translated into the ethically neutral language of psychoanalysis. According to Freudian theory, homosexuality (or, more precisely, male homosexuality) originated in an unsuccessful resolution of the Oedipus complex: a boy became excessively attached to his mother, ultimately identified with her (rather than with his father), and then sought in male sexual objects substitute selves whom he might love as he had been loved by his

4. Ibid., pp. 82–84, 265, 268.

5. Richard von Krafft-Ebing, *Psychopathia Sexualis,* twelfth (revised and enlarged) edition (1902), translated by Franklin S. Klaf (New York, 1965), pp. 222-368.

mother. Ellis doubted that this psychic mechanism could be demonstrated in the histories of more than a few inverts, and in any case the Freudian analysis ignored the indisputably hereditary character of inversion, as well as the fact that many young homosexuals felt attracted to their own sex long before the Oedipal crisis came to a head. He was prepared to acknowledge that the homosexual boy was often passionately fond of his mother, but this attachment, he believed, was not so much Oedipal as it was a reflection of the "community of tastes" the inverted boy naturally shared with his mother. Needless to say, Ellis took a dim view of all psychoanalytic claims about curing homosexuality. In fact, it was precisely the exaggerated therapeutic ambitions of the Freudians that inspired his critique. His case histories had convinced him that inversion was a permanent state of affairs, and indeed that the vast majority of homosexuals had no desire to be "cured."[6]

I have placed "cured" in quotes because Ellis himself did so.[7] It was a major contention of *Sexual Inversion*—second in importance only to Ellis's insistence on the congenital nature of inversion—that homosexuality could not properly be considered a disease. Here again Ellis was taking issue with Krafft-Ebing, who had characterized inversion (or at least congenital inversion) as "a functional sign of degeneration," implying thereby that it was but one manifestation of some more general process of deterioration. To be sure, Krafft-Ebing sometimes intended "degeneration" to carry the neutral evolutionary sense of "fallen away from the genus." For the most part, however, he was happy to surround homosexuality with an aura of sickness, and the terminology of "degeneration" served that purpose admirably.[8]

Ellis, by way of contrast, struggled to devise a language that avoided any suggestion of pathology. Thus he preferred to call homosexuality an "abnormality"—emphasizing that he used the

---

6. *Sexual Inversion*, pp. 301, 304–09, 330–31.

7. Ibid., p. 327, for example.

8. Krafft-Ebing, *Psychopathia Sexualis*, pp. 224, 267–68. Ellis, ever one for having all authorities on his side, claimed that Krafft-Ebing abandoned the theory of degeneration in the last edition of *Psychopathia Sexualis* (*Sexual Inversion*, pp. 70–71). This was a considerable exaggeration; it would be more accurate to say that the theory was presented in a somewhat gentler fashion.

word in a purely statistical sense—or, more frequently, an "anomaly," a label that, to my ears at least, is nearly devoid of pejorative overtones. On other occasions he termed inversion a "sport" or variation. He also proposed an ingenious analogy, borrowed from John Addington Symonds, that was obviously meant to subvert the pathological conception of homosexuality. Inversion, he argued, ought to be compared to color-blindness:

> Just as the ordinary color-blind person is congenitally insensitive to those red-green rays which are precisely the most impressive to the normal eye, and gives an extended value to the other colors,—finding that blood is the same color as grass, and a florid complexion blue as the sky,—so the invert fails to see emotional values patent to normal persons, transferring those values to emotional associations which, for the rest of the world, are utterly distinct.[9]

No sooner had Ellis submitted this analogy than he withdrew it in favor of an even more generous one. Color-blindness still implied some sort of deficiency. He therefore suggested instead a comparison with "color-hearing," the ability, that is, to associate sounds with particular colors. In terms of this final analogy, inversion appeared less a defect than a special talent.

At stake in this question of pathology was the very serious matter of whether homosexuals could function effectively in their nonsexual capacities. The theory of degeneration distinctly implied that they couldn't. Ellis, however, not only denied this implication, but sought to reverse its effect by repeatedly associating inversion with artistic and intellectual excellence. No fewer than thirty pages of *Sexual Inversion* were devoted to homosexuals "of exceptional ability,"[10] and Ellis also reported that over half of his case studies revealed unusual "artistic aptitudes." His tactic in this instance may have been ill-advised—to me it betrays something of the patronizing attitude that feminists have come to call "pedestalism"—but his intentions were clearly consistent with the larger apologetic purposes of the book. Far from being degenerates, homosexuals turned out to be responsible for some of civilization's finest achievements.

9. *Sexual Inversion*, p. 317.

10. Ellis's roster of famous homosexuals included Erasmus, Leonardo, Michelangelo, Cellini, Winkelmann, Kleist, A. von Humboldt, Marlowe, Francis Bacon, Byron, Wilde, Whitman, Verlaine, and Sappho. *Sexual Inversion*, pp. 30–57, 197.

Ellis completed his apology by seeking to relate homosexuality to two of the representative sexual doctrines of the early twentieth century. The first of these was the notion that sexual differentiation was a matter of degree—that each sex possessed the recessive characteristics of the opposite sex. As Ellis noted, the concept of latent organic bisexuality was not unknown to earlier thinkers. It had been employed by Plato, Schopenhauer, and, without reference to the question of homosexuality, by Darwin. But the theory became current among sexual theorists only at the beginning of the twentieth century. It was associated especially with Otto Weininger, Wilhelm Fliess, and, of course, Freud, and it gained in authority as physiologists began to discover that the extent of one's maleness or femaleness was a function of the body's complex internal chemistry. Ellis admitted he could not state the exact connection between latent organic bisexuality and overt homosexuality. But he felt that an awareness of our shared hermaphroditic constitution helped render homosexuality more comprehensible, and he surmised that future investigators would discover the causes of inversion in some disturbance of the body's internal secretions.[11]

Closely related to the argument concerning constitutional bisexuality was Ellis's effort to associate inversion with the relatively undifferentiated character of even the noninverted individual's sexual preferences during childhood and early adolescence. Here he joined in uneasy alliance with Freud, who regarded a homosexual phase as a normal feature of psychosexual development. Ellis was naturally reluctant to accept the Freudian inference that since the child failed to distinguish categorically among sexual preferences, he could easily be turned in the wrong direction by unfavorable circumstances. The early lack of discrimination in the choice of sexual objects might, he conceded, account for the casual forms of adult homosexuality encountered in prisons and in the military, but it could not explain true inversion.[12]

Ellis was prepared in this instance to adopt a tempered version of the Freudian doctrine, despite the threat it posed to his own belief in the congenital nature of inversion, primarily, I think,

11. *Sexual Inversion,* pp. 79–80, 310–17.
12. Ibid., pp. 75, 79–83.

because the theory of infantile ambisexuality, like that of organic bisexuality, could be put to good polemical use. He characteristically sought to legitimize tabooed sexual practices by showing their intimate relation to normal sexuality. In fact, he preferred to abandon the concept of sexual normality altogether, substituting instead the notion of a continuum of sexual behavior, on which the so-called perversions could be charted as simple exaggerations of the statistical average. The doctrines of bisexuality and ambisexuality suited this objective perfectly. They enabled Ellis to render homosexuality less objectionable by showing it to be a mere modification of a constitutional organization and a childhood inclination shared by all.

At the heart of *Sexual Inversion* stood Ellis's case histories—the biographies of thirty-three men, taking up, in the final edition, over one hundred pages of text. Most of these histories were presented in the first person, and they served Ellis's polemical objectives even more effectively than did the explicit theoretical apparatus of the book. If Ellis were not so transparently honest, one might suspect him of having manufactured these autobiographies expressly to confute the popular image of homosexuality. He conceded that his sample was hardly random. All his cases were British or American, and many of them were solicited from his literary and scientific acquaintances. Most important, almost none of the accounts was obtained because the individual in question had come into conflict with the law or had sought psychiatric help.[13] One might say that just as Krafft-Ebing's or Freud's case histories exhibited a pathological bias, Ellis's histories were biased in the direction of health.

No reader of *Sexual Inversion* could possibly have considered Ellis's homosexuals degenerate—in Krafft-Ebing's sense of the term. For one thing, they wrote too well. Almost without exception their life histories were set forth in lucid, graceful prose. Most of these men also had pursued remarkably successful careers as physicians, teachers, men of letters, and artists. Characteristically they claimed to be of sound heredity and to enjoy general good health. They had little to say about their families, thereby eliminating even the possibility of a Freudian interpretation of their sexual orientation, and not uncommonly

13. Ibid., pp. 91–92, 264, 301.

they themselves articulated Ellis's congenital explanation of homosexuality. Most of them also denied that they were in any obvious sense effeminate, and although Ellis professed to be unconvinced, he joined them in rejecting "the vulgar error which confuses the typical invert with the painted and petticoated creatures who appear in police-courts from time to time."[14] Neither were these men misogynists. On the contrary, the majority of them claimed to value female companionship highly.

Ellis's cases might be divided into two categories, according to whether they accepted or rejected their sexual orientation. The "self-approving" inverts were in the vast majority, but the autobiographies of both groups served Ellis's critical ends. The unhappy minority, for their part, emerged as towering sources of moral fortitude. They struggled manfully with their wayward passions, achieving an extraordinary degree of self-control, often at the cost of great suffering. On the other hand, those who accepted their sexual identity seemed equally heroic. They proclaimed the naturalness of their sexual feelings and grew eloquently indignant at the injustice of the law and public opinion. The accounts of both groups also belied the popular image of the invert's sexual life. Far from being universally addicted to anal intercourse (which in fact Ellis considered fairly rare),[15] these men indulged in at least as wide a variety of erotic activities as did heterosexuals, and seldom could their sexual behavior be classified unambiguously in terms of the familiar masculine-feminine, active-passive dichotomy. Perhaps most important of all, the autobiographies revealed the deeply emotional character of the inverts' sexual attachments. Repeatedly these men insisted that their relationships were as intense, as gratifying, and even as durable as any heterosexual romance.[16] Ellis did not accept this—or any other—claim of his correspondents uncritically. But his occasional dissent or qualification only lent an aura of judiciousness to his presentation, making the book all the more effective as a piece of sexual criticism.

14. Ibid., p. 285.
15. Ibid., pp. 282–83.
16. E. M. Forster's homosexual novel *Maurice*, written in 1913–14, exhibits the same emotional tone; it is, in a sense, the imaginative counterpart of *Sexual Inversion*.

Indeed, *Sexual Inversion* could be counted a complete polemical success were it not for Ellis's weak treatment of female homosexuality. The book dealt primarily with male inversion, and it is no doubt significant that even in matters of sexual deviation the masculine variant received the earliest and most elaborate examination. In *Sexual Inversion* women were confined to a single chapter, and although Ellis stated that homosexuality was just as common among women as men, he presented only six case histories. Even more bothersome than this disparity in the extent of his treatment was his apparent lack of interest in reconstructing the popular image of lesbianism. He was, for example, as emphatic about the mannishness of the typical female invert as he had been reserved about the effeminacy of the male invert.[17] Ellis's views on women and female sexuality were in general ambiguous, and I think the unequal treatment meted out to male and female homosexuals reflected this larger difficulty in his thinking.

II

What Ellis had achieved for homosexuality in *Sexual Inversion* he sought to do for masturbation in *Auto-Erotism*, which appeared in 1899 as part of the second volume of the *Studies in the Psychology of Sex*. The essay effectively defused what had become the most cherished anxiety of Victorian sexual ideology: the belief that masturbation invariably led to serious illness, even to insanity. The *locus classicus* of this doctrine was William Acton's *Functions and Disorders of the Reproductive Organs*, an enormously influential work first published in 1857. The theory, however, was remarkably pervasive. One can find it, for instance, even in the writings of a sexual reformer such as George Drysdale, whose *Elements of Social Science* (1854) was among the earliest apologies for birth control and a significant influence on Ellis's sexual thinking. The theory was also extraordinarily tena-

---

17. *Sexual Inversion*, pp. 244–57. Ellis's wife was homosexual, and this perhaps accounts for his ambivalence. It does not, however, explain why his treatment of lesbianism was so abbreviated. See Calder-Marshall, *The Sage of Sex*, pp. 136–39.

cious, and it was still plainly visible in the final edition of Krafft-Ebing's *Psychopathia Sexualis*.[18]

In *Auto-Erotism* Ellis took direct issue with this doctrine, and, as in the case of *Sexual Inversion*, his argument symbolized a major shift in opinion among early-twentieth-century sexual authorities. There was, he insisted, simply no evidence linking masturbation with any serious mental or physical disorder. The supposition of such a connection was in fact incompatible with "the enormous prevalence of masturbation." Ellis even argued that masturbation could be a legitimate source of mental relaxation. And he solidified his case, as he had done with homosexuality, by citing evidence of masturbation among animals, as well as among "nearly every race of which we have any intimate knowledge."[19]

More interesting than this direct assault on Victorian orthodoxy, and more revealing of Ellis's polemical subtlety, were his efforts to relate masturbation to a variety of activities and experiences that even nineteenth-century theorists considered relatively innocent. Thus he argued that masturbation was but one manifestation of a general psychosexual syndrome, for which he coined the term autoerotism. Under this rubric he included, alongside masturbation itself, such disparate phenomena as erotic dreams, daytime fantasies, narcissism, and hysteria, all of which, he suggested, involved "spontaneous sexual emotion generated in the absence of an external stimulus."[20] The grouping was significant, as Ellis's definition implied, precisely because each of these phenomena, except, of course, masturbation, was more or less involuntary. Indeed, Ellis claimed that the "typical" manifestation of autoerotism was the occurrence of orgasm dur-

18. Krafft-Ebing, *Psychopathia Sexualis*, pp. 47, 181, 226–27. On the nineteenth-century theory of masturbation see Steven Marcus, *The Other Victorians* (New York, 1966), pp. 19–22; Alex Comfort, *The Anxiety Makers* (New York, 1970), pp. 69–113; H. E. Hare, "Masturbation Insanity: The History of an Idea," *Journal of Mental Science* 452 (1962): 2–25; and Robert H. MacDonald, "The Frightful Consequences of Onanism: Notes on the History of a Delusion," *Journal of the History of Ideas* 28 (1967): 423–31.

19. *Auto-Erotism*, third (revised and enlarged) edition (1910), in *Studies of the Psychology of Sex*, Volume I, Part One, pp. 164–66, 246–58, 268–70.

20. Ibid., p. 161.

ing sleep, and to separate masturbation from such an obviously spontaneous sexual experience was, in his mind, to create "a special and arbitrary subdivision of the field."[21] Thus by means of an inference that might be called innocence by association, masturbation was transformed from a malignant vice into a benign inevitability. Moreover, throughout the essay Ellis seemed preoccupied with the purely conceptual matter of establishing the boundaries and internal contours of his new sexual category. This concern lent the argument a curiously abstract tone, which at once disguised and abetted Ellis's polemical intentions. Under closer scrutiny his category turns out to be rather flimsy. It does not represent a particularly useful or cogent grouping of psychosexual phenomena. Yet by creating a mood of dispassionate inquiry, even the essay's intellectual pretensions contributed to its critical effect.

Perhaps the most subtle feature of *Auto-Erotism* was Ellis's insinuation that autoerotic phenomena were especially common in women. Most of the examples he discussed involved female subjects, and he explicitly stated that adult masturbation was considerably more frequent in women than in men.[22] In one sense this contention served to undermine the nineteenth-century belief that women lacked sexual feelings. But in a paradoxical fashion the argument also drew upon that very prejudice for its emotional effect. Masturbation was robbed of its viciousness when it turned out to be no less prevalent among supposedly chaste middle-aged ladies than among sex-crazed adolescent boys.

I should not give the impression that Ellis considered masturbation completely innocuous. He was not yet Alfred Kinsey, and he was still farther removed from Masters and Johnson. The latter researchers, it seems to me, have made masturbation the ultimate criterion of correct sexual behavior. Not only do they suggest that the masturbatory orgasm is in some ways superior to that achieved in sexual intercourse, but they argue that proper coital technique should model itself on masturbation. Thus, for example, if the skillful lover wants to know how best to manipu-

21. Ibid., p. 162.
22. Ibid., pp. 244–46.

late the clitoris, he has simply to observe how women themselves manipulate it while masturbating.[23] Surely no sexual activity has undergone a more extraordinary reconstruction in the course of a mere century: from its pathogenic status among the Victorians, masturbation has risen to the position of final sexual arbiter.

Ellis stood at the beginning of this process of rehabilitation, and although he criticized the Victorian doctrine sharply, he did not abandon it altogether. He continued to believe, for instance, that masturbation might result in slight nervous disorders. However, his essential objection to masturbation was not medical but moral: masturbation entailed in a particularly extreme form the divorce of the physical and psychological dimensions of sexual expression. Consequently, Ellis argued, extensive masturbation in childhood and adolescence might leave the masturbator incapable of associating sexuality with affection.[24] It may well be that this same Romantic protest lay behind the Victorians' exaggerated fear of masturbation. But it remained for Ellis and other modernists to strip that protest of its fanciful medical encrustations.

III

I have begun by discussing Ellis's views on homosexuality and masturbation primarily because they offer an instructive introduction to his modernist tendencies. One cannot, however, do justice to Ellis as a theorist simply by rehearsing, in serial fashion, his opinions on the major sexual questions of the day. This might convey something of the breadth of his interests—and he obviously entertained the ambition to treat human sexuality in its totality—but it would fail to give an adequate impression of the conceptual unity that informed his survey. Admittedly, in any comparison with a major theoretical intelligence such as Freud,

23. William H. Masters and Virginia E. Johnson, *Human Sexual Response* (Boston, 1966). See especially pp. 63–64, 133: "Understandably, the maximum physiologic intensity of orgasmic response subjectively reported or objectively recorded has been achieved by self-regulated mechanical or auto-manipulative techniques. The next highest level of erotic intensity has resulted from partner manipulation, again with established or self-regulated methods, and the lowest intensity of target-organ response was achieved during coition."

24. *Auto-Erotism*, pp. 257–66; *Sexual Inversion*, p. 277.

Ellis is apt to appear somewhat ramshackle and eclectic. His style of argument was rather leisurely, and his organizational principles often opaque. Still, his sexual writings were bound together by a number of grand themes, which, though lacking the sharp contours of Freud's unifying doctrines, clearly reflected his intention to examine human sexuality in a systematic, theoretical fashion.

Among the most important of these recurring themes were the notions of tumescence and detumescence. Understood literally, these terms described the vascular congestion and decongestion that accompany orgasm. But Ellis also employed the concepts to signify the entire process of sexual arousal and release. In this larger sense, tumescence designated the "accumulation" of sexual energy during arousal, and detumescence the "discharge" of that energy at the moment of climax.[25] For Ellis this essential sexual process was comparable to any physical event in which energy was stored up and expended:

> Tumescence is the piling on of the fuel; detumescence is the leaping out of the devouring flame whence is lighted the torch of life to be handed from generation to generation. The whole process is . . . exactly analogous to that by which a pile is driven into the earth by the raising and then the letting go of a heavy weight which falls on the head of the pile. In tumescence the organism is slowly wound up and force accumulated; in the act of detumescence the accumulated force is let go and by its liberation the sperm-bearing instrument is driven home.[26]

I need hardly point out that this conception of the sexual process bears a striking resemblance to Freud's libido theory. Indeed, it was no accident that of all Freud's doctrines, only his hypothesis of a libidinal economy claimed Ellis's unqualified enthusiasm. The sexual energy postulated by Ellis was, like Freud's libido, extremely malleable. It could assume apparently nonsexual guises (as in sublimation), and it could combine with, or itself be reinforced by, other forms of human energy—attributes of considerable theoretical significance. In effect, both Freud and Ellis treated human sexuality according to the model of a closed

25. *Analysis of the Sexual Impulse,* second (revised and enlarged) edition (1913), in *Studies in the Psychology of Sex,* Volume I, Part Two, pp. 63, 65.

26. *The Mechanism of Detumescence* (1906), in *Studies in the Psychology of Sex,* Volume II, Part One, p. 142.

energy system, and both thereby revealed their loyalty to the assumptions of nineteenth-century positivism.[27]

The energy accumulated and released in sexual arousal was for Ellis a fundamental human substance, generated, he surmised, through internal chemical processes. It did not follow that tumescence was an automatic occurrence, comparable, say, to the accumulation of urine in the bladder. On the contrary, Ellis insisted that sexual arousal had to be pursued in a conscious and artful manner. There was, so to speak, a technique of tumescence, which Ellis called courtship. Courtship was thus not merely the original wooing of a sexual partner, but the requisite preliminary to every sexual act, "the process whereby both the male and the female are brought into that state of sexual tumescence which is a more or less necessary condition for sexual intercourse."[28] The bulk of Ellis's sexual writings addressed themselves to the process of courtship, so defined, and he argued that the whole of sexual psychology—including most of the sexual aberrations—evolved out of its exigencies.[29]

Certainly the most interesting implication of Ellis's emphasis on courtship was the suggestion that sexual arousal constituted a problem. In traditional theory it was not the stimulation but the control of sexual activity that posed difficulties: satyriasis and nymphomania rather than impotence or frigidity seemed to represent the greatest threats to sexual equilibrium. All modern theory, by way of contrast, makes exactly the opposite assumption, and, in characteristic fashion, Ellis's work stood at the beginning of this revolution in sexual perspectives.

Significantly, however, Ellis did not consider sexual arousal equally difficult for both sexes. On occasion—as in the passage I cited in the last paragraph—he suggested that courtship was as necessary to the passion of the man as to that of the woman. But he more frequently characterized the male's achievement of tumescence as simple, direct, and spontaneous. Ultimately, there-

27. "Psycho-Analysis in Relation to Sex," in *The Philosophy of Conflict* (London, 1919), p. 210; *Psychology of Sex* (1933) (New York, n.d.), pp. 255–56.

28. *The Sexual Impulse in Women,* second (revised and enlarged) edition (1913), in *Studies in the Psychology of Sex,* Volume I, Part Two, p. 239; *Analysis of the Sexual Impulse,* pp. 52–53.

29. *Analysis of the Sexual Impulse,* p. 59.

fore, courtship for him was grounded in the peculiar sexual psychology of women.

In many respects Ellis's treatment of female sexuality marked an important break with received opinion, most obviously in his refutation of the notion that women lacked sexual emotions.[30] Ellis documented both the novelty and the provincialism of this idea, revealing it to be a unique creation of the nineteenth century and limited in its appeal largely to English, German, and Italian authorities. More important, he established that the theory was without empirical foundation. His own researches had persuaded him that sexual desire was no less intense in women than in men, and that women's capacity for sexual enjoyment was likewise comparable to that of men.[31]

In quantitative terms, then, Ellis counted women at least the sexual equals of men, and he here articulated what was to become modern sexual orthodoxy. Yet he insisted that such quantitative comparisons were rather crude. There remained, he was convinced, important qualitative distinctions between the typical sexual responses of men and those of women. Ellis's analysis of these qualitative differences revealed his lingering Victorianism, and it also provided the basis for his sometimes reactionary opinions about the differences between men and women in the nonsexual sphere. On balance, his treatment of the entire matter of sexual differentiation can be called modern only in a highly qualified sense.

Ellis generally sought to veil female sexuality in mystery. The sexual instinct in women, he wrote, was "elusive," while male sexuality was "predominantly open and aggressive."[32] One reason for this elusiveness, he believed, was the greater complexity of the sexual process in women. Sexual excitement in men was wholly contained in a single event: penile erection, which Ellis characteristically described as "spontaneous." The corresponding

30. The principal representative of Victorian sexual theory, William Acton, had written that "sexual feeling in the female is in the majority of cases in abeyance." Cited by Marcus, *The Other Victorians,* p. 31. It should be noted that Carl Degler has recently questioned whether Acton's opinion was in fact the dominant one among Victorian sexual authorities. See "What Ought to Be and What Was: Women's Sexuality in the Nineteenth Century," *American Historical Review* 79 (1974): 1467–90.

31. *The Sexual Impulse in Women,* pp. 191–96.

32. Ibid., p. 189.

phenomenon in women was the clitoral erection, and Ellis implied that if women's sexual sensitivity were confined to the clitoris, their responses would probably exhibit the same direct, uncomplicated character found in men. But "behind" the clitoris was the "much more extensive mechanism" of the vagina and the womb, both of which demanded satisfaction. Ellis by no means accepted the Freudian doctrine that adult female sexuality was exclusively vaginal. In fact, he ridiculed the idea, suggesting it could have been conceived only by someone who lacked any direct knowledge of women's sexual experiences. But although the clitoris remained for him the chief focus of sexual pleasure in women, the involvement of the intricate and in a sense distant internal organs meant that arousal was more difficult and, above all, slower in the female than in the male. Here then was an important organic foundation of courtship.[33]

Ellis also claimed that female sexuality was more massive and more diffuse than male sexuality. By this he meant simply that a larger portion of the female body participated in sexual arousal. Ellis was among the architects of the theory of erogenous (or erogenic) zones—the notion that certain parts of the body, notably its entrances and exits, function as special centers of sexual responsiveness. In its Freudian guise this theory was to become a standard component of modern sexual doctrine. Curiously, Ellis seemed to consider these erogenous zones uniquely feminine. Erotic sensitivity in men, he suggested, was limited to the penis, "the point at which, in the male body, all voluptuous sensation is concentrated, the only normal masculine center of sex."[34] Indeed, he would not even allow that the scrotum might be sexually responsive. In women, by way of contrast, several nongenital areas, above all the breasts, participated in sexual excitement, and this greater diffusion of sexual sensitivity meant, once again, that arousal for the woman was a slower and more elaborate process than for the man.[35]

33. *The Mechanism of Detumescence,* pp. 129–32; *The Sexual Impulse in Women,* pp. 235–37; *Psychology of Sex,* p. 251.

34. *The Mechanism of Detumescence,* p. 123.

35. Ibid., pp. 132, 143; *The Sexual Impulse in Women,* pp. 249–50; "The Doctrine of Erogenic Zones," in *Eonism and Other Supplementary Studies* (1928), in *Studies in the Psychology of Sex,* Volume II, Part Two, pp. 116–20.

In Ellis's mind it followed from the greater diffusion of female sexuality that sex necessarily figured more prominently in the psychology of women than in that of men. That is to say, he believed that women were, to a greater extent than men, sexual beings. "In a certain sense," he wrote, in a particularly unfortunate turn of phrase, "their brains are in their wombs."[36] No doubt Ellis felt he was doing women a service in thus asserting their innate sexual expertise. He was in effect seeking to refute the Victorian doctrine of woman's asexuality by transforming her into the supreme representative of sex. Yet nothing reveals more dramatically the perils that the sexual revolution held in store for women: the revolutionaries threatened to convert them into sexual objects, creatures so preoccupied with their sexual needs as to be incapable of functioning in any other capacity.

Ellis also maintained that female sexuality was essentially passive. Men were propulsive, women receptive. In sexual relations the woman was the "instrument" from which the man "evoked" music.[37] Here Ellis was in complete accord with his Victorian predecessors, a rather surprising state of affairs in view of his sharp break with nineteenth-century tradition on almost all other sexual matters. In Ellis's defense I should point out that he considered female passivity only apparent, intended, through a policy of studied delay, to increase sexual desire both in the woman herself and in her partner. He also acknowledged that neither the vagina nor the womb was an entirely inert sexual organ: during intercourse the vagina to a certain extent drew the penis into itself, and the muscular action of the womb had a similar effect on the semen. But these matters were only lightly touched on in the *Studies,* while the natural sexual passivity of women received constant reiteration.[38]

In Ellis's opinion female passivity was so basic to the organization of human sexual life that it had given rise to a universal character trait among women: modesty. Modesty was thus for

36. *The Sexual Impulse in Women,* pp. 253, 106; *Analysis of the Sexual Impulse,* p. vii; *Sex in Relation to Society* (1910), in *Studies in the Psychology of Sex,* Volume II, Part Three, pp. 527, 547.

37. *Sex in Relation to Society,* pp. 525, 538–39, 542. The image came from Balzac's *Physiologie du Mariage.*

38. *The Sexual Impulse in Women,* pp. 228–29; *The Mechanism of Detumescence,* pp. 159–65; *Psychology of Sex,* pp. 78, 240–43.

him no mere refinement of civilization, but an almost instinctual component of feminine psychology, "an inevitable by-product of . . . the naturally defensive attitude of the female."[39] Not surprisingly, Ellis's insistence on the innate sexual passivity and modesty of women seriously prejudiced his thinking about their proper place in the larger order of things, and to a certain extent he must share with Freud intellectual responsibility for what Kate Millett has called the sexual counterrevolution.[40]

In sum, courtship—the conscious pursuit of tumescence—was made necessary, in Ellis's view, by the complex, diffuse, and essentially passive nature of female sexuality. We may now consider Ellis's notion of the contents of courtship—those procedures that succeeded in bringing the female to tumescence in the face of her organic resistance. Needless to say, the responsibilities of courtship fell largely to the male. In sexual relations, as in life as a whole, Ellis seemed to imply, biology had assigned man the more creative role. To a certain extent the male fulfilled his responsibilities simply by following his instincts. Thus in keeping with traditional sexual opinion, Ellis held that the forcefulness of the male's pursuit would normally overcome the female's biological inhibitions. Her own modest reactions merely prolonged the chase until tumescence had been achieved, at which point she naturally surrendered herself to the man. Ellis even made the improbable claim that women were never attracted to men by their beauty, but only by their physical vigor, which alone promised the "primary quality of sexual energy which a woman demands of a man in the sexual embrace."[41] As a sexual allurement beauty was an exclusively feminine attribute.

Ellis struck a more modern note when he argued that the male's natural aggressiveness ought to be tempered by a considerate attention to the woman's sexual needs. Since women were slow to arousal, it followed that sexual intercourse should be preceded by extensive foreplay, during which the man, while

39. *The Evolution of Modesty*, third (revised and enlarged) edition (1910), in *Studies in the Psychology of Sex*, Volume I, Part One, p. 40; also pp. 1, 41, 44–45, 70, 72; *Psychology of Sex*, pp. 35–36, 243.

40. Kate Millett, *Sexual Politics* (New York, 1970), especially pp. 176–220.

41. *Sexual Selection in Man* (1905), in *Studies in the Psychology of Sex*, Volume I, Part Three, pp. 192, 189–90.

remaining the active agent, assumed an essentially gentle, coaxing attitude. Normal foreplay, Ellis suggested, might even include cunnilingus, a practice Krafft-Ebing had condemned as a masochistic perversion. He also recommended *coitus reservatus* —prolonged intercourse in which the man held back his own orgasm, thereby allowing the woman to achieve repeated climaxes. Ellis found it difficult to reconcile this new emphasis on considerateness with the traditional need for masculine aggression. He simply stated that the proper balance of both attitudes was essential to "the art of love."[42]

We recognize in Ellis's plea for the sexual rights of women an important component of modern sexual consciousness. Ellis's long chapter on "The Art of Love" in the sixth volume of the *Studies* was in a sense the prototype for the countless how-to-do-it sexual manuals published over the last half-century. Moreover, this attempt to reorganize sexual relations in terms of the peculiarities of female sexuality represented an important historical advance. At the same time, we can regret that Ellis did not successfully eliminate the masculine bias of traditional sexual wisdom. There was an almost sinister note of manipulation in his exposition of the art of love, and it can be argued that the male's newfound solicitousness was in some ways even more demeaning to women than the simple neglect to which their sexuality had been subjected in the nineteenth century.

IV

Ellis often claimed that his sexual studies differed from those of earlier investigators primarily in the attention they devoted to normal sexuality. And in fact from William Acton's *Functions and Disorders of the Reproductive Organs* (in which the emphasis was unambiguously on the disorders) to Krafft-Ebing's *Psychopathia Sexualis*, nineteenth-century sexology had been largely preoccupied with sexual malfunctionings. It is also true that the bulk of Ellis's sexual writings dealt with what he himself considered nonpathological sexual processes.

42. *Sex in Relation to Society*, pp. 546, 548–49, 552; *The Sexual Impulse in Women*, pp. 237, 247; *Sexual Selection in Man*, p. 21; Krafft-Ebing, *Psychopathia Sexualis*, p. 154.

Still, Ellis obviously felt obliged to examine the sexual deviations that had loomed so large in the minds of his predecessors,
and in every instance he sought to render those deviations more
respectable. We have already observed him at this task in *Sexual
Inversion*. In his examination of the other sexual anomalies, he
followed the same procedure he had adopted in the case of
homosexuality: he attempted to relate each deviation to some
aspect of normal sexual experience. Furthermore, he insisted that
the theoretical constructs he had developed in his analysis of
normal intercourse—in particular the notions of tumescence and
courtship—also served to explain even the most obscure sexual
aberrations. Thus his treatment of deviant sexuality revealed not
only his familiar permissive bias, but a considerable theoretical
ambition as well—the intention, that is, to construct a truly systematic sexology.

Ellis's method of dealing with the sexual deviations is perhaps
best illustrated by his analysis of sadism and masochism, anomalies that had been extensively investigated by Krafft-Ebing
(who, in fact, invented the terms) and that were to assume an
important role in Freud's psychological system. The essential feature of both sadism and masochism, according to Ellis, was the
association of love with pain, and that association, he argued,
was based on the normal events of courtship among animals.
Pain came into intimate relation with sexual excitement first
through combat between males for the possession of the female,
and thereafter through the male's sexual pursuit and subdual of
his mate—a drama Ellis found reenacted among primitive tribes
in the practice of marriage by capture. Under civilized conditions, he believed, the emotional residues of animal courtship
could be observed in man's tendency to domination and woman's
delight in submission, proclivities that, even in normal relationships, sometimes led to actual cruelty.[43]

This argument was, of course, perfectly consonant with Ellis's
general analysis of male and female sexual psychology, and it
nicely achieved the apologetic purpose of grounding sadism and
masochism in normal behavior. At the same time, Ellis's reason-

43. *Love and Pain*, second (revised and enlarged) edition (1913), in
Studies in the Psychology of Sex, Volume I, Part Two, pp. 66–67, 71–74,
83, 89.

ing brought him into uncomfortable agreement with Krafft-Ebing, who had concluded that sadism was at bottom a pathological extension of the normal sexual psychology of men, and masochism an exaggeration of the distinctive sexual inclinations of women. It followed naturally that sadism was an essentially masculine disorder, masochism a feminine disorder, and when the inverse situation obtained (a female sadist or male masochist), Krafft-Ebing found himself forced to assume that the subject was a homosexual.[44]

Although Ellis's discussion of animal courtship seemed to lead to the same conclusions, he nevertheless explicitly rejected Krafft-Ebing's theory. His genuinely empirical temperament was troubled by several facts that simply did not fit Krafft-Ebing's neat equation. Against the predictions of the theory, for example, Ellis found that women were more often subject to sadism than masochism, and men more inclined to become masochists than sadists. And no evidence, he felt, justified Krafft-Ebing's explanation of this incongruity in terms of latent homosexuality. More important, Ellis discovered that sadistic and masochistic tendencies often occurred together in the same individual. The Marquis de Sade, he noted, was also a masochist, and the Austrian novelist Leopold von Sacher-Masoch, after whom Krafft-Ebing had named his clinical syndrome, was at the same time a sadist.[45]

In light of these considerations, Ellis sought to modify his image of the role of cruelty in animal courtship, arguing now that the infliction of pain was no more confined to the male than the suffering of it to the female. He suggested, for instance, that the female participated vicariously in the punishment her mate meted out to his rivals, and in the chase that followed she consciously tortured the male by eluding him. The male, for his part, experienced considerable pain and anxiety during the preliminary combat, and he also learned to savor the erotic denial imposed on him by the female. Thus under closer examination, Ellis concluded, animal courtship revealed no clear breakdown of sexual roles along sadistic and masochistic lines.[46]

44. Krafft-Ebing, *Psychopathia Sexualis*, pp. 103, 160, 167.
45. *Love and Pain*, pp. 84–86, 109–13, 119, 148, 171; *Psychology of Sex*, p. 153.
46. *Love and Pain*, pp. 67–69, 109.

On the basis of this analysis Ellis proposed to abolish the clinical distinction between sadism and masochism. Far from being opposites, as Krafft-Ebing had argued, they represented "complementary emotional states."[47] Ellis hoped to eliminate the categories altogether, substituting instead the covering term "algolagnia" (coined by Albert von Schrenk-Notzing),[48] which implied an undifferentiated connection between sexuality and pain, without regard to active or passive roles. This effort ultimately brought him into conflict with Freud, who sought to revive Krafft-Ebing's categorical distinction, although in terms of a much subtler psychology.

I should not give the impression that Ellis's objection to the antithesis between sadism and masochism was based solely on empirical scruples. He had theoretical—and polemical—reasons of his own for wishing to eliminate the distinction. The real importance of pain for sexual life, he argued, was that it gave rise to strong emotions—namely fear and anger—which served to supplement the energy of the sexual impulse itself. The underlying assumption of Ellis's argument was the notion of a unified human energy system, in which the different emanations of that energy could be converted from one form into another. The masochist or sadist, he theorized, was an individual whose supply of sexual energy was, perhaps for organic reasons, abnormally low, and who therefore could achieve tumescence only through extensive "borrowings" from the energies of fear or anger. The psychic mechanism implied here was in a sense inversely analogous to that of sublimation: where in sublimation sexual energy was converted to nonsexual ends, in sadism and masochism nonsexual energy was converted to sexual ends. In terms of this economic analysis, it obviously made no fundamental difference whether the additional energy was supplied by anger (sadism) or by fear (masochism).[49]

The net effect of Ellis's argument was to transform sadism and masochism from psychological into mechanical disorders, and this despite the fact that his own discussion of the topic had

47. Ibid., p. 159; also pp. 119–20, 166, 171, 186.
48. Erich Fromm, *The Anatomy of Human Destructiveness* (New York, 1973), p. 280.
49. *Love and Pain,* pp. 171–80.

been launched in largely psychological terms (i.e., those of domination and submission). Thus, where Krafft-Ebing's sadists had appeared as vicious, perhaps even murderous degenerates, and his masochists as pitiful, self-destructive neurotics, Ellis's subjects emerged as relatively normal human beings who suffered from a defect in their sexual plumbing. When cruelty entered a sexual relationship, it did not, in Ellis's view, necessarily reflect on the general psychology of the parties to that relationship. "We have to recognize," he wrote, "that sadism by no means involves any love of inflicting pain outside the sphere of sexual emotions, and is even compatible with a high degree of general tender-heartedness."[50] As definitive evidence, Ellis cited the Marquis de Sade himself, contrasting his enthusiasm for sexual cruelties with his hostility to the political cruelties of the Terror. Whatever the theoretical merits of Ellis's argument (and they are not to be dismissed lightly), one must admit that he had again brought off a remarkable piece of sexual apologetics.

Ellis elsewhere expanded that apology to incorporate all the major forms of sexual deviation, notably fetishism, exhibitionism, bestiality, and finally the scatological perversions, urolagnia and coprolagnia. These abnormalities had been classified and analyzed in considerable detail by Krafft-Ebing, who illustrated each perversion with case histories that ranged from the ludicrous to the disgusting. In characteristic fashion, Ellis attempted to soften Krafft-Ebing's portrayal, arguing, as he had in the case of homosexuality, that these anomalies were usually congenital and that each could be related to some aspect of normal sexual life. He noted, for example, that one could recognize the germs of exhibitionism in the ostentatious pride that nearly every adolescent male showed in his maturing genitals. Similarly, the coprolagnist's perverse desires were grounded in the universally appreciated attractions of the female buttocks. According to the same line of reasoning, the primitive belief that animals were in reality disguised men implied that for the simpleminded (among whom most cases of bestiality occurred) intercourse with animals was little different from intercourse with human beings. Finally, Ellis noted that even the normal lover was often fascinated by some

50. Ibid., p. 166; also pp. 159–60.

particular feature of his beloved, and such fixations, he suggested, represented the nonpathological equivalent of fetishism.[51]

Perhaps the most remarkable aspect of Ellis's analysis of the sexual deviations was his contention that they could all be understood as manifestations of a single psychological process, which he called erotic symbolism. In general, Ellis seemed to enjoy liquidating distinctions. The suggestion that all sexual deviations were in fact variations on the theme of erotic symbolism represented merely the most extravagant example of his reductive inclinations. Purely as a matter of intellectual style it placed him at the opposite end of the spectrum from Krafft-Ebing, who positively delighted in inventing new categories and subcategories of perversion, with ever more arcane labels. Krafft-Ebing's mind, one might say, resembled a cluttered Victorian mansion, while Ellis's intellectual style recalls the streamlined architecture of Frank Lloyd Wright or Mies van der Rohe. He was, in short, a modern.

I emphasize these formal matters because I'm afraid that the substance of Ellis's theory was less interesting than were his intentions. He justified the phrase "erotic symbolism" by arguing that all sexual deviations involved an imitation of both the actions and the emotions of normal sexual intercourse. He was perhaps most successful in demonstrating this "mimicry of the normal sexual act"[52] in his analysis of exhibitionism (which, curiously, he considered the most bizarre of all sexual anomalies, perhaps because it involved sexual gratification "at a distance"). The exhibitionist exposed himself, according to Ellis, with the intention of shocking, but ultimately pleasing, his "victim," and this desired reaction of embarrassment followed by gratification was, in both vascular and emotional terms, analogous to the tumescence and detumescence experienced by a sexual partner in actual intercourse. As Ellis expressed it, the exhibitionist "feels that he has effected a psychic defloration."[53]

Unfortunately, Ellis's efforts to find similar symbolic patterns in the dynamics of the other sexual deviations were not so ingenious. There was perhaps some merit in arguing that the scato-

51. *Erotic Symbolism* (1906), in *Studies in the Psychology of Sex*, Volume II, Part One, pp. 8–10, 28–29, 63–64, 79–81, 99, 106, 111, 113.
52. Ibid., p. 105.
53. Ibid., p. 94.

logical perversions imitated normal intercourse in that sexual excitement here became associated with activities involving the accumulation of pressures followed by sudden release and gratification. But what is one to make of the lame suggestion that in cases of bestiality, "the animal becomes the symbol of the human being," or that in homosexuality, the person of the same sex "symbolized" a person of the opposite sex?[54] These formulations simply revealed the poverty of Ellis's theory. And even in those instances, such as exhibitionism or urolagnia, where the notion of erotic symbolism proved illuminating, the theory offered no true explanation of these deviations. It merely described their libidinal dynamics.

Even though the theory of erotic symbolism resists close inspection, we should not overlook the polemical virtues of the phrase itself. It was perhaps the most spectacular example of Ellis's talent for euphemisms. What exhibitionist or coprolagnist, for instance, would not gladly call himself an erotic symbolist? The phrase was even better than neutral; it resonated with the aesthetic preoccupations of the day. It was precisely this artistic analogy, I believe, that Ellis had in mind in concocting the term. More than any other manifestation of human sexuality, he insisted, the erotic symbolisms involved "the potently plastic force of the imagination. They bring before us the individual man creating his own paradise. They constitute the supreme triumph of human idealism."[55] The erotic symbolist, in other words, was a sexual visionary. He was a man who, because of his extraordinary imaginative powers, succeeded in transcending—although at great peril to himself—the humdrum routine of sexual normality. Ellis was perhaps never more brilliantly tendentious.

V

From the outset of his career, Ellis assumed the role of sexual enthusiast. In his first published work, for example, he called sex "the chief and central function of life, . . . ever wonderful, ever lovely."[56] Later, in the *Studies*, he assured his readers that sexual

---

54. Ibid., p. 69–71.
55. Ibid., pp. 113–14.
56. *The New Spirit* (London, 1890), p. 129.

intercourse, under normal circumstances, was "entirely beneficial," and that even if sex were unrelated to procreation it would
remain indispensable to the fullest human development. Abstinence he considered unhealthy, and he cited with approval
Freud's critique of the ascetic tradition in "Civilized Sexual
Morality and Modern Nervousness." In short, what the world
needed, in Ellis's view, was not more restraint but more passion.[57]

In his reaction against Victorianism, Ellis often yielded to a
kind of soft-minded mythology of sexual release. He was much
given to lyrical talk about the naturalness and the beauty of sex,
in contrast with which Freud's austerity—or even the sexual ter-
rorism of the Victorians—seems almost refreshing. Still, Ellis
stopped well short of Wilhelm Reich. He never suggested that
sex was unproblematic—that were it not for the false anxieties
created by Christianity (or other ideological forces) we could
contemplate our sexuality with as little apprehension as we do
our nutritive or excretory functions.[58]

In fact, Ellis qualified his enthusiasm for sexual experience on
several grounds. To begin with, his energy theory committed
him, as it did Freud, to the notion that the higher human
achievements were purchased at the expense of direct sexual expression. "The stuff of the sexual life," he wrote, "is the stuff of
art; if it is expended in one channel it is lost for the other."[59]
Culture, therefore, involved sublimation, and although Ellis cannot be counted an uncritical advocate of sublimation, he was,
again like Freud, too much the connoisseur of art and literature
to preach uninhibited sexual abandon.

Even within the erotic realm itself, Ellis argued, the basic logic
of human sexuality demanded a certain amount of restraint. True
sexual fulfillment presumed a careful management of one's erotic
resources, and the most ecstatic sexual experiences were inaccessible to the man who expended those resources indiscriminately.
Indeed, Ellis maintained that without self-denial one's sexual life
would quickly degenerate into a series of trivial orgasms. Chas-

---

57. *The Mechanism of Detumescence*, p. 169; *Sex in Relation to Society*,
pp. 199, 201, 214, 216; "The Meaning of Purity," in *Little Essays of Love
and Virtue* (New York, 1922), pp. 60–61.

58. *Psychology of Sex*, pp. 105–06, 110, 249.

59. *Sex in Relation to Society*, p. 173; also pp. 172–77; *Psychology of
Sex*, pp. 260–64.

tity, therefore, had its legitimate claims—not in the sense of a total interdiction of sexual expression, but as a means of preparing oneself for ever more emphatic experiences of sexual release.[60]

Human sexual expression was further restricted, Ellis believed, by the fact that sexual relations merged into personal relations— they extended from the physical into the psychic realm as sexual lust evolved into sexual love. This uniquely human experience introduced enormous complications (as well as rich possibilities) that nearly always involved a check on impulse. Ellis was at his most thoughtful—and most radical—in his analysis of the function of sexuality in interpersonal relations. Indeed, his substantial writings on the subject constitute his most impressive achievement as a theorist, and they deserve extended exposition.

Basically Ellis was a romantic: he believed that the proper context for sexual relations was that complex emotional state we call love. Ideally sexual love should bind two (and no more) persons of the opposite sex together for life in a relationship he termed natural monogamy. It was "natural" simply because it answered to a need Ellis considered absolutely fundamental to human psychology: the desire for sustained erotic companionship. "Monogamy," he wrote, "is the most natural expression of an impulse which cannot, as a rule, be so adequately realized in full fruition under conditions involving a less prolonged period of mutual communion and liberty. . . . The needs of the emotional life . . . demand that such unions based on mutual attraction should be so far as possible permanent."[61]

Despite his enthusiasm for monogamy Ellis was a fierce critic of the traditional Western concept of marriage, which he felt sought to transform a substantive relationship into a formal one. He never tired of stating that true marriage was not a contract but a fact. It came into existence when sexual love caused two individuals to share a united life. It might survive the termination of sexual relations, provided the emotional commitment was sufficiently strong, but when both the physical and psychological attachments ended, so did the marriage. Such a relationship, Ellis insisted, was utterly private. It could never come within the prov-

60. *Sex in Relation to Society*, pp. 167–70.
61. Ibid., pp. 426–27. Ellis also maintained that the approximately equal number of men and women insured a statistical tendency to monogamy. See *Sex in Relation to Society*, pp. 421–26.

ince of the state—it could never be made a matter of legal arrangement—for the simple reason that no law, could command two individuals to love one another. Nothing, in Ellis's mind, was more senseless than a contract purporting to guarantee permanency of sexual inclinations, and nothing was more immoral than a legal system that forced people to continue living as man and wife when in fact their marriage no longer existed.[62]

Ellis acknowledged that a sexual relationship was sometimes attended by circumstances in which society took a legitimate interest, above all the birth of children. As citizens, children had a claim to parental support. Consequently some sort of formal registration of a sexual relationship was necessary if a couple intended to raise a family. Society could thus insist that all mothers and fathers be legally married, but not husbands and wives. In practice this meant that before lovers married in the traditional legal sense they would enter an experimental relationship, which, several decades before Margaret Mead, Ellis called a "trial marriage." But whether the marriage was merely informal or officially recognized, Ellis insisted that every provision be made for its termination when it ceased to be a real sexual and emotional relationship. Divorce was to be granted at the request of either party, the state merely insuring that economic responsibility for the children—if there were any—be fairly apportioned.[63]

As Ellis grew older his thinking about marriage deepened considerably. The basic concept remained the same (i.e., marriage should be an essentially private event, made public only for the sake of the children), but he developed a more complex notion of its sexual and emotional content. His early writings had made mutual sexual attraction the basis of any conjugal arrangement, although he recognized, of course, that marriage soon developed an elaborate emotional, familial, and economic superstructure. In his later work these nonsexual ties—a community of tastes, common parenthood, a shared household—assumed ever greater importance, and he suggested they might render a marriage viable even in the absence of sexual attraction. In fact, Ellis developed into a forceful critic of the romantic mythology of

62. Ibid., pp. 365, 374, 446, 475–76.
63. Ibid., pp. 379, 481, 487–89.

marriage that his earliest work had celebrated. It was a mistake, he now argued, to found marriage on the hope of exclusive and everlasting sexual love. The inevitable collapse of that foundation led many couples to conclude that their marriage had failed, when in fact it had merely shifted its basis. It was even incorrect, in Ellis's opinion, to assume that marriage should result in happiness, since from the beginning the relationship was detined to be tension-ridden. "Marriage," he wrote, "is essentially rather to be termed a tragic condition than a happy condition. It is by the intensity of life it produces that its success must be measured."[64]

Even in his early writings Ellis recognized that monogamy did not represent a completely adequate response to the human sexual condition. It satisfied the impulse for prolonged erotic companionship, but it ignored the equally basic desire for sexual variety. Ellis was never more tough-minded, or more subtle, than in his examination of what he characterized as modern man's need for erotic adventure. The basic premise of his analysis was a particular notion of the historical tendency of human sexuality. He was convinced that as man advanced from savagery to civilization his sexual instincts became both more intense and more refined. In fact, the sexual life of the savage was, in Ellis's view, a very modest affair when compared with that of his civilized brother. To a certain extent this disparity was a function of custom: the savage was subject to many sexual taboos that had disappeared with the advance of civilization, such as the prohibition on intercourse during war or during the hunting and fishing seasons. But Ellis believed the greater intensity of civilized sexual life was a matter of biology as well. Among civilized men—perhaps, he surmised, because of their larger pelvises—the sexual impulse itself had grown more demanding.[65]

64. "The History of Marriage," in *Eonism and Other Supplementary Studies*, p. 520; also pp. 516–20; *Psychology of Sex*, p. 207.
65. *Sex in Relation to Society*, p. 495; "The Sexual Instinct in Savages," Appendix A to *The Sexual Impulse in Women*, pp. 261–67, 275–76; *Man and Woman*, sixth edition (London, 1926), pp. 86–87. Ellis's emphasis on the "natural chastity" of savages reflected the early-twentieth-century reaction against the notion of primitive licentiousness. At the same time, his doctrine of the simultaneous advance of civilization and eroticism appeared to set him at odds with Freud, who argued that the development of civilization involved instinctual repression. The disagreement was only apparent, however. Freud did not claim that the sexual instinct itself became weaker

The desire for sexual variety was the most important manifestation of this intensified eroticism. Ironically, just as men and
women became increasingly sexual the modern marriage system
had confined human sexuality to a single outlet. The contradiction between the demands of monogamy and the increased desire
for variety had been "resolved," Ellis suggested, by the rise of
prostitution. He thus recognized prostitution as an inevitable by-
product of the marriage system, but he considered it an entirely
unsatisfactory response to the need for sexual adventure. For one
thing, in its historical forms prostitution met that need in men
only, and Ellis was convinced that the desire for variety was no
less intense in women.[66] But even the prospect of prostitution for
both sexes seemed to him unattractive. The relationship between
prostitute and client was by its very nature irredeemable, and
Ellis insisted it could satisfy only those who made extremely
humble demands on the sexual act. In effect, he recognized that
man's desire for sexual adventure was no mere mechanical matter
(to be contrasted with the deeply emotional need for sustained
erotic companionship), but a distinctly psychological inclination,
as unique to the human situation as the complementary impulse
to monogamy. Men and women sought not merely variety in
sexual intercourse, but variety in romance. For this reason alone
—even without taking into consideration the indignities suffered
by the prostitute—Ellis believed that prostitution would always
remain an unacceptable arrangement, and he opposed its legal-
ization.[67]

Ellis hoped that eventually the need for sexual variety would
be met by relaxing the bonds of monogamy. Since men and
women were fully capable of desiring—even loving—more than
one person at the same time, it followed that married couples
ought to learn to have affairs gracefully. In fact, in Ellis's ideal
sexual order a person might become simultaneously involved in a
number of relationships that were in some degree erotic. Such an
organization of sexual life promised both a richer emotional ex-

---

with the progress of civilization, but merely that its expression was increasingly inhibited. For his part, Ellis agreed that the greater intensity of sexuality under civilization introduced the need for moral restraints unknown
among savages.

66. *Psychology of Sex*, pp. 205–06.
67. *Sex in Relation to Society*, pp. 249–55, 287–97, 302–10, 314.

perience and a lower coefficient of exploitation than the established regime of monogamy-cum-prostitution.[68]

Ellis did not present this polyerotic vision glibly. He knew that multiple sexual arrangements had their liabilities. In particular he acknowledged that jealousy would remain an intractable, although useless, fact of emotional life. But he was persuaded that jealousy could be kept within bounds if husbands and wives were at all times completely frank with each other about their sexual inclinations. In effect, he proposed substituting a kind of psychological fidelity for the sexual exclusiveness that had traditionally provided the basis of marriage. Husbands and wives were to be true to each other in an intellectual rather than a physical sense—a responsibility, one might counter, that allowed for even less autonomy, certainly less privacy, than was the case under conventional monogamy.[69]

In arguing the case for sexual variety Ellis did not abandon his romantic principles. An extramarital affair, like marriage itself, involved for him a large psychological commitment, and he nowhere allowed that a sexual encounter might be legitimately casual. Thus although he seemed to pave the theoretical way for the more relaxed mores of our own day, the assumptions underlying his plea for sexual adventure were very different from those informing current sexual practice. For Ellis an extramarital experience was justified only by the intense physical and personal attraction of the individuals involved. The tendency of contemporary opinion, clearly, is away from this rather stringent romanticism.

VI

Ellis's advocacy of a freer sexual life was balanced, and in some instances contradicted, by his commitment to parenthood. He obviously believed that his thinking on this subject was at least as radical as his analysis of marriage. From our vantage point, however, his procreative and parental doctrines seem the most conventional aspect of his thought, distinctly more Victorian than modern.

68. Ibid., pp. 269, 312–27, 529.
69. Ibid., pp. 527–29, 564–09; "The History of Marriage," p. 527.

Ellis was strongly influenced by the eugenic theories of Francis Galton, whom he regarded as one of the supreme scientific geniuses of the nineteenth century. From Galton he drew the conviction that potential parents were obligated to consider whether their offspring would improve the quality of future generations. If a man and a woman were not fit "to be the fine parents of a fine race," then, Ellis suggested, they probably ought not to marry.[70] He implied that his main concern in taking this position was the welfare of individuals yet unborn: to bring inferior children into the world was an act of cruelty. For the modern reader, however, there hangs about Ellis's eugenic pronouncements rather too much of the unpleasant and dated rhetoric of racial purification. Moreover, it is difficult to reconcile his eugenic beliefs with his romanticism. If marriage was to be based on sexual passion and psychological affinity, there would seem to be little room left for a consideration of racial fitness. Ellis sought to meet this objection by arguing that the eugenic ideal would be "absorbed into the conscience of the community" in such a fashion that only the fit would appear sexually attractive.[71]

As a modernist, Ellis, of course, took a dim view of the Augustinian notion that sexual intercourse was justified only for the sake of reproduction. Yet he was reluctant to embrace the fully modern belief that the psychology of sex and that of procreation have little or nothing to do with one another. In fact, he maintained that a sexual relationship achieved its natural fulfillment in parenthood, and that in the absence of children the erotic life itself was apt to suffer. Parenthood was especially important for women. "In order to live a humanly complete life," he asserted, "every healthy woman should have, not sexual relationships only, but the exercise at least once in her life of the supreme function of maternity."[72]

It was this enthusiasm for motherhood, I believe, that underlay many of Ellis's reactionary opinions about women. He would

70. "The History of Marriage," p. 523.
71. "Eugenics and Love," in *The Task of Social Hygiene* (Boston, 1912), pp. 207–08; *Sex in Relation to Society*, pp. 1–2, 33–34, 581, 583–84, 597, 620–21, 627–29.
72. "The Changing Status of Women" (1888), in *The Task of Social Hygiene*, pp. 65–66.

have disputed this characterization vigorously, and it must be conceded that his position on most of the issues raised by the Women's Movement was unassailable. He advocated complete legal, political, and professional equality for women, insisted on their right to authority and independence within the family, and, as we have seen, defended their claim to equal sexual privileges. Yet despite these specific commitments, Ellis preferred to emphasize what he considered the fundamental differences between men and women, and he criticized contemporary feminists for seeking to minimize those differences. Thus he argued that the prime objective of the Women's Movement ought to be not equality with men but official recognition of the distinctive needs that resulted from woman's physical and psychological constitution.[73]

In practice this meant that Ellis advocated a number of reforms that, had they been adopted, would have considerably enhanced women's maternal functions. He suggested that during pregnancy and for a specific time after childbirth women ought to be released from all responsibilities and supported by the state or by their employers. Only such a "systematic endowment of motherhood" would eliminate the financial anxieties that frequently led young mothers to neglect their own and their children's welfare. He further underlined women's procreative role by proposing a four- or five-day period of rest during menstruation, as well as a year-long holiday for young girls at the onset of puberty. Throughout his writings he insisted on the enormous physical and psychological significance of menstruation—it was, he said, a manifestation of woman's "sexual invalidism"—and he questioned the femininity of those leaders of the Women's Movement who claimed to be little troubled by it.[74]

Like procreation, childrearing was in Ellis's view a much larger responsibility for women than for men. "It is the mother," he stated, "who is the child's supreme parent."[75] Therefore, the mother quite naturally achieved greater intimacy with the child

73. *Sex in Relation to Society,* pp. 3–4, 508; "The New Aspect of the Woman's Movement," in *The Task of Social Hygiene,* pp. 85–87, 95–96, 112.

74. *Sex in Relation to Society,* pp. 6–7, 20–21, 23–24, 67–71, 630; *Man and Woman,* pp. 347–49.

75. *Sex in Relation to Society,* p. 2.

than did the father. She, of course, looked after his physical needs (Ellis strongly urged that women breast-feed their children), and she was answerable for his intellectual development as well. It was to the mother, for example, that Ellis assigned the task of the child's sexual enlightenment. Thus, at precisely that moment in history when feminists were making their boldest move to expand woman's role in the world, Ellis seemed committed to maintaining, perhaps even enlarging, her domestic responsibilities. He never argued that a woman could be nothing else if she was a mother, but the essential tendency of his thought was to confine her to the home.[76]

Ellis's enthusiasm for motherhood seriously prejudiced his entire thinking about sexual differentiation. He addressed himself to this topic most explicitly in *Man and Woman*, among the more popular of his writings, having passed through six editions between 1894 and 1926. The book took note of a variety of secondary and tertiary sexual differences between men and women, most of them seemingly inconsequential, and it came to the agreeable-sounding conclusion that the two sexes were "perfectly poised"—meaning, I suppose, that if it were possible to compute the individual areas in which one sex surpassed the other, the result would be equal totals.

More interesting than the overt egalitarianism of the book was its implicit suggestion that women were designed to make children, men to make history. That childrearing was woman's destiny could be deduced from her more childlike nature: she was smaller, less hairy, and, according to Ellis, considerably more emotional than the adult male, all of which made her a more appropriate companion for the child. Ellis did not state expressly that the world of public events belonged by nature to men. He merely argued that men exhibited a greater tendency to variation than women, by which he meant that males were more subject to such biological anomalies as color-blindness, supernumerary digits, and—the significant item—genius. Ellis clearly believed he had discovered in the male's greater variational tendency the biological rationale for masculine cultural hegemony: it was, after all, genius that accounted for historical change—whether through artistic and technological creativity, or through political

76. Ibid., pp. 2, 24–27, 54.

and military leadership—and geniuses were more often men than women. Ellis patronizingly conceded that men had to suffer the consequences of their greater variational tendency: if there were more male geniuses, there were also more male idiots. But he failed to note that idiots were historically inconsequential.[77]

In later years Ellis became increasingly concerned with the problem of population control (as distinct from his earlier interest in population improvement), and this in turn partially undermined his commitment to motherhood. He now argued that some women could achieve psychological fulfillment without the experience of maternity, and that in such instances society should sanction nonprocreative relationships.[78] This was a significant concession, but it hardly represented a full-scale reformation of his thinking about parenthood and sexual differentiation. In his own gentler fashion Ellis remained as much a sexist as Freud. Moreover, it was no accident that the two thinkers who contributed most to liberating female sexuality from its Victorian fetters should have taken such essentially reactionary positions on the Women's Question. Under the circumstances there was an obvious tension between arguing for woman's sexuality and arguing for her humanity, and though Ellis nowhere said so expressly, I sense he feared the Women's Movement would bring a new Victorianism in its wake. Even today feminists find it difficult to defend both their sexual rights and their human rights, especially when their foremost adversaries are such obvious sons of the sexual revolution as Henry Miller and Norman Mailer. As an early-twentieth-century figure concerned primarily with dispelling the myth of woman's sexual insensitivity, Ellis probably deserves our tolerance.

VII

In 1910 Ellis completed the sixth and, he thought, final volume of the *Studies in the Psychology of Sex*. His subsequent sexual

77. *Man and Woman,* pp. viii–x, xiii, 65, 317–18, 404–24, 477–97, 511, 514, 522–24, 529; "The Mind of Woman," in *The Philosophy of Conflict,* p. 161; "The Mental Differences of Men and Women," in *Essays in War-Time* (Boston, 1917), p. 114.

78. *Psychology of Sex,* pp. 119, 121, 217; "The History of Marriage," pp. 499–500, 512–13; "The Renovation of the Family," in *More Essays of Love and Virtue* (New York, 1931), p. 47.

writings consisted of several articles on highly specialized subjects (published together in 1927 as Volume VII of the *Studies*),
numerous popular essays, and finally, in 1932, a one-volume
summary of the *Studies* entitled simply *Psychology of Sex*. For
the most part these post-1910 writings add little to our knowledge of Ellis's sexual opinions. Two subjects, however, do emerge
into greater prominence, one of personal importance for Ellis, the
other of considerable historical interest.

Arthur Calder-Marshall, whose treatment of Ellis's thought is
relentlessly *ad hominem,* argues that Ellis was drawn to the
study of human sexuality—and particularly sexual deviance—in
an effort to understand his own sexual difficulties. Apparently he
was impotent most of his life and a urolagnist as well.[79] Calder-
Marshall insinuates that Ellis's elaborate defense of the sexual
anomalies was a rationalization for his own perversion: he hoped
to apologize for himself by apologizing for all. I have chosen to
take Ellis seriously as a theorist—though I have stressed the
polemical nature of his theorizing—and I know of no way to
settle this question of where reasoned argument shades off into
self-justification. At the very least, however, one can note that in
later life Ellis no longer found it necessary to pursue the indirect
course he may have adopted up to 1910: the seventh volume of
the *Studies* contained a long essay entitled "Undinism," in which
he explored the intimate relation between urinary and sexual
psychology and sought to ground urolagnia in the primitive significance of water for human life—indeed, for all life.[80]

From a theoretical standpoint the most interesting feature of
Ellis's later work was the increased attention devoted to Freud.
Ellis claimed to have been the first to present Freud's ideas to the
English public.[81] But in the original six volumes of the *Studies,*
Freud figured only as one authority among many: his opinions
received no more pointed exposition than those of an Albert Moll
or an Iwan Bloch. By way of contrast, Ellis's later writings testify
eloquently to Freud's emergence as the most influential sexual
theorist of his time. Indeed, it is little exaggeration to state that

79. Calder-Marshall, *The Sage of Sex*, pp. 20–21, 39, 88, 249.

80. "Undinism," in *Eonism and Other Supplementary Studies*, pp. 379,
389–90.

81. "Freud's Influence on the Changed Attitude Toward Sex," *The
American Journal of Sociology*, 45, 3 (November 1939): 312.

those post-1910 writings represented a prolonged debate with the major contentions of psychoanalysis.

Ellis's attitude toward Freud was profoundly ambivalent. On the surface was a genuine—though often fulsome—expression of admiration, particularly for Freud's achievement as a sexual liberator. But these encomia did not succeed in disguising Ellis's deep-seated hostility. He showed uncharacteristic immodesty, for example, in emphasizing Freud's debt to his own *Studies,* from which, he insisted, Freud drew much of the inspiration for the epoch-making ideas set forth in *Three Essays on the Theory of Sexuality.* He was particularly sensitive about Freud's co-optation of the term "autoerotic," and he accused the psychoanalysts of distorting the concept to mean self-directed love (as opposed to self-induced, but essentially objectless, sexual excitement).[82] Underneath the specific disagreements one senses that Ellis resented Freud's rise to the position of modern sexual theorist *par excellence,* a preeminence he undoubtedly felt he had won for himself through the two decades of intellectual labor that went into the *Studies.*

Ellis never wrote a systematic critique of psychoanalytic theory. Instead, one finds throughout his later writings isolated objections and reservations that, taken together, add up to a refutation of Freud's entire project. Perhaps the most important area of disagreement was Freud's theory of infantile sexuality. Ellis, of course, did not deny that sexual life commenced long before puberty. Moreover, he was completely sympathetic with the essential theoretical presupposition of Freud's doctrine: the notion that each stage of psychosexual development represented simply a new organization of a single underlying human energy. Nonetheless, Ellis protested Freud's application of terms and concepts drawn from adult psychological experience to the sexual lives of children. Infantile sexuality remained for him essentially innocent. It was largely physiological in nature and could not bear the weighty psychological interpretation that Freud seemed determined to impose on it. Thus, for Ellis, it made no sense to speak of children as "polymorphous perverse," or to refer to manifestations of "homosexuality" in their behavior. As we know,

---

82. "Psycho-Analysis in Relation to Sex," pp. 200–01; "The Conception of Narcissism," in *Eonism and Other Supplementary Studies,* p. 363.

"perversion" was a term Ellis would gladly have abolished alto-gether, but if it had any legitimate meaning, it denoted a deeply ingrained adult sexual aberration, which bore little resemblance to the casual "perversities" of childhood. Even more objection-able in Ellis's mind was Freud's characterization of children as "incestuous." Indeed, he had no use whatsoever for the concep-tual centerpiece of Freudian theory, the Oedipus complex. Along with every common-sense critic of psychoanalysis, he maintained that the child's simple affection for his mother, and his natural resentment of those who would divert her attention from him, had been endowed with an unwarranted sexual connotation by Freud. In the same spirit of common sense Ellis rejected Freud's account of incest prohibitions in *Totem and Taboo*. The aversion to incest required no complicated explanation. It reflected the simple fact that familiarity always blunted sexual attraction.[83]

Ellis raised similar objections to such psychoanalytic doctrines as the death instinct, the theory of dream interpretation, and the oral-anal-phallic characterology.[84] Repeatedly he claimed that psychoanalysts preferred fanciful explanations where simple ones would do, and that they failed to support their contentions with evidence, particularly when it came to the sexual meanings they detected in various human actions. None of this, of course, was particularly trenchant or original. But these disagreements do illuminate the fundamental difference between Ellis's and Freud's intellectual styles.

In the end Ellis was too genuinely empirical, and too latitudi-narian in his intellectual sympathies, to appreciate Freud's ex-traordinary theoretical commitment. No doubt Freud's penchant for highly schematic psychological constructs and his distaste for pluralistic explanations help account for his greater influence. Ellis's theoretical aspirations were no less comprehensive, but the formulations he hit upon—such as the notions of tumescence and courtship—lacked the provocative outlines of Freud's central

83. *Sex in Relation to Society*, pp. 35–38. "Psycho-Analysis in Relation to Sex," pp. 202–03, 214, 219; *Psychology of Sex*, pp. 73, 76–77, 104–05, 116; "Eonism," in *Eonism and Other Supplementary Studies*, pp. 24–25; *Sexual Selection in Man*, pp. 205–06; "The History of Marriage," pp. 505–06.

84. *Psychology of Sex*, p. 153; "Undinism," pp. 431–32, 434–35, 455–57, 459; "The Synthesis of Dreams," in *Eonism and Other Supplementary Studies*, pp. 304–05.

doctrines. Nor did he possess the boldness (or, depending on your point of view, the intellectual rigidity) that allowed Freud to commit himself unequivocally to a single line of reasoning. Ultimately, then, Ellis's importance for modern sexual theory lies in the pervasive attitude of tolerance and enthusiasm with which he approached human sexuality. In effect, he established the atmosphere, though not the explicit theoretical context, in which later sexual thinkers were to pursue their tasks.

2 / Alfred Kinsey

Alfred Kinsey is rarely taken seriously as a thinker. In contrast to Havelock Ellis and Sigmund Freud, both of whom enjoy secure reputations as theorists, Kinsey is usually relegated to the category of enterprising empiricist. In the minds of most, I suspect, he belongs in the company of George Gallup: he was the scientist who found out what people actually do sexually. It is as if the modern sexual tradition had suffered a dramatic intellectual decline in crossing the Atlantic; as the mantle passed from Ellis and Freud to Kinsey and Masters and Johnson, sexual modernism was stripped of its theoretical pretensions.

Some critics, however, have noticed that there was more to Kinsey than raw empiricism. Lionel Trilling, for example, complained of *Sexual Behavior in the Human Male* that "it is full of assumption and conclusion; it makes very positive statements on highly debatable matters and it editorializes very freely."[1] He then proceeded to identify the book's presuppositions and to criticize them as materialistic. Kinsey, he suggested, was very much a theorist, indeed a disturbingly naïve and breezy arbiter of sexual propriety.

In at least one respect my own discussion of Kinsey resembles

1. Lionel Trilling, "The Kinsey Report," reprinted in *The Liberal Imagination* (New York, 1957), p. 218.

Trilling's: I, too, have been impressed by the systematic structure of assumption that underlies his examination of human sexuality. But my treatment differs in that it seeks to grant Kinsey's ideas a more sympathetic hearing. I don't find his materialism nearly so objectionable. In fact, I am inclined to admire his ability to put that materialism to critical use.

If Kinsey was not a simple empiricist, neither was he a truly original theoretician. Unlike Freud or Ellis, he does not command our attention because of the profundity or elegance of his thought. Rather, he is important because he has been influential, more influential probably than any other sexual thinker of the last thirty-five years. I have not, however, undertaken a study of Kinsey's influence (although I will return to that issue in the final section of the chapter) but an internal analysis of his sexual writings—of their presuppositions, tensions, biases, and implications. The justification for such an enterprise is not merely that Kinsey is sufficiently interesting to merit an examination of this sort, but that it will aid us in understanding his influence as well. His impact on modern sexual consciousness, I am persuaded, cannot be explained in terms of this or that empirical discovery. To a considerable extent, on the contrary, it reflects the structural characteristics of his thought with which this essay is largely concerned.

I

Kinsey was justifiably convinced that his sexual studies surpassed all early efforts primarily in the richness of their empirical base. It is, moreover, a tribute to his diligence that even today, nearly four decades after the project was launched, *Sexual Behavior in the Human Male* (1948) and *Sexual Behavior in the Human Female* (1953) remain the most reliable sources of information about American sexual behavior.[2] Alongside this achieve-

2. For instance, one of the most recent undergraduate texts on human sexuality, Herant A. Katchadourian and Donald T. Lunde's *Fundamentals of Human Sexuality* (New York, 1972), depends almost entirely for its generalizations about sexual behavior in this country on the two Kinsey volumes. Morton Hunt's *Sexual Behavior in the 1970's* (Chicago, 1974) is obviously more up-to-date, but it is much less thorough and in no sense replaces Kinsey.

ment the scientific procedures of Freud's and Ellis's sexual studies appear shabby indeed.

The centerpiece of Kinsey's research was the personal interview. The interview assumed for him the role that was assigned to written questionnaires in earlier sexual studies (such as those of Katherine B. Davis and Lewis M. Terman)[3] and that has been taken over by direct observation and experiment in the research of William Masters and Virginia Johnson. The interview was, in fact, Kinsey's most brilliant creation, an authentic tour de force in which every scrap of sexual information available to memory was wrenched from the subject in less than two hours.[4] Between 1938 and 1956 Kinsey and his three associates—Wardell Pomeroy, Clyde Martin, and Paul Gebhard—secured eighteen thousand such individual records. Kinsey personally conducted some eight thousand of the interviews.[5]

Kinsey's method of interviewing and his handling of the data compiled thereby were the subjects of considerable scholarly debate during his lifetime. Much of this literature was highly technical.[6] In essence, however, it focused on two issues: whether the information obtained in the interviews was accurate, and whether the sample interviewed was representative of the population as a whole. On both counts Kinsey defended himself vigorously and in the process revealed a number of his basic sexual assumptions.

Kinsey conceded that the accuracy of the interviews was threatened by two potential human failings: conscious deceit and the faultiness of recollection. Of these he considered the latter the more serious. He therefore developed several statistical procedures to test the reliability of his subjects' recall. For example, he conducted retakes on a limited number of histories, and he also compared selected pieces of information obtained from mar-

3. Katherine B. Davis, *Factors in the Sex Life of Twenty-two Hundred Women* (New York, 1929); Lewis M. Terman et al., *Psychological Factors in Marital Happiness* (New York, 1938).

4. *Sexual Behavior in the Human Male* (Philadelphia, 1948), p. 57.

5. Wardell B. Pomeroy, *Dr. Kinsey and the Institute for Sex Research* (New York, 1972), p. 4.

6. That debate is summarized in William G. Cochran, Frederick Mosteller, and John W. Tukey, *Statistical Problems of the Kinsey Report* (Washington, D.C., 1954).

ried couples. He was satisfied that these checks revealed a remarkable consistency—and therefore, presumably, accuracy—of
recollection. Memory, he was convinced, posed no significant
obstacle to the investigation of a subject's sexual past.[7]

In this conviction Kinsey stood at opposite poles from Freud,
who held that the most significant sexual experiences were often
inaccessible to memory because of repression. Behind these
different estimations of the power of memory lay a profound
disagreement about the nature of sexual experience itself. For
Freud sex was hedged about with danger, even with the possibility of psychic catastrophe. Kinsey, on the other hand, took an
entirely matter-of-fact view of human sexual experience. It might,
he allowed, be the source of considerable grief, but it utterly
lacked the demonic potential attributed it by Freud. Consequently he refused to entertain the notion that repression might
compromise the reliability of his data.

Kinsey recognized two possible forms of deceit in the interview: exaggeration and cover-up. He normally sought to minimize the importance of exaggeration and inflate that of cover-up.
Since he offered no justification for this preference, one is
tempted to see in it evidence of a desire to obtain higher incidence and frequency figures for all the forms of sexual activity he
investigated.[8] Partly because he enjoyed shocking his more puri-
tanical readers, and partly because he inclined to an ethic of
abundance in sexual matters, he suggested that many sexual
activities were even more common than his figures indicated. The
occurrence of cover-up in the interview, he maintained, accounted for this conservative bias in his findings.

Still, he hated to admit that even cover-up seriously tainted his
data. He had almost unlimited confidence in his ability to arrive
at the truth. Much like Freud, he believed that he had developed
a method of psychological investigation that broke through all
barriers of modesty and prejudice, even while it revealed the

7. *Male,* pp. 121–31; *Sexual Behavior in the Human Female* (Philadelphia, 1953), pp. 66–80.

8. Another manifestation of this desire was his insistence that no subject
be allowed to deny his involvement in a particular activity too easily: "We
always assume that everyone has engaged in every type of activity. Consequently we always begin by asking *when* they first engaged in such activity"
(*Male,* p. 53).

reality of those barriers. One of Kinsey's great discoveries, as we shall see, was that a person's sexual behavior was significantly influenced by his social class. It would seem to follow from this finding that a subject's willingness to admit to certain activities would reflect his class prejudices, and that cover-up, like performance itself, would be class-coded. Kinsey, however, refused to acknowledge such a possibility. He believed that all inhibitions must inevitably succumb to the nearly magical powers of his interrogation, just as Freud had maintained that unconscious resistances would ultimately collapse before the assault of the psychoanalyst.

Kinsey would have ridiculed the suggestion that mysterious forces were at work in the interview. It clearly never occurred to him that the relation between interviewer and subject might involve a peculiar chemistry, analogous to the transference that Freud detected between analyst and patient. For Kinsey the honesty of the subject's responses was guaranteed by the project's respect for certain obvious facts of human psychology. For one thing, the subject was given assurance of complete confidentiality. He was also never allowed to think that the interviewer in any way disapproved. Kinsey even affected a sympathetic interest in each subject's history, an interest that one is inclined to believe came quite naturally to him. Finally, he developed an ingenious coding system that enabled him to record the subject's responses without interrupting the flow of conversation, thus further contributing to the efficiency of the interview and to the subject's sense of well-being.

The assurance of confidentiality, the withholding of moral judgment, and the sympathetic manner of the interviewer may have served to allay the subject's most immediate anxieties, but they offered no positive inducement to full sexual candor. For Kinsey there was but one such inducement: he appealed to the commitment to scientific truth that he believed was shared by all modern men, even the most humbly educated. "Twelve thousand people," he wrote, "have helped in this research primarily because they have faith in scientific research projects."[9] The thought that more tortuous motives might have impelled his sub-

9. *Male*, p. 41. The figure twelve thousand represents the number of histories Kinsey had collected when the *Male* volume went to press in 1948.

jects' confessions did not seriously trouble him. "The psycho-analyst," he noted, "will incline to the view that most of those who have given histories have obtained some inflation of their egos by doing so."[10] Without further argument, however, Kinsey asserted that egoistic motives were outweighed by altruistic ones and in no significant way distorted his findings.

Sexual Behavior in the Human Male and *Sexual Behavior in the Human Female* give the impression of a powerful and sophisticated statistical technique. Yet Kinsey was curiously unsure of himself as a statistician.[11] In particular he was troubled by the charge that he had failed to secure a random sample of the American population in his interviews and that his findings therefore did not accurately reflect national patterns of sexual behavior.

This was an especially sensitive matter for Kinsey, since he had leveled a similar criticism at many of his predecessors. For example, he had taken both Freud and Ellis to task for the grossly unrandom character of the evidence on which they based their sexual doctrines. Freud he considered the greater offender in this respect, and he repeatedly stated that Freud's generalizations about sexual behavior, while sometimes correct, lacked any statistical foundation. Above all they were compromised by the selective factors that had induced Freud's patients to seek him out for psychiatric help. Thus Freud's pronouncements about the relation between sexual behavior and mental health were especially worthless.[12]

Ellis's sexual philosophy was more congenial to Kinsey's relentless hedonism than was Freud's, but Ellis was treated just as roughly for his statistical lapses. Much of Ellis's information, Kinsey noted, had been obtained through correspondence, either volunteered or solicited, and no effort had been made to test the representativeness of his informants—as Ellis himself readily admitted. Kinsey also faulted Ellis for not meeting his sources in person, a failing he attributed to Ellis's prudery.[13]

10. Ibid., p. 38.
11. See, for example, Cornelia V. Christenson, *Kinsey: A Biography* (Bloomington, 1971), pp. 103–04.
12. *Male,* p. 34; *Female,* p. 6.
13. *Male,* p. 619; Pomeroy, *Dr. Kinsey,* p. 69.

Kinsey had to temper his criticism by admitting that in sexual research a truly random sample was almost impossible to obtain. Such a sample would allow no volunteers and would rely instead on persuading randomly selected individuals to contribute a full account of their sexual experience. Kinsey's statistical critics urged him to undertake at least a small interviewing project along these lines in order to test the validity of his findings.[14] But he maintained that too much time would be required to persuade the more reluctant subjects to participate, and some of them, he believed, would resist all appeals, thereby undermining the logic of the entire enterprise. With regret and a certain intellectual discomfort he decided to stick to volunteers.

As a result, Kinsey's sample was overrepresented in some areas and underrepresented in others. It contained, for instance, too many Midwesterners, particularly Indianians, too many prison inmates, and too many homosexuals.[15] Above all, there was the suspicion that those who volunteered for the project were among the less inhibited members of society, and that the Reports thus registered an excessively licentious image of American sexual mores.

Kinsey was not without his statistical defenses. While acknowledging the liabilities of voluntary participation, he nevertheless argued that he had protected himself against unwanted selectivity. For one thing, he had classified his volunteers in terms of several nonsexual factors (such as age, social class, and religious persuasion), thus allowing him to identify any bias that might be introduced by the overparticipation of a particular segment of the population. Of course, he could control only so many factors, and an unidentified group with a distinctive sexual pattern still might be overrepresented in the interviews.

Kinsey's ultimate defense against undesired selectivity was his technique of hundred percent sampling. This entailed persuading all members of a given organization or group to volunteer their sexual histories. The groups themselves might be defined in any number of ways: a college fraternity, a social club, the residents of a particular apartment building, the students enrolled in a particular course—in short, any social unit not brought into exis-

14. Cochran, Mosteller, and Tukey, *Statistical Problems,* p. 23.
15. Pomeroy, *Dr. Kinsey,* pp. 138, 464.

tence by a common sexual interest. Since these groups were not based on sexual preferences Kinsey assumed that they would offer a faithful representation of the national sexual spectrum. This assumption ignored the possibility that the factors leading to the creation of such groups might have sexual correlates. Moreover, the groups from which Kinsey actually obtained hundred percent samples did not, by his own admission, constitute a cross section of the total population.[16] Nonetheless, I think one must agree that the hundred percent principle was an ingenious solution to the problem of selectivity in a voluntary sample.

Kinsey eventually obtained over a quarter of his histories from groups in which all members volunteered.[17] This was a remarkable achievement, often involving him in an exhausting courtship of the last reluctant members of the chosen organization. A comparison of the hundred percent samples with the rest of his histories revealed few significant differences,[18] and in this fashion Kinsey was able to use the hundred percent principle to establish the representativeness of his entire sample.

II

The Kinsey Reports were informed by a set of values and intellectual preferences that, taken together, could be said to constitute an ideology. In its essentials this ideology was not unique to Kinsey but the common property of the modern scientific establishment, as first enunciated in the tracts of the Enlightenment. Kinsey departed from his scientific predecessors only in the abandon with which he brought the values of science to bear on the delicate subject of sexuality.

The most visible trademark of the Kinsey style was an ostentatious avowal of both disinterestedness and incompetence wherever matters of ethics were at issue. "This is first of all a report on what people do," he wrote of the *Male* volume, "which raises no question of what they should do."[19] In reality, Kinsey held very strong opinions about what people should and should not do, and his efforts to disguise those opinions were only too trans-

16. *Female*, pp. 30–31.
17. Ibid., p. 30.
18. *Male*, pp. 93–102.
19. Ibid., p. 7.

parent. Thus throughout the Reports the reader was treated to an array of oblique moral posturings, ranging from indignation, as in his treatment of the repression of sexual minorities, to ironic condescension, an attitude he characteristically assumed when disabusing his audience about the supposed rarity of most illegal sexual practices.

The fundamental tenet of Kinsey's sexual ideology was tolerance. Repeatedly he stressed the need for "sympathetic acceptance of people as they are" and especially the need for recognizing the limits of man's ability to modify his sexual behavior.[20] To the scientist, he wrote, sex was "a normal biologic function, acceptable in whatever form it is manifested."[21] It seems not to have occurred to him that his insistence on tolerance was itself a moral judgment. "Moral" in his mind invariably implied condemnation.

The ethic of tolerance was based in part on Kinsey's discovery of the remarkable variety of human sexual experience. There were, he found, significant differences in the sexual behavior of various social classes, and yet greater differences in the sexual practices of separate cultures. Above all, there was the extraordinary extent of individual variation, including many different techniques of intercourse and an even wider variety of psychological attitudes associated with sexual acts. Kinsey was especially struck by the sheer quantitative range of individual sexual behavior. Some men, he noted, went for months without a single orgasm, while others climaxed daily. At the utmost extremes he uncovered two apparently healthy males, one of whom had ejaculated only once in thirty years, while the other had averaged more than thirty ejaculations a week over the same period of time. "This is the order of variation," he commented with evident irony, "which may occur between two individuals who live in the same town and who are neighbors, meeting in the same place of business, and coming together in common social activities."[22] Since the range of sexual behavior—and, presumably, desire—was so extreme, it followed that any attempt to establish uniform standards of sexual performance was both impracticable and unjust.

20. Ibid., p. 16; *Female*, p. 10.
21. *Male*, p. 263.
22. Ibid., p. 197.

The theme of individual variation was complemented by Kinsey's emphasis on what might be termed our common deviance: his revelation that many sexual practices generally considered rare were in fact quite prevalent. The classic example of such a secretly popular vice was homosexuality, which Kinsey demonstrated had been the source of at least one orgasm in the lives of 37 percent of the adult male population. Masturbation and premarital intercourse were also shown to be much more common than their official proscription would have led one to believe. The discovery of such widespread deviation from accepted sexual standards further confirmed Kinsey's commitment to sexual tolerance. It proved conclusively that any attempt to legislate sexual behavior was doomed to failure and that the only proper sexual policy was no policy at all.[23]

Kinsey's preoccupation with individual variation and common deviance found its intellectual basis in taxonomy, the science of classification. In fact, a concern with proper classification was his most fundamental intellectual drive and provided the link between his presexual and his sexual studies. The essential object of taxonomy, he believed, was to identify the significant subgroups of a particular population. Put another way, it sought to designate the important areas of congruence in a series of discrete individuals.

Before he turned to the examination of human sexuality Kinsey devoted twenty years of his life to a taxonomic study of the gall wasp, a tiny insect named for the fact that its eggs produce an abnormal growth, or gall, on plants. This research involved an analysis of the physical and behavioral characteristics of the wasps in order to distinguish authentic variations from hap-

---

23. Kinsey made the predictable exception of legislation outlawing sexual violence: "Society may properly be concerned with the behavior of its individual members when that behavior affects the persons or property of other members of the social organization, or the security of the whole group. For these reasons, practically all societies everywhere in the world attempt to control sexual relations which are secured through the use of force or undue intimidation, sexual relations which lead to unwanted pregnancies, and sexual activities which may disrupt or prevent marriages or otherwise threaten the existence of the social organization itself" (*Female*, p. 476). Of the three mentioned here, Kinsey approved fully of only the first category of prohibitions. His position was in effect identical to that of John Stuart Mill in *On Liberty*.

hazard sports. Kinsey identified several new varieties of the insect, and he also determined their frequency in the population and their position in the phylogenetic chain. At the same time, he undertook a critical examination of the received classification of gall wasp species. Significantly, he concluded that the system of classification was entirely arbitrary, the product of faulty taxonomic technique.[24]

Proper classification, Kinsey argued, depended on honoring two principles. First, one had to collect an adequate number of individual cases: "The taxonomist undertakes population sampling on such a scale as may involve hundreds of individuals from each locality, and tens of thousands of individuals from the species as a whole."[25] In the case of the gall wasp an adequate sample turned out to be four million insects, which Kinsey gathered over the years on field trips throughout the United States and Mexico.[26]

The second principle of modern taxonomy was that the sample be correctly distributed. Individuals were to be collected "in a fashion which includes material from every type of habitat and from the whole range of the species."[27] Unfortunately, this requirement introduced intellectual difficulties not present in the simple insistence on large numbers. In particular it raised the question of how one knew whether the whole range of the species was represented unless one had already determined the significant subcategories of the population under investigation. And since the very purpose of modern taxonomy was to arrive at an unbiased definition of such subcategories, the judgment that one's sample was properly distributed involved a circular and self-defeating inference.

Kinsey nowhere acknowledged this methodological difficulty. In the case of the gall wasp he apparently believed that the issue of proper distribution resolved itself into securing an adequate geographic spread in the sample. If one had insects "from every

24. The results of Kinsey's research were published in two large volumes, *The Gall Wasp Genus Cynips: A Study in the Origin of Species* (Bloomington, 1930) and *The Origin of Higher Categories in Cynips* (Bloomington, 1936). See Christenson, *Kinsey,* pp. 32–33, 38–39, 59–62, 70–87.

25. *Male,* p. 17.

26. Pomeroy, *Dr. Kinsey,* p. 16.

27. *Male,* p. 17.

type of habitat," then one could safely assume that all variations were represented. However, when he turned to the more complex subject of human sexuality, where it was no longer possible to rely on a simple environmental determinism, the philosophical difficulties inherent in his conception of distribution became much more vexed.

Kinsey recognized that if his study of human sexuality was to respect the principle of distribution, it too would have to be based on specimens drawn "from the whole range of the species." Only then could he generalize confidently about "sexual behavior in the human male" or "sexual behavior in the human female." In reality he limited his research to Americans and Canadians, and he also excluded black histories from his tabulations. Thus by his own admission his generalizations extended only to the white population of North America, despite the inclusiveness of his titles.[28]

Within the white American population Kinsey felt the principle of distribution would be satisfactorily honored if his sample included "persons of both sexes, of all ages, and from all sorts of socio-economic, educational and religious backgrounds."[29] In other words, just as an adequate geographic spread promised a full representation of the various species of gall wasp, so control over the factors of sex (that is, gender), age, social class, and religion guaranteed a complete representation of sexual styles. In the end Kinsey controlled for several other factors as well, including age at the onset of adolescence, marital status, decade of birth, and geographic origin. Nowhere, however, did he justify the choice of these factors to the exclusion of others, and nowhere did he prove that by controlling these particular matters he was assured of a properly distributed sample.

Consequently, it is quite easy to come up with a variety of factors whose neglect by Kinsey seems to violate his own principle of distribution. For example, he failed to control his sample on the basis of intelligence. He thereby assumed, without evidence, that dim-wittedness or brilliance has little bearing on sexual behavior—just as earlier sexual researchers had assumed that social class was irrelevant to sexual behavior. He also

28. Ibid., p. 76; *Female*, p. 4.
29. *Male*, p. 18.

neglected to control his sample in terms of personality character-istics.[30] Perhaps most important of all, he made no effort to classify his subjects according to their family experiences. He thus ignored such matters as whether a subject was the youngest or the oldest child, whether the subject's parents were living together or divorced, or whether his relationship with his parents had been gratifying or frustrating. In short, he ignored all those factors that would have interested a psychoanalyst and that may well have exercised a more profound influence on sexual behavior than any of the factors he did in fact consider.

The issue here is not that Kinsey ignored these matters in particular—although I think them significant—but rather that he never faced the philosophical problem inherent in his notion of distribution. Apparently he did not realize that any system of classification is in some degree arbitrary, resting on certain assumptions about what is important and what is not. His error lay not in choosing to examine the particular issues he did but in failing to recognize that he had in fact made a choice. One can't help feeling that some familiarity with the methodological litera-ture of modern sociology, and above all the writings of Max Weber, would have aided him in avoiding the hazards of his taxonomic approach.

In Kinsey's hands, however, taxonomy was intended more as a critical than a constructive tool. That is, he was more interested in undermining established categories of sexual wisdom than in creating new ones. Foremost among the objects of his criticism was the distinction between normal and abnormal sexuality. Here Kinsey completed the revolution launched by Havelock Ellis. He established beyond all doubt that sexual differences were matters of degree rather than kind. Almost any sexual style, he showed, could be placed alongside another that differed from it but slightly. In this manner all forms of sexual behavior, from celi-bacy to promiscuity, or from extreme homosexuality to extreme heterosexuality, could be charted along a single curve. "The most significant thing about this curve," he wrote, "is its continuity. It is not symmetrical, with a particular portion of the population set

---

30. At one point in the *Male* volume Kinsey mentioned that psychological tests were available for several thousand of his subjects. But he complained that the materials were too heterogeneous for statistical use (*Male,* p. 81).

off as 'normal,' 'modal,' 'typical,' or discretely different."[31] Abnormality thus became a taxonomically meaningless notion.

Kinsey recognized a legitimate medical use of the term abnormal to denote any condition that interfered with physical well-being, and he granted that by extension the term might be applied to activities that caused psychological or social maladjustment as well. But he flatly denied that sexual indulgence led to disturbances of this sort: "It is not possible to insist that any departure from the sexual mores, or any participation in socially taboo activities, always, or even usually, involves a neurosis or psychosis, for the case histories abundantly demonstrate that most individuals who engage in taboo activities make satisfactory social adjustments."[32] The occasional failure to make such adjustments reflected the psychic burden of hostile public opinion rather than anything intrinsically pathogenic about the sexual deviation itself. In this instance Kinsey was generalizing beyond the limits of his data, since he had made no systematic measurement of the social or psychological adjustment of his subjects. Nonetheless, his informal observations had convinced him that the distinction between healthy and neurotic sexuality was no more viable than that between normal and abnormal sexuality.

Lionel Trilling complained that Kinsey banished the concepts of normal and abnormal only to replace them with natural and unnatural.[33] The observation is somewhat misleading. It implies that Kinsey had committed the same taxonomic error he criticized in his predecessors, but with the evaluations now rearranged to conform with his own permissive philosophy. In fact, however, Kinsey used natural and unnatural in a very precise manner, and without statistical intent. Natural designated for him continuity between human behavior and that of the lower species, while unnatural implied the absence of such continuity.[34] The distinction was not, to be sure, a disinterested one. He believed that human fulfillment, in the sexual realm at least, lay in following the example of our mammalian forebears. But it is nonetheless incorrect to suggest that his use of natural was as arbitrary as earlier theorists' use of normal.

31. Ibid., p. 199.
32. Ibid., pp. 201–02.
33. Trilling, "The Kinsey Report," p. 227.
34. See, for example, *Male*, pp. 369, 373.

Kinsey's naturalism ran deep, and it was responsible for a good deal that humanists found objectionable in the Reports. Nothing was more characteristic of Kinsey than his reliance on the argument *de animalibus*. He evaluated every form of sexual activity in terms of its role in the sexual lives of the lower species, and he frequently concluded that outlawed sexual practices were entirely natural because they conformed to "basic mammalian patterns."[35] His naturalism received its most forcible expression in those chapters of the Reports treating sexual contacts between human beings and animals of other species, or interspecific contacts, as he preferred to call them. Not only did he maintain his usual aesthetic neutrality when discussing such relations, but he even sought to invest them with a certain dignity by suggesting that they could achieve a psychological intensity comparable to that in exclusively human sexual relations. Thus he found it entirely credible that a man might fall passionately in love with his dog, and that the affection could be returned in kind: "The elements that are involved in sexual contacts between the human and animals of other species are at no point basically different from those that are involved in erotic responses to human situations."[36] In effect, Kinsey refused to grant the human realm a unique place in the larger order of things. Indeed, it was precisely the pretension to such specialness, he believed, that accounted for most of our sexual miseries.

Because of Kinsey's uncompromising naturalism it has often been assumed that he was a materialist as well. Although the label is inappropriate in any rigorous philosophical sense, it is true that he was interested primarily in the physical aspects of sexuality. He paid scant attention to the emotional lives of his subjects. Of all the factors he controlled in gathering his histories only one—the degree of religiosity—was explicitly psychological. And even religiosity received a behavioral definition: it was measured in terms of how regularly the subject attended church.[37] In general, Kinsey placed little confidence in his subjects' statements about their sexual emotions. Such verbalizations, he felt,

35. Ibid., p. 59.
36. Ibid., pp. 676–77.
37. Ibid., pp. 79–81.

usually reflected the prevailing sexual orthodoxy and were a less reliable guide to a person's true feelings than were his actions.[38]

The most striking example of Kinsey's materialism—or, more precisely, of his behaviorism—was his decision to evaluate sexual experience strictly in terms of orgasms, and orgasms themselves strictly in terms of numbers. This meant he took no statistical note of how orgasms differed from one another in intensity or in the emotional values associated with them. It also meant that he ignored, at least in statistical terms, those sexual activities that did not culminate in orgasm. Kinsey defended this decision on purely pragmatic grounds. He argued not that orgasm was a completely adequate measure of sexual experience, but rather that it was the only measure distinct enough to allow of statistical treatment. In other words, the orgasmic standard was to a large extent a mathematical convenience.[39]

Even if he had been able to measure the psychological aspects of sexual experience precisely, I believe that Kinsey would have continued to count orgasms. He recognized that sex involved a larger emotional investment than any other physiological activity.[40] But he distrusted those who imputed that the physical reality of sex was somehow trivial when compared to its psychology. "Such thinking," he wrote, "easily becomes mystical, and quickly identifies any consideration of anatomic form and physiologic function as a scientific materialism which misses the 'basic,' the 'human,' and the 'real' problems of behavior."[41] The accusation of materialism he considered merely a front for the repressive values of his critics; it disguised their fear of sexuality in the high-minded language of humanistic philosophy. Moreover, he clearly believed that his critics' humanism was in fact inhumane. All their talk about the moral and psychological complexity of sex, while valid to a degree, served to rationalize enormous human suffering by lending intellectual respectability to the traditional Judeo-Christian prohibitions. For his own part, Kinsey was

38. Ibid., pp. 57–58.
39. Ibid., pp. 159–60, 193; *Female*, pp. 45–46, 510.
40. See *Male*, pp. 4, 42. Curiously, Kinsey never asked why sex should be so emotionally loaded. By way of contrast almost all of Freud's cultural writings were addressed precisely to solving this mystery.
41. *Female*, pp. 642–43.

happy to argue the cause of the flesh, and his materialism must be regarded not as a reflection of moral or intellectual insensitivity, but as a consciously adopted polemical stance.

III

Sexual Behavior in the Human Male rested on two basic concepts: outlet and factor. Outlet designated any activity that resulted in orgasm, while factor referred to any nonsexual circumstance that might affect the choice or frequency of outlet. Naturally these concepts also figured in the argument of *Sexual Behavior in the Human Female*, but only in the *Male* volume did they provide the center of dramatic interest.

The notion of outlet, for all its apparent innocence, performed important critical services for Kinsey. Principal among these was the demotion of heterosexual intercourse to merely one among a democratic roster of six possible forms of sexual release (the six, in order of their treatment in the *Male* volume, were masturbation, nocturnal emissions, heterosexual petting, heterosexual intercourse, homosexual relations, and intercourse with animals of other species).[42] What for centuries had been honored simply as "the sexual act" here found itself tucked away unceremoniously in slot number four, and its socially acceptable form, marital intercourse, was even more rudely confined to a single chapter toward the back of the book, where it received about one-third the attention devoted to homosexual relations. The notion of outlet thus allowed Kinsey to bring off a remarkable feat of sex-

---

42. *Male*, pp. 157, 193. The roster was as interesting for what it left out as for what it included. Among the missing were most of those forms of sexual activity that Richard von Krafft-Ebing had subsumed under the rubric "psychopathia sexualis." Their absence, moreover, was no mere oversight. Kinsey explicitly asserted that such sexual practices as transvestism, necrophilia, fetishism, and sado-masochism figured in but a statistically insignificant number of cases. In fact, the sole survivors of the psychopathia sexualis tradition in the Reports were homosexuality and animal contacts. The Reports also devoted remarkably little attention to venereal disease. Its neglect was a measure of Kinsey's break with the assumption that the only justification for studying sexuality was to do battle with the scourges of syphilis and gonorrhea. He utterly disdained such hygienic excuses (*Female*, pp. 88, 327, 502, 646).

ual leveling, and although he was elsewhere to reveal a lingering loyalty to the regime of marital heterosexuality, the fundamental categories of his analysis clearly worked to undermine the traditional sexual order.

Kinsey called the sum of the orgasms obtained from all sources "total sexual outlet." This concept, too, may have been inspired by a desire to put heterosexual intercourse in its place. It strongly implied that all orgasms were equal, regardless of how one came by them, and that there were accordingly no grounds for placing heterosexual intercourse in a privileged position. Thus in defending the notion of total outlet in the *Female* volume, he wrote that "there is a reality involved in any such summation of orgasms, for all orgasms appear to be physiologically similar quantities, whether they are derived from masturbatory, heterosexual, homosexual, or other sorts of activity. For most females and males, there appear to be basic physiologic needs which are satisfied by sexual orgasm, whatever the source."[43]

The notion of total outlet seemed to commit Kinsey to an essentially economic conception of sexual life. That is, it suggested that sexuality functioned according to the model of a closed energy system, such as had informed Freud's libido theory, Ellis's doctrine of tumescence, and the Victorians' notion of a spermatic economy. Each individual apparently came into the world with a fixed number of potential orgasms at his disposal, and he had merely to decide how to distribute those orgasms among the six possible forms of outlet. This, at least, was the sense implicit in Kinsey's surmise, in the *Female* volume, that the sum of an individual's orgasms constituted "a significant entity" in his life.

It would be a mistake, however, to put too much emphasis on the remnants of the economic metaphor in Kinsey's thought. He sometimes wrote as though he had such an economy in mind—suggesting that orgasms invested in one form of outlet were withheld from others—but much more often he took explicit issue with this conception of sexual functioning. Indeed, despite the hydraulic assumption implicit in his notion of total outlet, Kinsey must be considered among the severest critics of the economic metaphor that had dominated the sexual thought not only

43. *Female,* p. 511.

of the Victorians but of the first generation of modernists as well.

Kinsey's critique of the economic metaphor took several forms. Its most obvious manifestation can be seen in his analysis of nocturnal emissions (or nocturnal sex dreams, as he termed the comparable phenomenon in women). The traditional wisdom concerning this form of sexual outlet, as Kinsey noted, rested entirely on the hydraulic conception of sexual life. It assumed that nocturnal emissions occurred when other forms of sexual outlet, for whatever reason, were unavailable. Nocturnal emissions were thus thought to serve as a kind of safety valve for the release of accumulated sexual energy.[44]

Kinsey, however, found that the implied inverse relation between nocturnal emissions and other forms of outlets was entirely imaginary. Persons deprived of masturbation or intercourse did not in fact make up for it in wet dreams. On the contrary, in many instances the frequency of nocturnal emissions correlated positively with that of other outlets: less intercourse or less masturbation resulted in fewer not in more nocturnal emissions. Findings such as this left the compensatory theory of nocturnal emissions, and with it the economic metaphor, in considerable disarray.[45]

Kinsey took the hydraulic conception to task once again in his analysis of the effects of early adolescence on sexual behavior. At issue here was the assumption that if sexual life commenced early it must also end early, since the orgasms of youth were presumably subtracted from those of maturity. Victorian sexual theorists had depended heavily on this hypothesis in their campaign against masturbation. By means of it they sought to persuade adolescents that the price of self-abuse, in many instances, was impotence in later life.[46]

Kinsey dismissed this variation of the economic argument outright. Against the predictions of the theory, all his evidence pointed to a positive correlation between adolescent and adult sexual athleticism. The earlier one matured, and the more one indulged one's passions in adolescence, the richer one's adult experience. Unhappily for the cause of chastity, lusty boys did

44. Ibid., p. 207.
45. *Male*, pp. 476, 511–13, 527–30; *Female*, pp. 194–95, 208–10.
46. Alex Comfort, *The Anxiety Makers* (New York, 1970), pp. 69–113.

not turn into impotent men. On the contrary, they made the most demanding of lovers.[47]

In its modernist guise, such as it appears in the writings of Freud and Ellis, the economic hypothesis suggested not merely that the different forms of sexual release were related to one another on a zero-sum principle, but that sexual life as a whole bore an essentially economic relation to many nonsexual aspects of experience. Freud and Ellis maintained that cultural enterprises were supported by energies originating in the sexual realm, and that those enterprises were undertaken only at the expense of direct sexual expression. In short, the economic hypothesis emerged among early-twentieth-century theorists as the doctrine of sublimation.

Kinsey was as hostile to the idea of sublimation as he was to the cruder variants of the economic hypothesis. It too, he believed, had been inspired by repressive motives, and he took caustic note of "the speed with which moral leaders of all denominations have adopted the term to cover everything that Freud originally intended, and abstinence, self-control, stern suppression, and the rest of the ascetic virtues as well."[48] At the same time, he found it somehow fitting that the notion of sublimation should have lent itself so readily to moralistic exploitation, since the original conception, he was persuaded, amounted to little more than a pseudoscientific repackaging of ancient religious prejudice.

As Kinsey was well aware, sublimation is an extremely elusive notion. Since it is basically a relative phenomenon, its existence in any given instance cannot be established without knowing the full sexual capacity of the individual in question. The fact that a productive artist copulates at an impressive rate does not rule out the possibility of his sublimating, since he might copulate even more vigorously if only he would abandon his art.

Acknowledging the difficulty of testing the concept empirically, Kinsey nonetheless argued that the most likely examples of sublimation would be found among individuals with extremely low rates of outlet. Accordingly, he proceeded to analyze the histories of 179 young men who had experienced orgasm no more often than once a fortnight over a five-year period, with a view to

47. *Male,* pp. 297, 307, 319–23.
48. Ibid., p. 206.

determining whether they might have channeled their sexual energy into "higher" activities. No evidence, however, suggested that they had. Their low rates of outlet appeared to result not from sublimation but from physical incapacity, or sexual apathy, or in some instances pure timidity. "There are simply no cases which remain as clear-cut examples of sublimation," he concluded, and he happily dismissed the concept as yet another scientifically meaningless creation of Judeo-Christian moralism. Like the compensatory theory of nocturnal emissions and the economic equation of adolescent abstinence with adult potency, it served merely to rationalize sexual repression.[49]

IV

Kinsey's argument in the *Male* volume was organized in terms of a complex promotion and demotion of the different factors and outlets, in which he repeatedly took issue with the prevailing wisdom concerning their relative significance. In general, he was anxious to augment the importance of those forms of outlet proscribed by the official morality and to belittle those that were officially tolerated. Similarly, he sought to demonstrate that the factors usually believed to have the greatest impact on sexual life were in fact relatively insignificant, while others, some without any apparent sexual significance at all, figured prominently in determining the contours of erotic experience.

Of the six forms of outlet, two can be said to have suffered a substantial demotion, either in significance or in value, at Kinsey's hands: animal contacts and nocturnal emissions. I have already indicated that Kinsey treated interspecific sexual relations sympathetically, but he also emphasized that they were the least important source of outlet for American males, increasingly so as society became more urbanized. Rather surprisingly, he found that nocturnal emissions were nearly as insignificant as animal contacts. At the same time, Kinsey's treatment of nocturnal emissions revealed an animus entirely absent from his discussion of interspecific relations, an animus inspired no doubt by the fact that nocturnal emissions had provided traditional sexual morality

49. Ibid., pp. 207–13.

with an excuse for repressing most other forms of sexual expression. Hence his judgment, for which he offered no statistical support, that "emissions are most often depended upon by the male who has not made what the psychiatrists would call a good socio-sexual adjustment."[50]

Inhabiting a more ambiguous position in the roster of outlets was heterosexual petting. As a source of actual outlet—that is, of orgasm—petting appeared even less important than nocturnal emissions. But Kinsey recognized that it was, nonetheless, one of the most prominent features of American sexual life, and thus despite its failure to register in his statistical calculations, he devoted considerable attention to it. Moreover, no feature of the Kinsey Reports is more responsible for their piquant historical flavor than this emphasis on petting, a word that has virtually disappeared from our sexual vocabulary. Indeed, one cannot read Kinsey's discussion of petting without being immediately transported into the distinctive sexual ambience of the 1940s and 1950s, with its uniquely frustrating synthesis of permissivism and restraint, of which petting was the characteristic expression.

Kinsey's feelings about petting were divided. On the one hand, he granted it an important educational function. In fact, he documented a positive correlation between petting and the effectiveness of sexual relations in marriage. He noted in particular that women with little experience in premarital petting were more likely to become frigid wives. The distinctive virtue of petting was that it provided a very gradual introduction into the mysteries of sexual response, whereas after marriage the initiation was bound to be more precipitous and therefore potentially more traumatic.[51]

On the other hand, Kinsey also believed that the reliance on petting as a sexual outlet involved making the best of a fundamentally bad situation. It was the peculiar form of sexual exercise that the young had been forced to devise because sexual intercourse was prohibited them. Furthermore, its psychological effects were often most unfortunate. "The evidence is now clear," he wrote, "that such arousal as petting provides may seriously

50. Ibid., p. 525.
51. Ibid., pp. 543–46; *Female*, pp. 265–66.

disturb some individuals, leaving them in a more or less extended nervous state unless the activity has proceeded to orgasm."[52] Petting was also associated in Kinsey's mind with the excessively self-conscious and unmanly emphasis on foreplay that, as we shall see, he deplored in the sexual lives of the middle and upper classes. Thus, like nocturnal emissions—the other sexual outlet that official morality tolerated in place of intercourse—petting was the frequent object of his scorn.

Of all the forms of outlet, heterosexual intercourse elicited Kinsey's most ambivalent evaluation. "Heterosexual coitus," he noted with delicious but probably unconscious irony, "is, in many ways, the most important aspect of human sexual behavior."[53] Significantly, intercourse always remained, without his being fully aware of it, the standard by which he judged most other forms of sexual expression, as is evident from his treatment of petting. At the same time, heterosexual intercourse suffered a relative eclipse simply because of the prominence Kinsey assigned to masturbation and homosexuality, both of which were objects of his partiality.

Kinsey must unquestionably be counted among the foremost modern defenders of autoerotism. Not only did he reveal its near universality among American males, but he also disputed, with even fewer qualifications than had Havelock Ellis, any suggestion that the practice might be harmful. "On the basis of our previous review of more than five thousand cases of males who had masturbated," he wrote in the *Female* volume, "and on the basis of the data now available on nearly twenty-eight hundred cases of females with masturbatory experience, we may assert that we have recognized exceedingly few cases, if indeed there have been any outside of a few psychotics, in which either physical or mental damage had resulted from masturbatory activity."[54] Masturbation was harmless, moreover, no matter how often one indulged in it; "excessive" masturbation simply didn't exist. Indeed, masturbation became pathogenic only when repressed, and Kinsey claimed to have observed tremendous psychic damage in those who had fretted over their masturbation or attempted

52. *Male*, pp. 541–42; *Female*, pp. 263–64.
53. *Male*, p. 479.
54. *Female*, p. 167.

vainly to give it up.[55] As with most of his statements about the relation between sexual activity and personal well-being, this claim was largely impressionistic. He had undertaken neither a systematic survey of his subjects' health nor any controlled experiments that might have established the etiological significance of masturbation. Yet his commitment to autoerotism was such that he spoke as though his generalizations were supported by unimpeachable statistical evidence.

Kinsey took particular issue with the aspersions cast on masturbation by the Freudians, who, while granting that the practice was physically innocuous, insisted that it was regrettable from a psychological point of view. To be precise, the Freudians had suggested that masturbation in adulthood indicated psychic immaturity and a narcissistic fixation of the libido. Kinsey denied both allegations. There were many individuals, he insisted, for whom masturbation was an essentially interpersonal experience, since it was accompanied by heterosexual or homosexual fantasies, and there were likewise many adults who masturbated and yet were not immature "in any realistic sense." Freud's error was in regarding masturbation merely as a substitute for sexual intercourse. Statistical evidence indicated that it functioned as such in the lives of some males (its frequency declined as males grew older and, presumably, had access to other means of sexual release), but other males continued to masturbate simply for the sake of variety or because of "the particular sort of pleasure involved." In the end Kinsey attributed Freud's aversion to masturbation to the persistence of "Talmudic traditions" in his thinking, and he spoke proudly of the greater tolerance for masturbation shown by the American psychiatric community.[56]

Kinsey completed his defense by arguing that masturbation actually helped the individual achieve a satisfactory sexual adjustment in marriage. This was particularly true, he argued, in the case of women. The girl who did not masturbate was at a serious sexual disadvantage. She became accustomed to tensing her muscles and withdrawing from physical contact, and such habits were not easily unlearned after marriage.[57] Kinsey thus

55. *Male*, pp. 503–06, 513–14; *Female*, pp. 167–70.
56. *Male*, pp. 239, 511, 515; *Female*, pp. 170–71.
57. *Female*, p .172.

exactly reversed Havelock Ellis's judgment that masturbation might adversely affect one's ability to establish successful sexual relationships. On the contrary, it was the first and, in some respects, most important vehicle of sexual adjustment.[58]

V

Kinsey accorded homosexuality a no less enthusiastic and considerably longer treatment in the *Male* volume than he had masturbation. At the same time, his analysis of homosexuality revealed a characteristic intellectual weakness, which for want of a better label might be called his nominalism. The exposition of the taxonomic method at the beginning of the *Male* volume had suggested a certain insensitivity to the difficulty of establishing viable analytic categories. In his examination of homosexuality that insensitivity became glaringly apparent.

One of the most widely publicized findings of the *Male* volume was that 37 percent of the male population in America had had at least one homosexual experience to orgasm sometime between adolescence and old age. "This," editorialized Kinsey in characteristic fashion, "is more than one male in three of the persons that one may meet as he passes along a city street."[59] A number of practical considerations followed from this revelation, the most important being that law enforcement officials should bear in mind, when dealing with a male arrested for homosexual activity, that over a third of all males in the society could be brought to trial for similar offenses. Thus there can be no doubting Kinsey's intention in the *Male* volume of dramatically promoting the significance of homosexuality in the total sexual experience of American men, even though he was at pains to refute the contention of certain Freudians that *all* persons must have experienced homosexual feelings on some occasion in their lives.[60]

58. I came across only one passage in Kinsey that revealed any doubts about the benefits of masturbation. The passage in question noted that the relation between masturbation and "socio-sexual adjustments" had yet to be determined (although elsewhere, as I have mentioned, he wrote as if this question had been definitively resolved), and he conceded that a heavy reliance on masturbation might be considered "an escape from reality" (*Male*, pp. 515–16).

59. Ibid., p. 623; also pp. 261, 610, 650.

60. Ibid., pp. 622, 627, 664.

Ironically, in view of the importance Kinsey attributed to homosexual outlet, the principal theoretical contention he wished to make about homosexuality was that, properly speaking, it did not exist. That is, he argued that homosexuality was neither a clinical syndrome nor a sexual identity. There were no homosexual persons, but only homosexual acts. Thus the word "homosexual," he insisted, was properly used only as an adjective, not as a noun.[61]

Kinsey adopted this position in order to dispute the popular belief that anybody involved in a homosexual act must in fact be a homosexual. At the same time, he wished to disabuse certain persons of the notion that their behavior in this or that instance was not homosexual because they had entered upon it with psychological reservations. An example of such self-delusion would be the male who, while allowing others to fellate him, never performed the act himself and thus pretended to have kept his heterosexual credentials intact. For Kinsey any sexual act involving persons of the same sex was homosexual, regardless of what those persons might be doing or thinking. Conversely, he insisted that it was incorrect to consider acts such as fellatio and cunnilingus inherently homosexual; when practiced by persons of the same sex they were homosexual, when practiced by persons of the opposite sex they were heterosexual.[62]

The common element in these criticisms of prevailing opinion concerning homosexuality was Kinsey's aversion to the notion of sexual identity, the notion, as he expressed it, "that homosexual males and females are discretely different from persons who merely have homosexual experience, or who react sometimes to homosexual stimuli."[63] A person, for Kinsey, was what he did, and nothing more. In sexual terms, he was the sum total of his sexual acts. If all those acts, including mental acts, happened to involve members of the opposite sex—as was the case, Kinsey believed, for about half of the male population—then the person

61. Ibid., pp. 617, 657. Throughout both the *Male* and *Female* volumes Kinsey followed the awkward practice of referring to manifestations of homosexuality as "the homosexual," indicating that, for all his theoretical objections, he found it syntactically impossible to do without some sort of substantive.

62. *Male*, pp. 193–94, 615–17.

63. Ibid., p. 616.

might legitimately be called heterosexual, although Kinsey was inclined to think that even many of these individuals had at least a capacity for homosexual response. Since, however, only a tiny minority of the male population was exclusively homosexual, the substantive "homosexual" was of little value and might well be dispensed with.

In rejecting the notion of homosexual identity Kinsey simply made explicit the assumptions underlying Havelock Ellis's hypothesis of a sexual continuum: if in sexual matters there were no differences of kind but only of degree, then categories such as homosexuality and heterosexuality were obviously meaningless, except perhaps as ideal types.[64] Thus without, I'm sure, his being aware of it, Kinsey came to conclusions that recall the radical empiricism of David Hume. Just as Hume had dissolved the self into a series of discrete moments of consciousness, Kinsey dissolved sexual identity into a series of discrete orgasms. Both thinkers stood poles apart from an essentialist psychologist such as Freud, who insisted that one might very well "be" something quite other than what one did—in this instance, that one might be a homosexual without ever having committed a homosexual act or even entertained a homosexual thought.

Occasionally Kinsey seemed to acknowledge the difficulties inherent in his extreme nominalist position. He was troubled, for example, by the case of a man who reported "an extensive homosexual history," but whose dreams remained entirely heterosexual. Since, as Kinsey recognized, such a person would have little reason to misrepresent the content of his dreams, one might reasonably suspect that he was not in fact homosexual. Anomalies of this sort, however, did not lead Kinsey to concede that the self might be more than the sum of its experiences. He continued to insist that a just estimate of a man's sexuality could be arrived at by counting sexual acts, both physical and mental, without attempting to distinguish the significant from the trivial, the substantial from the accidental.[65]

64. Ibid., pp. 647, 650; Female, pp. 469, 469n.
65. Male, pp. 526–27. Kinsey's hostility to the notion of sexual identity, and his insistence on a strictly behavioral definition of homosexuality, may have reflected anxiety about his own sexuality. In the 1930s he had become deeply attached to a student named Ralph Voris, who died of pneumonia two years after the sexual project was launched. Pomeroy writes that "Voris

Kinsey's principal motive in undermining the notion of sexual identity seems to have been a desire to combat the popular stereotype of the homosexual personality. If there was no such thing as a homosexual, it clearly made no sense to speak of that nonexistent entity as effeminate, temperamental, or artistically gifted. No effort was made, in either the *Male* or *Female* volume, to test whether there might be a correlation between such character traits and the inclination to perform homosexual acts. But Kinsey made it quite evident that he doubted any correlation existed. Apparently it was enough for him that such traits could not be attributed to the 37 percent of the male population that had enjoyed one homosexual experience to orgasm, and still less to the 50 percent that had responded at some point to homosexual stimuli.[66]

Despite his criticism of the notion of homosexual personality, Kinsey was surprisingly tolerant of the belief that individuals involved in homosexual behavior exhibited distinct sexual proclivities. In this respect he was a good deal less progressive than Havelock Ellis. Thus he argued that homosexual relations were characterized by promiscuity and instability, and that "homosexually experienced males" were unusually finicky in their sexual preferences. He was forced to these conclusions, probably against his will, in order to explain a particular statistical anomaly: namely that while the incidence of homosexuality was remark-

---

became the closest friend Kinsey ever had; their relationship probably meant more to him than any other" (*Dr. Kinsey*, p. 46). If the relationship had a sexual content, it was apparently a highly sublimated one and as such would have failed to meet Kinsey's behavioral criteria for a homosexual experience. Hence those criteria may have served to protect Kinsey's own sense of heterosexual identity. I have speculated in greater detail about Kinsey's possible homosexual inclinations in a review of *Dr. Kinsey and the Institute for Sex Research* in *Atlantic* (May 1972), 99–102.

66. *Male*, pp. 614–15, 636–38; *Female*, p. 486n. Elsewhere Kinsey argued that the affectations associated with homosexuality were in fact the exclusive property of certain urban homosexual groups, which, he maintained, represented only "a small fraction" of the males with homosexual experience. He contrasted these citified homosexuals with a type that he apparently considered no less prevalent: what might be called cowboy homosexuals— "hard-riding, hard-hitting, assertive males," who enjoyed sexual relations with women (when they were available), but who turned to other males when "outdoor routines" brought them together in exclusively male society (*Male*, pp. 457–59).

ably high the frequency of homosexual outlet was very low. That is, while 37 percent of the male population had had at least one homosexual experience, homosexual contacts accounted for only 6 or 7 percent of all male orgasms.[67]

This disparity was all the more mysterious to Kinsey in view of the enormous potential of homosexual outlet. He was convinced that the sexual capacity of men was considerably greater than that of women. From this it seemed to follow that the sexual needs of males were better met by other males than they were by females. In other words, Kinsey's quantitative preoccupations led him to imply that the mathematics of sexual life were more conducive to homosexuality than to heterosexuality. And since at least half of the males in the population were known to be capable of homosexual response, one would have expected the frequency of homosexual outlet to be a good deal higher than it was.[68] Kinsey's line of reasoning in this instance represented a striking example of his tendency to conceive of the ideal sexual universe according to a homoerotic model.

Two factors, Kinsey surmised, kept homosexual outlet from reaching its natural level. The first of these was the social prohibition on homosexuality, which he believed prevented many men from acting on their desires and kept others ignorant of the channels through which homosexual partners might be found. But he maintained that social taboos were not in themselves sufficient to account for the low frequencies; hence his acceptance of the traditional wisdom concerning the characteristic pattern of homosexual relations. Since homosexual alliances were rarely stable, homosexuals lacked the regular source of outlet that marriage provided for heterosexual couples. The typical promiscuity of homosexuals, while it obviously meant a greater variety of sexual experiences, therefore entailed a substantially lower overall frequency of outlet than was enjoyed by heterosexuals (or at least by married heterosexuals). Similarly, the extreme finicalness of the homosexually experienced male—his preference for partners "of a particular age or a particular social level, of a particular height or weight, with hair of a particular color, with

67. *Male*, pp. 610, 633–36.
68. Ibid., pp. 631–32.

particular genital qualities, or with other particular physical aspects"—also prejudiced his ability to find sexual outlets. Together, the pressures of society and the homosexual's own idiosyncrasies resulted in a considerably impoverished sexual experience.[69]

It will be noticed that I have not been able to expound Kinsey's argument in this instance without speaking of "homosexuals" as if they were an identifiable sexual type. Neither was Kinsey himself.[70] In fact, the argument makes no sense unless one assumes that there are persons who can be identified, in some essential fashion, as homosexuals. In short, Kinsey's argument found him betraying not only his usual progressive instincts but his nominalist principles as well.

Pursuing the same logic he had adopted in his critique of the notion of homosexual personality, Kinsey also dismissed the controversy over the causes of homosexuality. Here again, I suspect, he sensed the tendentiousness of the traditional etiologies, all of which inclined to assume that homosexuality was a disease. Since, however, it made little sense to seek the causes of a condition that didn't exist, Kinsey ruled the entire debate out of order.

He was particularly disdainful of efforts to provide homosexuality with a biological foundation. In fact, his first publication in the field of human sexuality was an article, written in 1941, in which he refuted the hypothesis that homosexuality had hormonal origins. He demonstrated that endocrinologists and sexual theorists drawing upon endocrinal evidence had misconstrued the role of hormones in sexual life. Experiments with animals had shown that the injection of gonadal hormones could induce an animal to adopt the mannerisms of the opposite sex—passivity in the case of the male, aggressiveness in the case of the female. But such modifications of sexual behavior had been misrepresented, he argued, when they were taken as evidence of homosexuality, since the choice of a sexual partner remained unaffected. There was simply no recorded instance of hormonal injections causing an animal to alter its preference of sexual object, and thus no

69. Ibid., pp. 632–33.
70. On page 632 of the *Male* volume, for instance, he refers explicitly to "homosexual individuals," as well as to "homosexual males."

scientific evidence to suggest that homosexuality originated in a peculiar hormonal imbalance.[71] In effect, Kinsey cast doubt on Havelock Ellis's prediction that science would one day discover the causes of homosexuality in some disturbance of the body's internal chemistry.

Kinsey was no less firm in his rejection of the psychological explanations of homosexuality, including the Freudian explanation. "It does not suffice," he wrote, "to find that the homosexual offenders preferred their mothers to their fathers, when a survey of non-offenders shows that most children, for perfectly obvious reasons, are more closely associated with their mothers."[72] Here Kinsey's critique exactly echoed Ellis's. Like the hormonal explanation, that of the psychoanalysts lacked any statistical confirmation, and Kinsey evidently felt that none would be forthcoming.

In the end Kinsey stuck to his contention that homosexuality required no explanation whatsoever. The ability to respond to homosexual stimuli was a universal human, indeed a universal biological, capacity. The fact that some persons showed a greater affinity for homosexual relations than did others could be attributed to the accidents of individual experience (in particular whether one's first sexual experience happened to be with a person of the same or the opposite sex) or to the mysteries of individual choice:

> This problem is, after all, part of the broader problem of choices in general: the choice of the road one takes, of the clothes that one wears, of the food that one eats, of the place in which one sleeps, and of the endless other things that one is constantly choosing. A choice of a partner in a sexual relation becomes more significant only because society demands that there be a particular choice in this matter, and does not so often dictate one's choice of food or of clothing.[73]

Whence it followed that the greater prevalence of homosexuality in certain societies simply reflected a greater tolerance of homosexual relations in those societies. In the *Female* volume Kinsey allowed that certain facts of physiology and psychology con-

71. Kinsey, "Criteria for a Hormonal Explanation of the Homosexual," *Journal of Clinical Endocrinology* 1 (1941): 424–28; *Male*, pp. 615, 658–59; *Female*, pp. 757–59.

72. *Female*, p. 19; *Male*, p. 315.

73. *Male*, p. 661; see pp. 659–61, 666; *Female*, pp. 447–49.

spired to make heterosexuality the more common form of sexual
expression in all societies, and in the animal world as well.
Among such facts were "the greater submissiveness of the female
and the greater aggressiveness of the male," which implied a
psychological valence that promoted heterosexual intercourse
and frustrated homosexual intercourse, and also "the greater ease
of intromission into the female vagina and the greater difficulty
of penetrating the male anus." Nonetheless, he maintained that
the real problem was to explain not why an individual preferred
a partner of one sex rather than the other, but why he failed to
become involved "in every type of sexual behavior," a conclusion,
one must admit, that followed with absolute consistency from his
nominalist presuppositions.[74]

Sensing perhaps that his denial of the very existence of
homosexuality created a number of conceptual difficulties, Kinsey
proposed to replace the distinction among heterosexuals,
homosexuals, and bisexuals with what he called "the heterosexual-
homosexual rating scale." This device established a seven-way
classification of persons according to their sexual preferences.
Kinsey defined his seven categories as follows:

0. Exclusively heterosexual with no homosexual
1. Predominantly heterosexual, only incidentally homosexual
2. Predominantly heterosexual, but more than incidentally homosexual
3. Equally heterosexual and homosexual
4. Predominantly homosexual, but more than incidentally heterosexual
5. Predominantly homosexual, but incidentally heterosexual
6. Exclusively homosexual

Psychological as well as physical reactions were taken into consideration in determining whether a person belonged in one category or another, although Kinsey confessed that the proper
weighting of psychological and behavioral factors in any given
instance was a delicate matter.[75]

The heterosexual-homosexual rating scale was arguably the
most pathetic manifestation of Kinsey's philosophical naïveté. He
was clearly unaware that from a theoretical standpoint a seven-

74. *Female,* pp. 449–51.
75. *Male,* pp. 638–55.

way breakdown differed in no significant respect from a three-way breakdown. The former might conceivably prove more useful, more responsive to the facts, than the latter, but it involved the same basic assumption: it presumed that at some point differences of degree became differences of kind. Kinsey managed to ignore this theoretical consideration entirely. He suggested, in other words, that one might reasonably say of a person, "He's a 3," while to call that same person a bisexual was illegitimate. He thus failed to anticipate that some future sexual critic, mindful of his own insistence on the infinite gradations of sexual behavior, might well argue that the seven categories of the heterosexual-homosexual rating scale, no less than the three they were meant to replace, represented the illicit hypostatization of an essentially fluid reality.

Wardell Pomeroy has called the heterosexual-homosexual rating scale one of Kinsey's eight major contributions to modern sexology. At the same time, Pomeroy laments the fact that the scale never caught on as Kinsey expected it would.[76] That failure should surprise no one. It was from the start a hopelessly mechanical contrivance, which sought to promote a system of classification that bore little relation to reality. The operative terms of Kinsey's seven-way breakdown—"predominantly" and "incidentally"—simply did not carry enough psychological weight to allow his categories to emerge as essential types. There thus seems little reason not to collapse category 1 into 0, category 5 into 6, and categories 2 and 4 into 3, leaving of course the traditional scheme of heterosexuals, homosexuals, and bisexuals. In short, the heterosexual-homosexual rating scale failed to meet the only significant test of any new system of classification: it failed to establish its practical superiority to the existing system. And most students of human sexuality continue to write as though the distinction among heterosexuals, homosexuals, and bisexuals—a distinction that emerged at the beginning of the century[77]—is as useful as anything one might reasonably hope for.

I should not leave the impression that Kinsey's enthusiasm for homosexuality knew no bounds. Forced to choose, he would, I

76. Pomeroy, Dr. Kinsey, p. 467.

77. The third edition of Havelock Ellis's Sexual Inversion makes clear that this terminology was firmly established as early as 1915. See Sexual Inversion, pp. 2–4, 88.

suspect, have given the nod to heterosexuality. Thus in the *Female* volume, after stressing that men had much to learn from lesbians about female sexual response, he remarked, in his inimitable manner, that "with the additional possibilities which a union of male and female genitalia may offer in a heterosexual contact, and with public opinion and the mores encouraging heterosexual contacts and disapproving of homosexual contacts, relationships between females and males will seem, to most persons, to be more satisfactory than homosexual relationships can ever be."[78] An ambiguous endorsement, to be sure, but an endorsement nonetheless. Moreover, Kinsey was not above using the threat of homosexuality to argue implicitly for greater sexual freedom among the young: "Our case histories show that . . . disapproval of heterosexual coitus and of nearly every other type of heterosexual activity before marriage is often an important factor in the development of homosexual activity."[79] The argument, as he probably would have admitted, appealed to the worst instincts of his audience, but it clearly implied that homosexuality was in some sense undesirable. Nevertheless, the overwhelming impression created by the Kinsey volumes was one of extraordinary tolerance, and homosexuals have rightly come to consider him among their warmest friends.

VI

Just as he had done with the various sexual outlets, Kinsey subjected the factors that affected the choice and frequency of outlet to critical reappraisal, promoting the importance of some and demoting others. The factors to which he devoted the most attention in the *Male* volume were marriage, religion, history, age, and social class. In general, he sought to cast doubt on the significance of marriage, religion, and history—in other words, those factors that popular opinion credited with the greatest impact on sexual behavior—and to emphasize the importance of age and social class, especially the latter, which he felt had been inexcusably neglected by previous sexual investigators.

No fewer than three chapters of *Sexual Behavior in the Human*

78. *Female,* p. 468.
79. Ibid., p. 285; also pp. 14, 460.

Male were addressed to the effect of marriage on sexual life. The main point Kinsey sought to establish in these chapters was that marriage counted for a good deal less than our official morality would lead one to expect, at least as far as males were concerned. With the relish of a prizefighter setting up his opponent for the killing blow, he imputed that if the Judeo-Christian proscriptions were truly honored, all orgasms, save for those obtained through nocturnal emissions, would result from marital intercourse. In fact, however, he showed that fewer than half of the orgasms achieved by American males were derived from intercourse with their wives, which meant that more than half were derived from sources that were "socially disapproved and in large part illegal and punishable under the criminal codes."[80] Even married males secured only 85 percent of their orgasms from marital intercourse, and in the upper social classes that figure sometimes dropped as low as 62 percent. In effect, Kinsey established that a man's overall rate of outlet could be charted along a curve from adolescence to old age, a curve that was not dramatically affected by marriage and whose contours were determined primarily by metabolic rather than by institutional factors. With barely concealed glee he concluded that "marital intercourse, important as it is in the lives of most of the population, falls far short of constituting the whole of the sexual history of the American male."[81]

Among nonmarital sources of heterosexual outlet, Kinsey was most concerned with premarital intercourse. In fact, the sexual predicament of the young elicited his most indignant reaction, and no group in American society, unless it be the homosexual community, was the object of greater sympathy on his part. Appropriately, those portions of the *Male* volume that treated premarital intercourse were devoted not so much to establishing its prevalence—although he demonstrated that most males had experienced intercourse before marriage[82]—as to challenging the reasonableness of its interdiction.

Kinsey's efforts in this cause were more remarkable for their passion than their cogency. He deployed all the familiar argu-

80. *Male,* p. 568.
81. Ibid., p. 568; also pp. 257, 293, 296, 565–66.
82. Ibid., p. 549.

ments based on animal behavior and the practice of non-Western cultures. Premarital abstinence was unnatural, in the first instance, because among every other species of animal intercourse commenced immediately upon sexual maturity, if not earlier. This said no more than that marriage was a distinctly human phenomenon and that the prohibition of premarital intercourse was thus by definition unique to man. But even within the human community, Kinsey argued, nearly all cultures other than our own made some allowance for sexual intercourse prior to marriage. Thus the unqualified proscription of fornication, like that of homosexual relations, appeared to be an exclusive injustice of our Judeo-Christian, or, more precisely, Anglo-American, heritage.[83]

Kinsey also sought to reconstruct the popular image of premarital intercourse. In most instances, he found, it was not the clandestine, sordid, and guilt-ridden affair portrayed by its moralistic critics. He showed, for instance, that the greater portion of premarital intercourse occurred not in the back seats of automobiles or behind the school gymnasium but in the home of one of the parties: "The data do not justify the general opinion that pre-marital coitus is, of necessity, more hurried and consequently less satisfactory than coitus usually is in marriage."[84] Premarital intercourse emerged in Kinsey's treatment as a distinctly romantic experience, at once more exciting and more tender than its routine marital counterpart. Nor was it usually followed by pangs of conscience; between 69 and 77 percent of the women with premarital experience said that they saw no reason to regret their transgression. Finally, Kinsey dismissed any suggestion that the threat of pregnancy was sufficient justification for forbidding premarital intercourse. Pregnancy, like venereal disease, had become largely preventable, and in any case the chances of impregnation resulting from a particular sexual encounter were fairly remote.[85]

Kinsey's ultimate defense of premarital intercourse exactly paralleled his defense of masturbation and petting: he argued that premarital experience contributed to sexual success in mar-

83. Ibid., pp. 547, 549, 559; *Female*, p. 284.
84. *Female*, p. 311.
85. Ibid., pp. 311–12, 316–19, 327; *Male*, p. 562.

riage. Here again he was concerned primarily with the sexual adjustment of women: "The record on our sample of married females shows that there was a marked, positive correlation between experience in orgasm obtained from pre-marital coitus, and the capacity to reach orgasm after marriage."[86] He recognized that this correlation might involve selective factors. That is, he admitted that the women who regularly achieved orgasm in marriage might simply be those who were more highly sexed, which would also account for their greater premarital experience. But he insisted that "psychologic and sociologic data" had established the unparalleled importance of early experience in forming adult patterns of behavior, both in the sexual realm and elsewhere, and he thus doubted that selective factors alone could explain the correlation.[87]

The very fact that Kinsey chose to defend premarital intercourse in terms of its importance for sexual adjustment in marriage documented his loyalty to the traditional marital ideology of our culture. In spite of his intention to discredit the usual monogamous pieties, marriage remained, in the back of his mind, the norm in terms of which he evaluated most other sexual outlets. Theoretically he might have made marital intercourse the variable and some other practice, such as masturbation, the constant. That is, he might well have asked whether frequent and problem-free intercourse with one's spouse made one a better masturbator. The suggestion is admittedly fanciful, but it serves to underscore the degree to which the Kinsey studies were informed by an essentially marital perspective.

Further evidence of Kinsey's commitment to marriage was provided by his treatment of extramarital intercourse. In general, he showed less sensitivity to the need for sexual variety than had Havelock Ellis. In fact, Pomeroy reports that he was so naïve in this regard that not until 1948 did he begin asking his subjects about extramarital petting.[88] He tended to think that when a

86. *Female*, p. 328.
87. Ibid., pp. 329–30, 385–88.
88. Pomeroy, *Dr. Kinsey*, p. 121. Pomeroy also reveals that the atmosphere surrounding the Kinsey projects was an extraordinarily monogamous one. Among the criteria that Kinsey established for prospective interviewers was that they be happily married (Pomeroy, p. 101).

person married the problem of sexual outlet was largely resolved. Once alerted to the extent of extramarital intercourse (he found that it occurred in the histories of about half the married men in the population),[89] Kinsey seemed prepared to defend it, although never with the enthusiasm that he brought to his defense of premarital intercourse. His reserve made perfect sense, moreover, in view of his inclination to treat human sexuality in basically quantitative terms. The prohibition on premarital intercourse meant that a person was denied intercourse altogether, while that on extramarital intercourse meant merely that he was denied a certain kind of intercourse. The former deprivation was for Kinsey by far the more serious.

Given the uproar that greeted Kinsey's expressed doubts about the viciousness of extramarital intercourse, notably on the part of Reinhold Niebuhr,[90] one is struck by the tentativeness of his remarks on the subject. He simply questioned the assumption that extramarital intercourse always undermined the stability of marriage. Although "the public record" was filled with infidelities that had wrecked homes, he wondered whether the full story was not perhaps more complex than the most highly publicized cases led one to assume. His interviews had turned up instances of infidelity, particularly among the lower classes, that had not led to the breakup of the marriage or even interfered in any apparent way with the mutual affection of the spouses. Kinsey seemed to feel that the most appropriate extramarital affair, from the viewpoint of preserving the marriage, was an alliance in which neither party became overly involved emotionally. In this respect his apology, if it can be called such, diverged markedly from Havelock Ellis's, who, it will be remembered, held that an extramarital affair was justified only if there was a substantial psychological investment.[91]

Kinsey completed his brief by suggesting that under certain

89. *Male*, p. 585.

90. Reinhold Niebuhr, "Kinsey and the Moral Problems of Man's Sexual Life," in Donald Porter Geddes, ed., *An Analysis of the Kinsey Reports* (New York, 1954), pp. 62–70.

91. *Male*, pp. 591–92. Significantly, the Kinsey volumes contained but a sole reference to group sex, and that an extremely perfunctory one (*Male*, p. 572).

circumstances extramarital intercourse, like premarital intercourse, might actually contribute to the viability of marital relations:

> There are some individuals among our histories whose sexual adjustments in marriage have undoubtedly been helped by extramarital experience. Sometimes this depends upon their learning new techniques or acquiring new attitudes which reduce inhibitions in their marital relations. Some women who had had difficulty in reaching orgasm with their husbands, find the novelty of the situation with another male stimulating to their first orgasm; and with this as a background they make better adjustments with their husbands. Extra-marital intercourse has had the effect of convincing some males that the relationships with their wives were more satisfactory than they had realized.[92]

In the end even infidelity was subjected to the marital standard, and Kinsey was unquestionably wronged when he was made the prophet of "anarchism in the field of sex."[93]

Some readers will find my emphasis on Kinsey's marital enthusiasms exaggerated, if not perverse. I ought to concede that he thought of marriage largely in pragmatic terms. That is, he showed little sympathy for the residual romanticism that characterized Havelock Ellis's conception of marriage. In general, he regarded marriage less as a companionship than as a convenient arrangement for the regular satisfaction of sexual desire. "Convenience" was in fact the word he most often used to describe the advantages of marriage. Marriage provided a man and a woman with an extremely sensible means of coping with their sexual needs, and its convenience accounted for the fact that a person's rate of outlet nearly always increased after marriage. Of course, Kinsey acknowledged that there was more to marriage than sex. But more consistently than Ellis he viewed marriage as an erotic institution, and he emphasized that sexual incompatibility was

92. Ibid., p. 593.
93. Niebuhr, "Kinsey," p. 68. In the *Female* volume Kinsey took a more conventional position on extramarital intercourse. While still insisting that its benefits ought not to be overlooked, he conceded that it probably "contributed to . . . divorces in more ways and in a greater extent than the subjects themselves realized" (*Female*, p. 435; also pp. 431–36).

very often the cause of marital failure.[94] I remain impressed therefore by the degree to which he unconsciously assumed that marital intercourse was the most important aspect of a person's sexual experience. Even his defense of premarital intercourse should be read not as an argument against marriage itself but rather as a plea to extend the advantages of marriage to the unmarried. He was, in short, a good deal more conventional than he himself or his critics ever realized.

VII

I said at the beginning of the last section that religion, like marriage, was one of the factors whose importance for sexual life Kinsey tended to belittle. The statement must be understood in a relative sense. By no means did he wish to deny religion all significance for sexual behavior, but only to demote its influence vis-à-vis that of age and social class and to deflate its popular reputation as a major force for sexual restraint. These intentions were less evident in the *Female* volume than in the *Male*, and he ultimately found that religion exercised a greater influence on sexual behavior, at least among women, than he had anticipated.

Even in the *Male* volume Kinsey's treatment of religion was far from consistent. In fact, his argument was informed by two incompatible points of view. Sometimes he emphasized the relative ineffectiveness of religious sanctions. He suggested, in other words, that the sexual life of the religious was not remarkably different from that of the irreligious. This enterprise found him pointing up the hypocrisy of the devout in an ironic, often smirking manner. More frequently, however, he chose to stress the sexual hardships that religious conviction imposed upon the faithful, an argument that obviously credited religion with a substantial—and deleterious—influence on erotic behavior. In this instance his line of reasoning called forth not irony but indignation and pathos. The two perspectives, the ironic and the pathetic, subsisted uneasily alongside one another, although the contradiction between them was in a sense resolved in favor of the latter when Kinsey came to assess the historical impact of

94. *Male*, pp. 281, 296, 562–63; *Female*, p. 266.

religion on sexual life. That is, while he sometimes questioned the power of religious conviction to mold sexual behavior in the contemporary world, he never doubted that religion was the original source of the sexual values we supposedly lived by.

Kinsey found that piety had the effect of reducing a man's sexual performance by about a third. It had the same influence, moreover, on all forms of outlet save nocturnal emissions.[95] This finding allowed of two interpretations. A straightforward reading of the data would lead one to conclude that religion functioned as an important deterrent to sexual expression. On the other hand, the fact that religion affected merely the rate and not the choice of outlet cast doubt on its true efficacy. Although the frequency of orgasm from all sources was lower among serious Christians and Jews than among the secular, the percentage of orgasms derived from the outlets explicitly proscribed by the Judeo-Christian code, such as masturbation, homosexuality, and premarital intercourse, was approximately the same for believers as for nonbelievers. Kinsey never drew explicit attention to this paradox, but the matter-of-fact way in which he contemplated the masturbatory, homosexual, and premarital involvements of the devout positively reeked of irony. He seemed to take secret delight in this triumph of nature over conviction.

The fact that piety reduced the rate of marital intercourse by the same amount that it reduced that of other outlets posed a theoretical difficulty for Kinsey. Since intercourse within marriage was not regulated by any of the major American religions—except perhaps indirectly by the Catholic Church through its condemnation of birth control—the lower frequency of marital intercourse among the religious raised the possibility that the devout were not chaste because of their religion but, rather, religious because of their chastity. It suggested, in other words, that a selective factor might be at work and that the religious were simply those with less sexual drive. Kinsey, however, chose to interpret the data otherwise. He argued that the lower rate of marital intercourse among the religious showed the effects of conditioning in the years before marriage. Since these individuals tended to repress any desires they had for masturbation, homosexual relations, and premarital intercourse during adolescence,

95. *Male*, pp. 472–83.

they established a generally inhibited sexual pattern that was not easily abandoned after they married. Thus he remained persuaded that religious conviction and not metabolic incapacity accounted for their lower frequencies of outlet.[96]

Nonetheless, Kinsey also argued that the influence of religion, important though it might be, was utterly "dwarfed" by that of social class. And some of the most dramatic statistics in the *Male* volume were those showing the powerlessness of religion in the face of class prejudice. Thus, for example, he established that the rate of premarital intercourse among devout Protestants of the lower class was six or eight times as high as that among merely nominal Protestants of the middle and upper classes. A similar pattern could be detected in homosexual and extramarital relations. Such findings testified to the malleability of conscience, and they supplied powerful ammunition for deflating the claim of religion to be a preeminent factor in determining sexual behavior.[97]

The real importance of religion, in Kinsey's opinion, lay in its historical role as the source of our official sexual values. In fact, he suggested that the inhibitions of the religious clearly documented the origin of those values in ancient theological prejudice.[98] The very looseness of this argument was testimony to the strength of Kinsey's anticlerical sentiments. He was anxious to pin the blame on religion, no matter what the evidence.

In general, Kinsey's conception of history was appallingly simpleminded, although it was not without its Voltairian charms. He viewed the historical process as a great moral drama, in which the forces of science competed with those of superstition for the minds and the hearts of men. He had little appreciation of

---

96. Ibid., p. 571. He might have resolved the issue definitively if he had undertaken a comparison between religiosity and age at the onset of adolescence. He found that early sexual maturity corresponded with high rates of outlet in adulthood. In other words, age at the onset of adolescence was a measure of "the intensity of a male's sex drive" (*Male*, p. 569). Therefore, had Kinsey shown that no correlation existed between religiosity and age at the onset of adolescence, the hypothesis that the devout were simply the undersexed could have been eliminated. On the other hand, the discovery of such a correlation would cast serious doubt on his argument.

97. Ibid., pp. 477–79, 482–83, 589.

98. Ibid., pp. 408, 470, 486, 589.

social and economic influences in history—a rather surprising blindness in view of the importance he attributed to social class as an index of sexual behavior in the contemporary world—and he tended to assume that ideas were the ultimate determinants of historical change. He was a kind of amateur intellectual historian.

Like Nietzsche, Kinsey believed that our sexual values originated largely with the Jews, from whom they had been taken over by the Christians. But unlike Nietzsche, who regarded all of Western civilization as heir to the peculiarly repressive morality of the Jews, Kinsey seemed to think that Jewish asceticism had in the modern world become the more or less exclusive property of Englishmen and Americans. Continental Europe remained in his imagination an almost Polynesian sexual paradise.[99]

If he were asked why the Jews, and after them the Christians, had adopted such repressive sexual values, he would have answered that they did so for religious reasons. And in Kinsey's mind this meant that they did so for largely unintelligible reasons: "Mores, whether they concern food, clothing, sex, or religious rituals, originate neither in accumulated experience nor in scientific examinations of objectively gathered data. The sociologist and anthropologist find the origins of such customs in ignorance and superstition, and in the attempt of each group to set itself apart from its neighbors."[100] This judgment did extraordinary violence to the actual opinions of most modern sociologists and anthropologists, who have emphasized not the irrationality but precisely the logic of religious values and practices. Kinsey's treatment of religion was refreshingly innocent of the functionalist perspective that has dominated sociological and anthropological studies in the twentieth century. Durkheim he seems never to have heard of, and Malinowski he knew only as the man who had celebrated the sexual bliss of the Trobriand Islanders.[101]

Like a good *philosophe*, he saw no reason to seek the rationale of any system of sexual legislation. It did not enter his mind, consequently, that Jewish asceticism might have answered to

99. Ibid., pp. 263, 465, 473, 483, 486–487, 593. Shortly before his death Kinsey traveled to Europe. His observations there confirmed him in the belief that the English and Americans were, sexually speaking, a race apart. See Pomeroy, *Dr. Kinsey*, pp. 401–38, especially p. 419.

100. *Male,* p. 203; also p. 365.

101. Ibid., pp. 4, 22, 373, 547; *Female,* p. 413–14.

some social, political, or psychological need. On the contrary, all sexual regulations, he insisted, reflected only human folly and willfulness. They were, in short, a kind of madness. In Kinsey's defense, it should be said that while he lacked the sophistication of the functionalists, he also avoided their conservatism. He would never have tolerated the proposition that sexual taboos were justified because they guaranteed social stability.

The introduction of Judeo-Christian sexual morality thus marked a major watershed in human history for Kinsey. In fact, it marked the *only* watershed, and he frequently implied that from that fateful moment to the present little had changed in the sexual values and behavior of the West. He was particularly anxious to disprove the widespread assumption that there had been a dramatic transformation in sexual mores since the end of the First World War. As far as the sexual habits of American males were concerned, history, he argued, was a factor of negligible importance.

Since he was to reverse himself on the significance of history in the *Female* volume, it should be noted that the data from which he drew his conclusions in the *Male* volume were not strictly speaking historical. He did not group his subjects according to birth dates, but instead divided them into two categories on the basis of their age at the time they contributed their histories. One group contained all those under thirty-three at the date of the interview, while the other contained all those thirty-three and older.[102] Since, however, the sample was gathered over a ten-year span there was some confusion about the exact historical significance of the comparison thus undertaken.

On first examination Kinsey's statistics seemed to reveal a number of important changes in the sexual behavior of his two generations. Among the younger group there was, for example, more masturbation (at least in lower-class circles), more premarital petting and intercourse, and fewer contacts with prostitutes.[103] Indeed, an impartial reader might have concluded from Kinsey's data that a veritable sexual revolution had occurred among the young. But Kinsey himself rejected such an interpretation. The changes that had taken place involved, he insisted, only "minor details of behavior" and touched on "nothing . . .

102. *Male*, pp. 395–96.
103. Ibid., pp. 401–05, 411, 416, 537–39, 603.

deeply fundamental in overt activity": "These comparisons of the sexual activities of older and younger generations provide striking evidence of the stability of the sexual mores. They provide scant justification for the opinion harbored by some persons that there are constant changes in such mores, or at least a constant flux—perhaps an 'evolution' toward something better, or a constant degeneration in behavior."[104] The few shifts that could be detected he attributed largely to metabolic factors, in particular the tendency of the younger generation to mature at an earlier age, rather than to any conscious transformation in sexual values.

Kinsey seems to have been determined at all costs to deny history its wonted role as a major influence on sexual behavior, and this endeavor found him belaboring his data as he did nowhere else in the Reports. He was motivated, one senses, by two considerations. The first was his desire to defend the young against their adult critics. He hated the moralism of the old, and he was convinced that their notions about the sexual excesses of the young were inspired by waning sexual prowess and simple envy. He therefore went out of his way to argue that the older generation had been equally libidinous in its own youth and, as a result, had no right to criticize.

Kinsey's deeper reason for denying the impact of history on sexual behavior sprang from his continuing desire to discredit religion. The absence of a historical pattern drew attention to the stranglehold of Judeo-Christian values on the American libido. It proved conclusively "that many of our present-day attitudes on sex are matters which were settled in the religious philosophy of the authors of the Old Testament."[105] Thus, even though belief itself might be on the wane, and even though Kinsey's own investigation had shown that religious conviction was less important than social class in determining one's erotic experience, religion remained, in his opinion, a powerful and repressive force in American sexual life.

VIII

The two most important influences on male sexuality, according to Kinsey, were the biological factor of age and the cultural

104. Ibid., pp. 414–15; also pp. 397–99, 556–57.
105. Ibid., p. 415.

factor of social class. More than anything else age determined how much sexual activity a man enjoyed, while social class determined what kind of sexuality he enjoyed. In effect, age and social class defined, respectively, the quantitative and qualitative contours of a man's sexual response.

"In the sexual history of the male, there is no other single factor which affects frequency of outlet as much as age."[106] Stated thus in its most general form, Kinsey's conclusion was not particularly startling. In fact it conformed to popular opinion. Everyone knew that a man's sexuality changed dramatically in the course of his lifetime. It existed only in a dormant form during childhood; it emerged properly at adolescence; blossomed in the twenties and thirties; began declining in the forties; and burnt out definitively in the fifties or sixties. In the particulars of his analysis, however, Kinsey contradicted this conception at every point. Indeed, he revolutionized our notion of the sexual aging process.

For one thing, sexual life, he showed, did not begin at adolescence. One might be tempted to respond that Freud had exploded that myth half a century earlier. But the infantile or childhood sexuality that Kinsey discovered was very different from that posited by Freud, and he was in fact unsympathetic to the explicitly Freudian doctrine.

Kinsey's criticism of Freud was by no means original. It bore close resemblance to the strictures of Havelock Ellis and was the common property of many anti-Freudians, despite Freud's effort to disarm the criticism in his *Three Essays on the Theory of Sexuality*. Briefly, Kinsey maintained that most of the childhood activities called sexual by Freud were not demonstrably such. Freud, he argued, was guilty of extending the notion of sexuality to cover almost all forms of tactile stimulation, and for his part, Kinsey was not prepared to consider "every occasion on which a babe brings two parts of its body into juxtaposition" a sexual event.[107] In effect, his definition of what was sexual remained much more conventional than Freud's. As a result his examination of childhood sexuality addressed itself only to those activities that would be considered sexual in adult life. That is, he was interested exclusively in genital activities, and he thereby re-

106. Ibid., p. 218.
107. Ibid., pp. 163, 180, 498; *Female*, pp. 133–34.

jected the most distinctive feature of the psychoanalytic interpretation of infantile sexuality, namely its emphasis on the pregenital organization of the libido in childhood.

Kinsey found that over half of his male subjects recalled some form of preadolescent sex play, and he argued that it was "not improbable" that practically all boys had indulged in such play. He also found that the greater portion of children's erotic play was homosexual. Nevertheless, he expressly disputed Freud's hypothesis of a distinct homosexual phase in libidinal development. The data revealed no such sequential pattern, and Kinsey attributed the popularity of homosexual play simply to "the greater accessibility of the boy's own sex." Needless to say, he defended the essential innocence of these childhood activities and cautioned parents against inducing guilty reactions in their children.[108]

More significant than the discovery of widespread sexual play among children was the revelation that such play resulted in arousal and sometimes even orgasm. From the testimony of nine adult males who had had sexual relations with younger boys, Kinsey obtained information about the sexual response of 317 preadolescents. Of these, half had achieved orgasms by seven years of age and two-thirds by twelve. Orgasms had even been recorded in infants of four or five months. "There is no essential aspect of the orgasm of an adult which has not been observed in the orgasms which young children may have,"[109] he announced, thereby demoting ejaculation to the status of a mere accident. He concluded that in a truly uninhibited society half of the male population would probably achieve orgasm by age four, and the proportion would approach a hundred percent as much as five years before adolescence. In other words, a nonrepressive civilization would see the distinction between infantile and adult sexuality dissolved, an anticipation that Kinsey found confirmed in the sexual behavior of animals.[110]

Even in existing society, Kinsey showed, adolescence was not the watershed it had once been thought to be. Among about half of his male subjects, pre-adolescent sex play had led directly into comparable adolescent activities, and he argued that the hiatus

108. *Male*, pp. 165–68; *Female*, pp. 107, 109, 115.
109. *Female*, p. 104.
110. *Male*, pp. 175–81; *Female*, pp. 103–05.

between childhood and adult sexual life in the remaining 50 percent of the cases was "clearly a product of cultural restraints." Thus throughout the two Reports he stressed the continuity between pre-adolescent and adolescent sexual behavior, and this, in turn, led him to reject Freud's notion of a latency period.[111]

On the other hand Kinsey acknowledged that sexual behavior did undergo a transformation during adolescence. For one thing there was a distinct acceleration in the rate of sexual activity, at least among males, and regular means of outlet were established for the first time. Kinsey was not satisfied, however, with this purely quantitative characterization of adolescent sexual development. In untypically subtle fashion he insisted that the essential difference between childhood and adolescent sexuality was psychological: the adolescent male perceived his sexual activity in an entirely different manner from the child. Where the sexual life of a boy was "more or less a part of his other play," that of the adolescent became "an end in itself."[112] Adolescent sexuality was thus not merely more regular than its preadolescent counterpart, it was also more self-conscious. At the same time, Kinsey suggested that sexual life achieved a new specificity during adolescence:

> Originally the pre-adolescent boy erects indiscriminately to the whole array of emotional situations, whether they be sexual or nonsexual in nature. By his late teens the male has been so conditioned that he rarely responds to anything except a direct physical stimulation of genitalia, or to psychic situations that are specifically sexual. . . . The picture is that of the psychosexual emerging from a much more generalized and basic physiological capacity.[113]

Although Kinsey would have been reluctant to admit it, this conception bore a certain resemblance to Freud's notion of an evolution from polymorphous perversity to genital tyranny—the belief, in other words, that adolescence witnessed the genital organization of impulses that had earlier expressed themselves in nongenital ways.

111. *Male*, pp. 167, 171, 174, 180–82; *Female*, p. 116. Kinsey's reference to the Freudian doctrine was curiously inaccurate. He spoke of "a sexually latent or dormant period in the later adolescent years" (*Male*, p. 180). I assume, however, that he meant the later *pre*adolescent years.

112. *Male*, pp. 182, 191.

113. Ibid., pp. 165; *Female*, p. 102.

Kinsey's most stunning revision of the traditional model of sexual aging was his demonstration that adolescence itself marked the peak moment in the sexual history of the male. He showed that the sexual decline generally thought to set in during the forties in fact began before the twenties. "The high point of sexual performance is, in actuality, somewhere around 16 or 17 years of age. It is not later."[114] Kinsey even argued that in terms of *capacity* the male was already in decline by the onset of adolescence. Perhaps only his revelation of widespread involvement in homosexual activities caused as much surprise as this documentation of youth's sexual preeminence.

The discovery had a number of disturbing implications, the most obvious being that the marriage system stood at odds with the hard facts of sexual aging. Kinsey found that marital intercourse provided married men with their most regular source of sexual relief. Yet for various reasons (primarily economic in nature) marriage in America usually occurred after adolescence. This meant that the most important sexual outlet accessible to men in their twenties and later, and the only outlet (except nocturnal emissions) deemed a legitimate source of gratification by the official morality, was generally unavailable to those in greatest need of it. And since intercourse nonetheless remained the principal sexual activity even of unmarried men, many teenagers were of necessity involved in illegal and clandestine activities.[115]

It was not only the legal system that had lost touch with the realities of sexual aging. Kinsey argued that many of the institutional arrangements for dealing with teenagers also served to aggravate the problem. In particular he suggested that teenage boys were too often placed at the mercy of middle-aged women—whether mothers, teachers, or simply voting citizens—whose own repressed lives made them uniquely unqualified to comprehend the sexual needs of the adolescent male. He dramatized this dilemma in picturesque fashion by contrasting the sexual life of the typical teenager with that of his teacher:

Many of these women, including some high school biology teachers, believe that the ninth or tenth grade boy is still too young to receive

114. *Male,* p. 219.
115. Ibid., pp. 221–23.

any sex instruction when, in actuality, he has a higher rate of outlet and has already had a wider variety of sexual experience than most of his female teachers ever will have.[116]

An equally serious problem arose from the different patterns of sexual aging in men and women. Women, Kinsey found, pursued a course of sexual development that corresponded roughly to the popular conception of male sexual development. That is, they learned to respond only gradually during adolescence, did not reach their maximum level of activity until the early thirties, and tended to remain close to that maximum well into middle age, when there was a gradual tapering off. It followed that from a sexual standpoint men and women were like ships passing in the night. The male's years of greatest sexual capacity came at a time when women were relatively unresponsive, while the female's sustained years of maximum activity corresponded to the man's years of sexual decline. The mathematics of sex, it seemed, were unfavorable to marriage.[117]

Kinsey's examination of sexual aging generally found him pleading the cause of the young. He did not, however, lack all sympathy for the old. Admittedly, he never developed the enthusiasm for geriatric sexuality that has characterized the work of William Masters and Virginia Johnson. But he did seek to correct a number of misconceptions about sex in old age. Moreover, in those instances where the old might be said to have advanced the cause of hedonism, he was quick to take their side.

Sexual Behavior in the Human Male sometimes left the impression that older males were sexually depleted. But Kinsey expressly disputed the notion that men passed through a climacteric, perhaps in late middle age, after which sexual life suddenly ceased. Sexual decline in the male, he showed, was gradual, not abrupt, and the rate of decline in the later decades of life was the same as that in the twenties and thirties. He also established that sexual activity among males came to a complete halt much later than was generally thought to be the case. Only a quarter of his subjects had become impotent by seventy years of age, and one man was still having regular intercourse at eighty-eight.[118] No more than childhood was old age a sexual wasteland.

116. Ibid., p. 223; *Female*, pp. 526–27.
117. *Male*, p. 229; *Female*, p. 353.
118. *Male*, pp. 227, 235, 237.

Kinsey complemented his defense of the old by putting in a good word for child molesters. This represented the only instance in the Reports where adults appeared in the role of victims and children in that of oppressors. The threat posed by middle-aged and elderly men to the sexual integrity of young girls, he argued, had been greatly exaggerated: "Many small girls reflect the public hysteria over the prospect of 'being touched' by a strange person; and many a child, who has no idea at all of the mechanics of intercourse, interprets affection and simple caressing, from anyone except her own parents, as attempts at rape."[119] Only a small portion of the sexual approaches made to children, Kinsey found, eventuated in actual physical contact, and if those approaches sometimes caused psychological damage, that was to be attributed to cultural conditioning rather than to anything pathogenic in the experience itself. Indeed, he was brazen enough to suggest that children sometimes enjoyed their sexual encounters with adults. Throughout this discussion, it should be noted, Kinsey assigned the villainous role not to children as such but specifically to female children, just as in his examination of the sexual hardships endured by teenagers he assigned the role of repressor to mothers and female teachers. Inevitably one feels that his sympathies went out not so much to the young in general as to those among them who happened to be males.

IX

I have mentioned that Kinsey was deeply impressed by the influence of social class on sexual behavior. Indeed, one senses that from his own standpoint the most startling finding of his study related not to sexuality but to social structure, namely the discovery that America was, to an unanticipated degree, a class-ridden society. His pronouncements about class and its impact on sexual behavior, especially in the *Male* volume, were delivered in a tone of wonderment and disbelief that implied he had been only painfully disabused of his democratic assumptions. In this respect *Sexual Behavior in the Human Male* must be placed alongside certain sociological writings of the 1930s and 1940s that

119. Ibid., p. 238; *Female*, pp. 116–22.

revealed the depth of class distinctions in America. It bore particularly close resemblance to Robert and Helen Lynd's community study *Middletown*. In fact, the *Male* volume might almost be read as a sexual appendix to *Middletown*. Just as the Lynds established that differences in wealth and social background condemned Americans to radically divergent familial, educational, and cultural experiences, Kinsey showed that class distinctions found their way even into the bedroom, indeed into the most intimate details of erotic life.[120]

Like the Lynds, Kinsey adopted a two-way breakdown of American society. He referred to his two groups as the lower level and the upper level. In occupational terms this distinction corresponded roughly to the Lynds' distinction between the working class and the business class:

> Members of the first group, by and large, address their activities in getting a living primarily to *things*, utilizing material tools in the making of things and the performance of services, while the members of the second group address their activities predominantly to *people* in the selling or promotion of things, services, and ideas.[121]

In terms of educational criteria Kinsey sometimes shifted into a three-way classification of those who had gone only to grade school, those who had gone to high school, and those who had gone to college. For the most part, however, the college group was identified with the upper level and the grade-school and high-school groups with the lower level. "Upper level" thus called to mind well-fixed professional people living in the suburbs,

---

120. *Sexual Behavior in the Human Male* and *Middletown* also shared a common geographical focus: each was Indiana based. Kinsey, of course, worked out of Indiana University, and students at the university as well as local residents were heavily represented in his sample. *Middletown* was a study of Muncie, Indiana, which the Lynds argued was "as representative as possible of contemporary American life" (*Middletown* [New York, 1929], p. 7). Other studies that shared Kinsey's and the Lynds' preoccupation with class structure included W. Lloyd Warner and P. S. Lunt, *The Social Life of a Modern Community* (New Haven, 1941) and *The Status System of a Modern Community* (New Haven, 1942); Carl Withers, *Plainville, U.S.A.* (New York, 1945); A. B. Hollingshead, *Elmstown's Youth* (New York, 1949); and J. Dollard, *Caste and Class in a Southern Town* (New York, 1937).

121. Lynds, *Middletown*, p. 22.

while "lower level" implied relatively hard-pressed manual laborers living in the inner city.[122]

At the time he composed the *Male* volume, Kinsey clearly believed that social class was more important than any other factor affecting sexual life. The differences between lower- and upper-class sexual behavior were as great, he contended, as those found between separate national cultures, and they could be detected even in the sexual activities of young children. Furthermore, the mores of the class held such powerful and mysterious sway over the individual that a socially mobile person would adopt the sexual habits of the class into which he ultimately moved well before the end of adolescence.[123]

What were these differences in sexual behavior that so divided the rich from the poor? They were not, be it noted, differences in the overall rate of activity. Although the poor seemed to have a slight edge in total performance, Kinsey argued that the truly important differences between the classes pertained to the choice of outlet and the "style" of execution.[124] The sexual life of the poor was characterized by its singleminded commitment to genital relations, above all heterosexual intercourse, while that of the rich tended to more diffuse and narcissistic forms of expression. Put grossly, though not wholly inaccurately, the poor copulated while the rich masturbated.

Kinsey found that the poor diverged most strikingly from the rich in their addiction to premarital intercourse, prostitution, and homosexuality. Between the ages of sixteen and twenty boys with only a grade-school education experienced seven times as much premarital intercourse as did boys who went to college, and they experienced it with a wider variety of partners as well. A member of the grade-school group was also about three times as likely to go to a prostitute as a member of the college group, and he would probably have four or five times as many homosexual experiences. Kinsey further discovered that lower-class males were quite promiscuous in the early years of marriage but grew

122. *Male*, pp. 77–79, 329–35. As Kinsey himself noted (p. 333), his categories were not, strictly speaking, economic; one comes closer to the truth in characterizing his social classes as status groups.
123. Ibid., pp. 205, 329, 419, 441, 447.
124. Ibid., pp. 335–37.

faithful with age, a pattern that was exactly reversed among upper-class males.[125]

While the poor were copulating the rich characteristically busied themselves not only with masturbation but with such other noncopulative activities as petting and nocturnal emissions. Between the ages of sixteen and twenty unmarried males of the college group masturbated twice as often as grade-school graduates, and the disparity between the autoerotic activities of the two classes increased with age. In the same late adolescent years an upper-class male also had three times as many nocturnal emissions and petted to climax three times as frequently as a typical representative of the lower class.[126]

Alongside these important differences in the outlets chosen by the two classes were differences no less remarkable in what might be called their sexual styles. The rich, Kinsey found, were great adepts of sexual sophistication. The poor, on the other hand, preferred directness and simplicity. The difference could be characterized as that between an intellectual and an instinctual sexuality, and it found expression particularly in the divergent attitudes of the two classes toward foreplay. The poor, Kinsey showed, proceeded directly to intromission with little regard for preliminaries. They considered nudity obscene and oral eroticism perverse. Even kissing was of doubtful propriety in lower-class circles, and Kinsey noted that a boy from the working class was likely to have had intercourse with hundreds of girls, only few of whom he had kissed. Finally, sexual intercourse among the poor was usually conducted in the missionary position, since the lower-class male was inclined to be scandalized by any experimentation in such matters.

The upper-level male, by way of contrast, was a devotee of Havelock Ellis's "art of love." A confirmed reader of marriage manuals, he was aroused by a variety of nongenital activities that the lower-class male found at best indifferent and at worst positively abhorrent. He believed it his responsibility to prepare the slower-responding female for intercourse and did so conscientiously. He was especially preoccupied with the female breast and with manual or oral stimulation of the vagina. In effect, he

125. Ibid., pp. 347–63, 587.
126. Ibid., pp. 339–47.

brought to sexual intercourse many of the techniques that he had learned in the years when intercourse was prohibited him and he had been forced to rely on petting as a source of outlet.[127]

Kinsey's sympathies were divided in this conflict of sexual styles. In some passages he appeared as heir to the tradition of Ellis. Here he criticized the narrowness of the lower-class male's sexual conceptions and argued that most of the practices condemned by the poor had been observed in the sexual behavior of animals. In other words, he suggested that the rich were in some respects closer to nature.[128]

More often, however, Kinsey abandoned the tradition of Ellis in order to defend the greater sexual wisdom of the lower orders. He loved to hobnob with the poor and to display his familiarity with their manners and lingo. Not surprisingly, this addiction to slumming resulted in a partiality for lower-class sexual habits. In fact, he became a formidable critic of the sexual sophistication of the rich. He argued, for example, that the upper-class male's interest in the female breast was far out of proportion to the breast's true erotic significance for the female. He also obviously approved of the poor's preference for intercourse over masturbation and their high tolerance for homosexuality. Above all he was convinced that their direct, even blunt approach to sex was in the end more sensible than the mannered, self-conscious style of the rich. In this regard he noted that lower-class women—precisely those women who were not the objects of the male's solicitations—achieved orgasm in intercourse more regularly than did upper-class women. In other words, he suggested that the foreplay ethic of the rich rested largely on superstition. Thus although he might have wished the poor to show greater forbearance for the so-called perversions of the rich, he seemed to imply that their bigotry was not without its foundation in reality.[129]

Kinsey made several attempts to explain the differences he

127. Ibid., pp. 363–74, 386.
128. Ibid., pp. 369, 371, 540, 573–74, 577–78; *Female,* pp. 228–31, 257, 365.
129. *Male,* pp. 52, 367, 572–73, 575–76; *Female,* pp. 253–55, 365, 384–85. In the *Female* volume Kinsey was forced to reverse himself on the relation between social class and the female's ability to achieve orgasm. On the basis of a larger sample and a "more adequate method of analysis," he concluded that upper-class women were the more likely to reach climax in intercourse (*Female,* pp. 354, 378–79).

found between lower- and upper-class sexual behavior, as well as to explore their implications. He felt that some of those differences could be ascribed to the intellectual advantages of the rich. The upper-class male, he surmised, had a more highly developed imagination than the lower-class male, and this superiority probably accounted for his greater receptivity to nongenital stimuli:

> The higher degree of eroticism in the upper level male may . . . be consequent on his greater capacity to visualize situations which are not immediately at hand. In consequence, he is affected by thinking about females, and/or by seeing females or the homosexual partner, by burlesque shows, obscene stories, animals in coitus, and sado-masochistic literature. . . . None of these are significant sources of stimulation for most lower level males, who may look on such a thing as the use of pictures or literature to augment masturbatory fantasies as the strangest sort of perversion.[130]

Kinsey also employed this hypothesis to account for the upper-class male's high rate of nocturnal emissions. Emissions, he suggested, depended on erotic dreams, which in turn depended on the capacity to fantasize.[131]

If Kinsey had been asked to explain why the poor lacked the imaginative faculty of the rich, he would have responded that the deficiency was due in part to their inferior education. But he also believed that in the sexual realm at least the poor had no need to develop such a faculty. Since sexual intercourse was easily accessible to them, they had little reason to cultivate the imaginary substitutes that figured so prominently in the sexual repertory of the well-to-do:

> The very fact that upper level males fail to get what they want in socio-sexual relations would provide a psychologic explanation of their high degree of erotic responsiveness to stimuli which fall short of actual coitus. The fact that the lower level male comes nearer having as much coitus as he wants would make him less susceptible to any stimulus except actual coitus.[132]

In other words, Kinsey's hypothesis of a differential in imaginative capacity already presumed the existence of significant differences in the sexual behavior of his two classes. It was not in any

130. *Male*, p. 363.
131. Ibid., pp. 345, 521.
132. Ibid., p. 363.

sense a fundamental explanation and did not even address itself to such differences as existed in the homosexual and extramarital patterns of the two classes.

In the end Kinsey fell back on the contention that differences in the sexual habits of rich and poor simply reflected their divergent "sexual philosophies." Like his treatment of the impact of religion on sexual life, this explanation betrayed what can best be called an intellectualistic bias. Rich and poor behaved dissimilarly, he argued, because they held dissimilar values. Beyond that one could not go.[133] Thus, although he insisted emphatically on the intimate connection between social situation and sexual behavior, Kinsey could not specify the nature of that connection. He explained neither how the differences between lower- and upper-class life led logically to the differences in the sexual mores of the two classes, nor, conversely, how those mores themselves influenced the nonsexual aspects of existence. He never, for instance, considered how the divergent sexual patterns of rich and poor may have served to buttress the existing social system. If we can believe Herbert Marcuse and Norman O. Brown, the almost exclusively genital nature of lower-class sexuality is of enormous significance for the organization of social and economic life. Marcuse in particular has maintained that the desexualization of the body and the confinement of erotic pleasure to the genitals is a precondition for transforming the body into an instrument of labor.[134] Nothing comparable to this hypothesis was to be discovered in Kinsey. Apparently he did not consider it within his purview to speculate on the ultimate social logic of his findings.

Kinsey recognized, however, that the existence of two distinct class patterns of sexual behavior created a number of social problems. The two patterns, he showed, did not exist in innocent isolation of one another but were locked in mortal combat. Conflict arose when the representatives of the upper class sought to impose their sexual standards on the poor. With undisguised indignation Kinsey reviewed the efforts of upper-class psychiatrists, marriage counselors, employers, teachers, social workers, army officers, judges, and prison wardens to force working-class

133. Ibid., pp. 379, 383–85, 572.
134. Herbert Marcuse, *Eros and Civilization* (second edition; Boston, 1966), pp. 38, 48.

persons under their care or jurisdiction to honor the sexual code of the affluent. By way of contrast the instances of working-class standards being imposed on the upper class were extremely rare; he mentioned only the single hypothetical example of the policeman of lower-class origins who happened to discover a boy masturbating in a back alley and meted out excessive punishment. Since the power holders in our society were nearly all members of the upper class, and since they had effected the codification of their own sexual values in the various legal statutes of the country, Kinsey found it quite easy to side with the poor in this sexual class war. He was, if you will, a kind of genital Marx, charging that class prejudice condemned the poor to "loss of social standing, imprisonment, disgrace, and the loss of life itself" if they failed to conform to the sexual standards of the wealthy. He left little doubt, moreover, that he looked forward to the day when the poor would be liberated from the sexual tyranny of their betters.[135]

X

Sexual Behavior in the Human Female appeared five years after *Sexual Behavior in the Human Male,* and it differed from its predecessor in a number of ways. For one thing, Kinsey took advantage of the interlude to refine many of his ideas. The second volume therefore showed greater polish and discernment than the first. There was less emphasis on the brute material fact of orgasm (although this modification was made necessary in part by the not uncommon failure of women to achieve orgasm in their sexual encounters), and he paid closer attention to questions of attitude and motivation.[136]

Kinsey also sought to broaden the empirical base of his project. The bulk of the evidence still came from interviews—the case histories of 5,940 white females—but this material was supplemented by what he referred to as "recorded" and "observed" data. The recorded data consisted of sexual calendars, correspondence, fiction, and graffiti, as well as "some 16,000 works of art." Observed data referred to studies conducted by gynecologists, obstetricians, urologists, and other clinicians, along with informa-

135. *Male,* pp. 384–93.
136. *Female,* pp. 45, 65–66.

tion gathered "from the direct observation of mammalian sexual activities and human socio-sexual relationships."[137] The text of the *Female* volume contained no clear reference to these direct observations, but Pomeroy has reported that Kinsey made films of a number of sexual activities, thus anticipating the procedures of Masters and Johnson.[138]

Not surprisingly, Kinsey also took advantage of the *Female* volume to answer some of his critics. As a result the book was more explicit in its assumptions and more candid in its prejudices than the *Male* volume had been. He admitted, for instance, that his research was not concerned solely with determining the facts about human sexuality but had been directed toward resolving certain sexual dilemmas as well, particularly those experienced by married couples, young people, and so-called sex offenders. Nevertheless, he maintained that this interest in problem solving had not prejudiced the objectivity of his findings.[139]

If the differences between the *Male* and *Female* volumes were limited to such refinements and modifications as these, it would hardly make sense to insist, as I have, that the two volumes be accorded separate analyses. But *Sexual Behavior in the Human Female* undertook to examine several issues that had never been raised in the first volume, and, conversely, many of the questions that had figured prominently in the earlier study slipped from view in its successor. Thus, although the *Female* volume was every bit as argumentative as the *Male* volume, its arguments were, to a surprising extent, unprecedented.

The most serious casualty of the half-decade separating the two books was the elaborate system of factors that had provided *Sexual Behavior in the Human Male* with its organizational backbone. The factors were still there in the *Female* volume, but they had become shadows of their former selves and were not even afforded the amenity of separate chapter headings. Furthermore, those factors that had exercised the greatest influence on male sexual behavior turned out to be the least significant as far as women were concerned, while those that had touched men only lightly appeared to have a rather more marked effect on women. Of all the factors, social class and age suffered the most dramatic demotions. Indeed, it comes as rather a shock after the

137. Ibid., p. 89; also pp. 3, 83–92.
138. Pomeroy, *Dr. Kinsey*, pp. 172–87.
139. *Female*, pp. 7–21.

passion Kinsey had expended on class distinctions and their invidious implications in the *Male* volume to find him dismissing
class as all but inconsequential with respect to the sexual behavior of women. Not even premarital intercourse, which among
men was the outlet most spectacularly affected by social class,
showed any variation among women of different social levels.
The same held true for nocturnal sex dreams, masturbation, petting, and marital coitus. In each of these areas the experiences of
women from different classes were for all practical purposes indistinguishable. Only with respect to two outlets—extramarital
intercourse and homosexual relations—could Kinsey discern any
class pattern among his female subjects. The extramarital pattern
conformed to that found among men: in their mature years lower-
class women tended to be more faithful than upper-class women.
Curiously, the homosexual pattern was exactly the opposite of
that among men. It was the upper-level female who was more
likely to have had homosexual relations, a tendency Kinsey attributed to the fact that girls from wealthy families married later
than poor girls and thus were forced to accept homosexual substitutes for heterosexual intercourse in the years before marriage.[140] The explanation seems plausible enough until one
recalls that males from the upper class also married later than
their lower-class counterparts, and yet they had the less extensive
homosexual experience.

The picture with regard to age was similar. Kinsey, of course,
did not deny that age had an effect on female sexual behavior.
But he stressed that it influenced women much less powerfully
than it did men. There was nothing in the female's history comparable to the sudden rise in outlet that the male experienced at
adolescence. Rather, what changes occurred were invariably
gradual. It was almost as if the female's aging pattern had been
modeled after the popular conception of femininity: female sexual
aging was, so to speak, smooth and rounded, with none of the
angularity or propulsiveness of the typical masculine pattern.[141]

A woman's sexuality, then, rose and declined with utmost
decorum. Furthermore, in the middle of her life there was a long

140. Ibid., pp. 150, 200–01, 206–07, 239–42, 293–95, 354, 421, 459–60.
141. Ibid., pp. 110, 125, 511–12; *Male*, p. 183. Even the graphs on
which Kinsey charted the aging patterns of men and women seemed to
reflect these contrasting images of masculinity and femininity: the male
curves were angular, the female curves rounded. See *Female*, pp. 126, 141.

period, lasting sometimes more than thirty years, during which her sexual performance changed virtually not at all. From the late twenties until the fifties or sixties she remained on a kind of sexual plateau. The male, by way of contrast, enjoyed no such period of stability, since his sexual capacity was constantly on the decline from the late teens. Kinsey found, moreover, that the plateau effect held not merely for a woman's total performance but for most individual modes of outlet as well. Only those activities that involved a male partner, such as heterosexual intercourse or petting, revealed a distinct aging pattern, and he argued convincingly that the pattern in question was in reality the man's, not the woman's.[142]

The image of female sexual behavior that emerged from Kinsey's discussion of age and social class was one of extraordinary uniformity. Or, as he himself expressed it, female sexuality seemed to be distinguished from male sexuality by its lesser conditionability. On the other hand, some of Kinsey's findings pointed to the opposite conclusion, suggesting, that is, that female sexuality was if anything more responsive to outside influences than male sexuality. This was true with regard to two factors in particular, religion and history.

In the *Male* volume Kinsey had hedged on the matter of religion. He admitted that its influence was palpable, but when placed alongside that of social class or age it seemed to him relatively insignificant. In the *Female* volume, however, religion emerged as the only factor of unquestioned importance. Religious conviction, Kinsey found, had a powerful inhibitive influence on the sexual behavior of women, an influence that seemed all the more impressive in view of the female's imperviousness to most other factors. Not only were religious women much less likely to become involved in sexual activities, but when they did become involved their rates of outlet were nearly always lower than those of nonreligious women. Kinsey also discovered that religious women achieved orgasm in intercourse less often than nonreligious women, and he blamed their frigidity on the moral restraints that led them to avoid sexual relations before marriage.[143]

142. *Female,* pp. 144–45, 200–01, 206–07, 234, 237, 251, 289, 348–54, 518, 528.
143. Ibid., pp. 154, 247–48, 304–06, 424, 463, 515–16, 521–24, 529.

The treatment of the historical issue in the *Female* volume showed a marked advance in precision over the comparable effort in the *Male* volume. Instead of dividing his sample according to age at the time of the interview, Kinsey grouped his subjects into those born before and those born after 1900. In the *Male* volume he had found that history was of little importance; his younger and older generations exhibited almost identical patterns. Female sexuality, on the other hand, appeared to be more susceptible to changes in the historical atmosphere. Women coming of age during and after the First World War were found to be consistently more liberated than their mothers. Kinsey seemed particularly impressed by the statistics on premarital intercourse, which showed twice as many women of the younger generation involved. In fact, the post-1900 group registered higher incidence figures for every form of outlet save homosexuality. It also contained fewer frigid wives.[144]

Kinsey attributed this new libidinousness among women to several causes, including the Progressive campaign against prostitution, the writings of sexual modernists like Havelock Ellis and Sigmund Freud, and the general liberalizing effects of the war. At the same time, he contended that the changes were not so revolutionary as they appeared to be. He drew particular attention to the fact that the increased participation of women in various sexual activities had not been accompanied by a rise in the frequency with which they indulged in those activities. A larger percentage of the younger generation might be masturbating, petting, and enjoying premarital and extramarital intercourse, but those women who engaged in such practices did not exercise their newfound freedom any more often than did the active population of the older generation.[145] In effect, Kinsey sought to minimize the significance of the historical pattern he had discovered. He did so, in my opinion, because the existence of such a pattern threatened to undermine what was to become the central theoretical contention of the *Female* volume, namely that women were sexually less conditionable than men.

If I may summarize Kinsey's findings with respect to the factors influencing female sexual behavior, he suggested that social

144. Ibid., pp. 55, 110, 151, 202, 242–44, 253, 298–301, 356–58, 365, 373, 422, 461–62.
145. Ibid., pp. 151–52, 202–03, 301–02, 424.

class had practically no effect on female sexuality, that age had considerably less effect on women than it had on men, and that the influence of history, while discernible, was not to be exaggerated. One senses that he would gladly have denigrated the significance of religion as well. But the statistics on religion were intractable, and he had to be content with drawing as little attention to them as possible. In general, the examination of factors had not shed much light on female sexuality, and the entire issue was disposed of in one-third the space required in the *Male* volume.

XI

As I've just indicated, the question that most concerned Kinsey in *Sexual Behavior in the Human Male*—i.e., how sexual behavior was influenced by such factors as age, social class, and religious persuasion—played only a minor role in *Sexual Behavior in the Human Female*. Instead, the second Kinsey Report addressed itself to an entirely different issue. Its overriding preoccupation was with the similarities and differences between the sexuality of women and that of men. Put another way, it posed the question, "How is sexual behavior affected by the unique factor of gender?"

Kinsey fully recognized the hazardousness of this inquiry. "Comparisons of females and males must be undertaken with some trepidation and a considerable sense of responsibility," he wrote, and he carried on a running battle with the glib analyses of male-female differences that had been proffered by earlier sexual theorists, including Freud and Ellis. He also confessed that it would be "surprising" if he had succeeded in liberating himself from the prejudices of his forebears. The admission was both candid and accurate.[146]

Perhaps the most striking feature of Kinsey's prolonged comparison of male and female sexual behavior in the *Female* volume was the hostility he showed toward received opinions on the subject. He was certain that differences existed, but he was equally certain that they were not what most people thought they were. Above all he believed that they bore little relation to the

146. Ibid., p. 567.

immediately observable anatomical differences between men and women. A substantial portion of the *Female* volume, accordingly, was devoted to proving that, in physical terms, male and female sexual responses were remarkably similar.

Without doing excessive violence to the complexity of Kinsey's argument, I think he can be said to have concentrated on three topics. There was, first, a series of issues concerning the role of the penis in the sexual arousal of both men and women. Second, there was the question of the relative diffusion of sexual response in the male and the female, and in particular the role of the breasts. Finally, there was the matter of the differing reproductive functions of the two sexes and their supposed influence on sexual behavior.

Kinsey was a great debunker of the penis. *Sexual Behavior in the Human Female* represented the absolute nadir of phallic consciousness. It showed Kinsey at his most militantly feminist and in his most consistent opposition to Freud. Not only did he challenge various notions about the advantages supposedly accruing to the male through possession of a penis, but he also cast doubt on the importance of the penis for the sexual pleasure of the female.

Kinsey summarized the prevailing phallic wisdom:

It has . . . been suggested that the larger size of the male phallus accounts for most of the differences between female and male sexual response, and that a female who had a phallus as large as the average penis might respond as quickly, as frequently, and as intensely as the average male.[147]

This hypothesis, Kinsey showed, rested on at least two false empirical premises: first, that men responded more intensely than women, and second, that they responded more quickly (the issue of frequency he was willing to concede). No anatomical evidence suggested that the penis, despite its larger size, was any more sensitive than the homologous organ in the female, the clitoris, and whatever unspecified advantage the larger size of the penis guaranteed the male was more than compensated by the extreme sensitivity of the labia minora and the vestibule of the vagina. The notion that women responded less quickly than men was, according to Kinsey, a delusion fostered by the modern foreplay

147. Ibid., p. 573.

mystique. He acknowledged that women were often slower to achieve orgasm in intercourse, but their slowness, he believed, was attributable largely to miscues on the part of the male, and when women masturbated to orgasm they required little more time than men.[148]

Just as misguided as the folklore concerning the intensity and speed of female response was the notion that the male's possession of a penis accounted for the differences between male and female sexual psychology. Here Kinsey seemed to be taking issue with the Freudian theory of penis envy, although Freud was not explicitly mentioned. Nevertheless, he insisted that there were "fundamental psychologic differences between the two sexes which could not be affected by any genital transformation."[149] This opinion was confirmed, he argued, by the fact that the same psychosexual differences could be detected in male and female primates, yet the clitoris of the female primate was often as large as the penis of the male.

In short, Kinsey maintained that sexual arousal and climax were physically identical in men and women. The rhythmic muscular movements that he considered the single most important feature of sexual response were, he argued, indistinguishable in the two sexes, and the same held true for such other physiological evidence of arousal as the loss of sensory perception and the increases in respiration, blood pressure, and pulse rate. In fact, the only sexual process physiologically unique to one sex was ejaculation. And when it was borne in mind that the female among most other species of animal did not even possess the capacity for orgasm, one had to be impressed by the virtual identity of male and female response.[150]

Having established that the penis brought no unusual benefits to the male, Kinsey went on to argue that it brought none to the female either. He could accept the notion that a woman might gain peculiar psychological satisfaction from the deep penetration of the vagina by the penis, and he also admitted that penile pressure on the clitoris, the labia minora, and the vestibule of the vagina could effect distinct sexual gratification. But he insisted

148. Ibid., pp. 163–64, 572, 576–79, 591–92, 625–27.
149. Ibid., p. 574.
150. Ibid., pp. 160–61, 373–74, 594, 631, 635–36, 640–41, 688.

that in most women the walls of the vagina lacked end organs of touch, and thus there was no reason to believe that penile insertion was uniquely important in female sexual satisfaction. All the evidence from female masturbatory and homosexual practices, which rarely involved deep vaginal penetration, argued to the contrary. Thus Kinsey, like Masters and Johnson after him, took exception to the Freudian distinction between the clitoral sexuality characteristic of immature females and the vaginal sexuality supposedly appropriate to fully adult women. Indeed, he denounced as "a biologic impossibility" the Freudian imperative that women transfer their response from clitoris to vagina.[151]

Havelock Ellis had argued that female sexuality was more diffuse than male sexuality, by which he meant that a larger portion of the female body participated in sexual arousal than was the case with the male. To this traditional doctrine Kinsey also took exception, although he was not completely consistent on the matter. He agreed that many nongenital areas of the body, above all the anus, mouth, and breasts, shared in sexual response. But he argued that none of these organs, not even the breasts, had been shown to be any more responsive in women than in men.[152]

On the other hand, Kinsey sometimes suggested that male sexuality seemed to be more genital than female sexuality. He reported, for example, that female subjects often criticized men for their exclusive preoccupation with the genitals, while women themselves appeared to be more responsive to generalized body contacts. This difference could also be detected in the homosexual activities of the two sexes, male homosexuals emphasizing genital manipulation, female homosexuals preferring a more diffuse eroticism. Kinsey seemed to imply that the difference was psychological in origin, since he had explicitly denied that any physical basis existed for assuming that sexual response was more concentrated in one sex than in the other.[153]

Finally, Kinsey sought to cast doubt on the notion that the different reproductive functions of men and women had any

151. Ibid., pp. 162, 576, 580–84, 592, 632; *Male*, p. 576. For an interesting critique of Kinsey's discussion of the vaginal orgasm, see Irving Singer, *The Goals of Human Sexuality* (New York, 1973), pp. 93–97.

152. *Female*, pp. 585–87, 591–92; *Male*, p. 575.

153. *Female*, pp. 467–68, 573, 658–59.

bearing on their sexual behavior. "Ejaculation may constitute a spectacular and biologically significant event," he wrote, "but it is an event which depends on relatively simple anatomic differences, rather than upon differences in the basic physiology of sexual response in the female and the male."[154] He also devoted remarkably little attention to the effect of pregnancy or menstruation on female sexuality. The fact that a woman's sexual desire seemed to be most intense just before the onset of menstruation, when she was at her most sterile, showed, he argued, that evolution had effected a radical separation of sexual and reproductive functions in the human animal.[155] In this opinion he assumed what can only be described as the most extreme modernist position.

XII

Despite his contention that sexual arousal in the female was physically indistinguishable from sexual arousal in the male, Kinsey nevertheless asserted that "the female is generally less responsive than the male."[156] Clearly he did not mean by that that women respond less intensely than men. Neither did he seem to think that the desire for sexual release, when it occurred, was any less imposing in women than it was in men. Rather, the charge of the female's lesser responsiveness referred to her lower frequencies of outlet; while women wished for and enjoyed orgasm as emphatically as men, that wish apparently came upon them less often than it came upon the male of the species.

As evidence for this generalization Kinsey cited the statistics on masturbation and nocturnal sex dreams. The female's rate of outlet for both of these activities was substantially below the male's. Moreover, Kinsey argued that masturbation and nocturnal sex dreams provided the most reliable guides to the female's true sexual capacity, since neither was compromised by desires originating with the male. Both showed how women responded when acting solely on their own impulses. This assumption was at variance with his finding in the *Male* volume that rates of

154. Ibid., p. 636.
155. Ibid., pp. 213, 593, 609–10. Kinsey also denied that the menopause resulted in any diminution in female sexual response (*Female*, p. 735).
156. Ibid., p. 575.

masturbation and nocturnal emissions were profoundly affected by social class and therefore hardly a faithful measure of biological capacity. He would have responded, no doubt, that women had been shown to be relatively insensitive to social influences and that the statistics on female masturbation and nocturnal sex dreams thus accurately reflected their natural propensities.[157]

Kinsey also drew upon phylogenetic evidence to support his contention. Studies of animal behavior suggested that females among the lower species were likewise less responsive than males. Indeed, among the majority of animals the female never achieved orgasm, and in those species where masturbatory activities had been observed it was the male that was more often involved. Kinsey admitted, however, that the available phylogenetic data were "fragmentary."[158]

Finally he argued that evidence from heterosexual relations confirmed the female's lesser responsiveness. Here he noted in particular the not infrequent failure of women to achieve orgasm in sexual intercourse, an almost unheard of occurrence among men. Nine percent of his female subjects had never reached climax, and 2 percent had never consciously experienced sexual arousal. The disparity between male and female performance was especially striking among the unmarried. He found, for instance, that the average male had over 1,500 orgasms before marriage, while the average female had fewer than 250. He also argued that the tendency of wives to give higher estimates than their husbands of the frequency of marital coitus evidenced their desire for less sexual activity.[159]

As I have noted, Kinsey was convinced that the female's lesser responsiveness did not originate in any physical distinction between the sexes. Neither did he believe that it resulted from an inherent modesty or natural morality supposedly characteristic of women. He thus felt himself forced to the conclusion that the female's lower frequencies of outlet reflected her lesser sensitivity to psychological influences, although he ultimately suggested that the differences in male and female sexual psychology were themselves based on fundamental neurological differences.

157. Ibid., pp. 132–33, 146, 192.
158. Ibid., pp. 134–35; *Male,* pp. 128, 571.
159. *Female,* pp. 76, 250, 512–13, 519–20, 526–27; *Male,* pp. 128, 157, 223, 571.

Kinsey assembled a considerable body of evidence to support this hypothesis. His most impressive data bore on the role of observation and fantasy in the sexual lives of men and women. With remarkable consistency men were found to be more susceptible to visual and imaginary stimulation. Twice as many men as women confessed to be aroused by seeing members of the opposite sex, and twice as many men as women preferred to have sexual relations in the light. Males were four times more likely to respond to pornography, which accounted for the rarity of pornography designed for a female audience. Men were also more inclined to fantasize while masturbating, and they were more given to such sexual practices as sado-masochism, fetishism, and transvestism, which, following Havelock Ellis, Kinsey argued were dependent for their appeal on the power of the sexual imagination. The female's lesser psychological involvement was likewise reflected in her tendency to be easily distracted during sexual relations. In fact, the sexy talk with which many men embellished their ministrations often served to divert rather than further arouse the female, whose successful progress toward orgasm depended primarily upon "the continuity of physical stimulation."[160]

Kinsey also argued that his examination of the various "factors" affecting sexual behavior supported the hypothesis of the female's lesser psychological responsiveness. In particular the female's failure to be influenced by social considerations indicated a relative insensitivity to the psychological pressures that arose from class prejudice. Women, it seemed, were oblivious to the sexual opinions of their neighbors. Indeed, it was almost as if their indifference to psychological influences had entirely removed them from the class system. As sexual creatures, they were a race apart, sharing a common psychic deprivation that transcended all social barriers.[161]

The conclusion was inescapable: male sexuality was predominately mental, female sexuality predominately physical. Or as Kinsey expressed it, female sexuality appeared to be less subject to conditioning, meaning by that, less subject to influences of a psychological nature.[162] This verdict had the ironic effect of re-

160. *Female*, pp. 165, 384–85, 502, 651–81, 687; *Male*, p. 581.
161. *Female*, pp. 685–86.
162. Ibid., pp. 649–50, 688.

versing the popular belief that sex for women was somehow more an emotional than a physical reality, more bound up with ineffable psychological considerations (such as love) than with the brute fact of physical stimulation. It also left the impression that women were in a sense less fully human than men, since their sexual responses were determined by material rather than by cerebral considerations.

The male's greater sensitivity to psychological stimuli served to explain his higher rates of outlet. Since he was constantly subject to visual and imaginary influences that the female found indifferent, he experienced regular inducement to sexual activity. Indeed, it was virtually impossible for him to escape such inducement; even the most innocent activities—such as walking down the street—were fraught with temptations. The female, on the other hand, rarely experienced sexual desire before being directly stimulated physically. Until she found herself actually locked in the embrace of her lover she remained relatively unaware of her need for sexual release.

Kinsey believed that the more intensely psychological nature of male sexuality also accounted for a number of other differences between male and female sexual patterns. It explained, for instance, why the male responded not merely more frequently but also more regularly than the female. Men, he found, rarely went for long without some form of sexual outlet. Women, by way of contrast, seemed to alternate between periods of great sexual activity and periods of sustained abstinence. He reasoned that the periods of abstinence simply represented those times in a woman's life when she experienced no direct physical stimulation. Such periods occurred rarely in a man's life, since the psychological sources of arousal were ever-present. At the very least, the male's greater sensitivity to the charms of fantasy meant that nocturnal emissions would continue to provide a sexual outlet even when all other modes of release were cut off.[163]

The female's lesser sensitivity to psychological stimuli also explained her sexual passivity. In both the animal and the human worlds it was usually the male that initiated sexual activities, for the very simple reason that the male was more inclined to feel sexual arousal before experiencing actual physical contact. The

163. Ibid., pp. 65, 199–200, 289–90, 350, 456, 666, 681–82; *Male*, p. 192.

disparity in psychological responsiveness further accounted for the male's greater interest in oral sex and in experimenting with different coital positions and techniques. At the same time, the male's susceptibility to psychic stimuli meant he was more interested in sexual variety. Men, Kinsey found, had much higher rates of extramarital intercourse than women, and they were much more inclined to approve such behavior. In agreement with Havelock Ellis he argued that the desire for sexual variety reflected a psychological rather than a physical need. But against Ellis he maintained that men were considerably more responsive than women to the psychological temptations that led to infidelity. As he himself put it, the double standard was firmly grounded in real psychological differences between the sexes.[164]

In the last two chapters of *Sexual Behavior in the Human Female* Kinsey considered the possible organic sources of the differences he had detected in the psychosexual responses of men and women. His primary concern in this discussion was to discredit the suggestion that those differences originated in some hormonal distinction between the sexes. For the most part he distrusted the claims of endocrinology, largely because they had given rise to a popular hormonal mystique whose implications he considered dangerously manipulative:

> A general knowledge of the hormones has become widespread in the population as a whole, but in regard to certain critical matters this knowledge is quite incorrect. Journalistic accounts of scientific research, [and] over-enthusiastic advertising by some of the drug companies . . . have led the public to believe that endocrine organs are *the* glands of personality, and that there is such an exact knowledge of the way in which they control human behavior that properly qualified technicians should, at least in the future, be able to control any and all aspects of human sexual behavior.[165]

The individuals most immediately threatened by this hormonal mystique were of course homosexuals, but Kinsey clearly feared that attempts would be made to eliminate every form of socially unacceptable sexual behavior by means of an endocrinal attack. Such efforts to manipulate personality he considered no more

164. *Female*, pp. 109, 230, 250, 256, 258, 322, 409, 456, 458, 666, 682–83; *Male*, pp. 577–79, 589.
165. *Female*, p. 721.

scientific, and little more humane, than the ancient practice of treating rapists and child molesters by castrating them.[166]

According to Kinsey only one significant difference between male and female sexual response—namely the sexual aging pattern—was attributable to hormonal factors, and even in this instance the evidence was far from conclusive. A few studies had indicated a correlation between the aging patterns in men and women and the levels of both pituitary secretions and the 17-ketosteroids in the two sexes. But Kinsey cautioned that no causal relation had been established between these phenomena, and he explicitly stated that the correlation might simply reflect the dependence of both the hormonal and aging patterns on some third (and as yet undiscovered) physiological process.[167]

Having eliminated the hormonal explanation for all male-female differences save possibly the sexual aging pattern, Kinsey proceeded to speculate that the divergence between psychological responsiveness in men and women, upon which so many behavior patterns seemed to depend, might reflect some difference in the cerebral chemistry of the two sexes. Damage to the cortex of the cerebrum, it had been found, could reduce the capacity to respond to psychosexual stimuli. And since Kinsey had established that there were marked differences in the effectiveness of such stimuli in the two sexes, it was not unreasonable, he argued, to assume that the female's lesser responsiveness to psychological influences depended on "cerebral differences between the sexes." Once again he admitted that the experimental evidence for this conclusion was as yet slight, but that did not prevent him from positing the existence of what was in effect a distinct female brain.[168]

Kinsey's hypothesis of the female's lesser sensitivity to psychological stimuli is open to the criticism that he had not given sufficient weight to the social pressures shaping female sexual psychology. A number of his own findings suggested that, were it not for those pressures, women might be even more receptive than men to psychological influences. He discovered, for instance, that some women were able to achieve climax simply by

166. Ibid., pp. 727–29, 744–45, 748, 757–59.
167. Ibid., pp. 751–53, 755–56.
168. Ibid., pp. 710–12.

thinking about sexual situations. By way of contrast, not one of the more than nine thousand men he interviewed reported that he was capable of reaching orgasm on the basis of fantasy alone.[169] Moreover, while it was true that women had proven less susceptible to class prejudice than men, they were if anything more sensitive to the psychological influences that arose from religious conviction. Similarly, female sexual patterns had proven more responsive than male patterns to the influences of history: the liberalization of sexual values brought about by the First World War and other historical developments had had little impact on the sexual behavior of men, but it had substantially altered the female pattern. One might well ask whether these evidences of the female's sensitivity to influences that Kinsey himself would have recognized as distinctly psychological did not suggest that woman's sexuality was less dependent on physical considerations than he believed to be the case.

Expressed in terms of Kinsey's own analytic categories, he had failed to take into account the possibility that women had been conditioned to be unconditionable, that their relative insensitivity to visual and imaginary stimuli was itself a product of conditioning. His response to such a criticism would have been that the sexual behavior of animals seemed to corroborate the distinction he had drawn between the physical sexuality of human females and the psychological sexuality of human males.[170] However, a careful reading of *Sexual Behavior in the Human Female* shows that Kinsey's phylogenetic evidence was extremely impressionistic; it lacked the statistical rigor that he demanded for his generalizations about the sexual life of men and women. Clearly he gave in too readily to the proposition that the differences he discovered between male and female sexual behavior were biologically determined. In this respect, his discussion of male-female differences represented the one serious weakness in an otherwise solidly liberal and humane front. And it is enormous tribute to the power of sexual prejudice that this most consistent critic of Western sexual values, the scourge of Reinhold Niebuhr and Lionel Trilling alike, should have articulated a theory of male-female sexual differences that, for all its sophistication,

169. Ibid., pp. 200, 540.
170. Ibid., pp. 650–51, 656, 662, 669.

tended to confirm popular opinion. Significantly, not even his most outspoken detractors took issue with him on the matter.

XIII

Kinsey has had probably a greater influence on modern sexual consciousness than any other thinker since Freud. In this final section I would like to offer some speculations about the precise nature of his influence. In particular I want to comment on the relation of that influence to the characteristic assumptions, biases, and modes of argument in his work that I have drawn attention to in this chapter.

One must concede that many aspects of Kinsey's thought to which he attached great importance have had little apparent impact on contemporary sexual attitudes. A prime example would be his findings about the relation between sexual behavior (at least male sexual behavior) and social class. I doubt that the general public, or even the educated public, is significantly more aware today than it was thirty years ago of the existence of radically divergent sexual mores in different social classes. Conceivably the differences are no longer as great as they once were. The fact remains that Kinsey was unsuccessful in his effort to make Americans class conscious in sexual matters. His qualified endorsement of lower-class sexual forthrightness and his criticism of the elite ethic of foreplay fell on equally deaf ears. Havelock Ellis's art of love, of which Masters and Johnson must be counted the latest proponents, has clearly carried the day.

Another element of Kinsey's thought that has made little impression on popular sexual lore is his theory of male-female sexual differences. It is perhaps not surprising, and certainly not regrettable, that his distinction between the physical sexuality of women and the psychological sexuality of men should have failed to become a conscious component of today's sexual ideology. The doctrine was simply too abstract for ready absorption. (The belief that men enjoy pornography and women don't predates Kinsey. What has not entered the public realm is the explicit theoretical distinction that Kinsey drew from the data on pornography and related phenomena.) It is, however, surprising that his attack on phallic consciousness and on the theory of the vaginal orgasm, an attack that so obviously anticipated the teachings of

Masters and Johnson, also appears to have gone largely unappreciated. Women need not have awaited the publication of *Human Sexual Response* in 1966 to launch a feminist critique of received sexual opinion. Kinsey had supplied all the necessary resources as early as 1953, and yet they remained untapped. In general, one can say that his findings about female sexuality have had less impact on popular attitudes than his findings about male sexuality. I have no ready notion why this should be the case, but it is perhaps related to his own greater interest in and sympathy for male sexuality. Just the opposite, incidentally, has happened with Masters and Johnson, who have influenced thinking about female sexuality much more than that about male sexuality.

One must also concede that certain issues that loom large in the contemporary sexual universe were of only marginal interest to Kinsey. The most important of these is the matter of sexual adventure: swinging, group sex, and the like. If this preoccupation has intellectual origins at all, they lie outside Kinsey, who, as noted, paid even less attention to sexual adventure than Havelock Ellis. The same holds for the intellectual pedigree of today's interest in the so-called byways of sex. Ellis, Krafft-Ebing, and Freud were all more avid students of sadism, masochism, transvestism, voyeurism, and exhibitionism than Kinsey. He justified this neglect by arguing that such practices were statistically insignificant. One senses, however, a certain reserve; the more extravagant and picturesque expressions of human sexuality simply didn't capture his imagination. Finally, Kinsey's almost complete lack of concern for such traditional sexual issues as pregnancy and venereal disease was clearly well ahead of his time, and of ours as well. V.D. continues to be a popular bugaboo, and Masters and Johnson, writing a decade after Kinsey, have devoted a great deal of attention to the relation between sexual response and reproduction.

In three areas Kinsey's influence has been significant. First, there can be little doubt that, to his everlasting credit, he helped create a more tolerant attitude toward homosexuality. This liberalizing influence derived most obviously from his simple empirical demonstration of exactly how many people are involved in homosexual activities. At the same time, his dissolution of the very category of homosexuality may have worked an even deeper effect. It suggested not merely that homosexual acts are extremely common, but that homosexuality, since it is not a state of being, exists as a potentiality in all persons. Put another way, it helped give rise to the sentiment "We're all bisexual, it's just a matter of degree."

Perhaps I have judged Kinsey's treatment of sexual identity, and the popular attitude that it has, in part, inspired, too harshly. Let me admit therefore that the proposition "We're all bisexual" has its political uses, and I applaud whatever contribution this piece of fuzzy thinking has made to improve the lot of homosexuals. It should be noted, however, that the concept often serves as a source of self-delusion for individuals who refuse to accept their homosexuality. Armed with the conviction that they are "really" bisexual, they fancy themselves more manly than true homosexuals and sometimes even undertake to marry, with tragic results. All this is not to deny that there are persons whom it would make genuine psychological sense to call bisexual, although I think the breed exceedingly rare.

One can also sense Kinsey's influence in the increasing tolerance with which the sexual activities of the young, especially the unmarried young, are contemplated. As with homosexuality, this liberalizing influence has stemmed in part from a simple empirical discovery, namely that a great deal of sexual activity, among young and old alike, occurs outside marriage. More important was Kinsey's demonstration of the preeminent role of age as a factor in sexual life. While he may have failed to make Americans sexually class conscious, he succeeded brilliantly in making them sexually age conscious. In particular he helped make them aware of the extraordinary sexual needs of adolescent males. Somewhat surprisingly, his revelations about the genital capacities of children have gone virtually unnoticed.

Kinsey's admirable effort to relieve the sexual agonies of the young has had a less happy effect on the sexual well-being of those beyond youth. In fact, his findings about the role of age in sexual response have given rise to two much resented myths: first, that most middle-aged men are sexually exhausted and, second, that most middle-aged women are nymphomaniacs. It is perhaps less interesting that both notions represent wild distortions of Kinsey's actual findings than that they mirror a real bias in his work: his compassion, I would even say love, for the young. The concern that Masters and Johnson have shown for the sexual adjustment of older couples might well be regarded as the predictable reaction to both Kinsey himself and the myths he generated.

The final area in which I detect Kinsey's influence is more amorphous and concerns the frame of reference in which we regard sexual experience. If I am not mistaken, sex is in the process of being demystified. That is, it is coming to be thought of as an essentially commonplace experience rather than something mysterious or prohibited. In Durkheim's terms, it is being transported from the realm of the sacred into that of the profane.

Kinsey, I would argue, is this century's foremost sexual demystifier. Freud, for all his desire to liberate mankind, never suggested that sex could be tamed. If anything, he heightened our sense of its perils and its opposition to the values of civilization. Similarly, Ellis, while he took a less austere view than Freud and contributed magnificently to the assault on Victorianism, continued to associate sexuality with profound and complex human emotions. He was separated from Kinsey, in other words, by his romanticism. By way of contrast, not only did Kinsey lack Freud's sense of the demonic element in human sexuality, he was also as untainted by romanticism as any major sexual theorist I can think of, with the possible exception of the Marquis de Sade. Not even Masters and Johnson approach his purity in this regard. Indeed, no one else has more consistently associated sexual experience with dispassion.

Kinsey was fully conscious of the demystifying motif in his work. He brandished it proudly in his homilies on scientific method and in the heavy irony with which he recorded the sexual opinions of established authorities. I would suggest, however, that the demystifying impact of his work stemmed less from such overt gestures than from certain structural features of his thought. Above all it stemmed from his decision to examine sexual behavior in terms of the concept of outlet, a concept essentially quantitative, morally indifferent, and—no unimportant matter—colorless. The notion of outlet stripped sexual experience not only of its nuance but of its magic and its terror as well. At the same time, it effected a kind of democratization of human sexual affairs. It brought the most tabooed activities under the same conceptual roof as marital relations and in the process rendered them innocuous.

Ultimately one's judgment of Kinsey will depend on how one evaluates the human sexual condition (or, less grandly, the American sexual condition) at mid-twentieth century. If, on the one hand, one is convinced that we still live in the shadow of Victorianism, that ignorance and prejudice in sexual matters continue to create unacceptable levels of anxiety, then Kinsey will earn our admiration as a person who did as much as any intellectual can to make sexual life less painful, freer, and perhaps even happier. If, however, one believes that, in the process of demystification, sex has become trivialized, that in eliminating the anxiety we have also eliminated the ecstasy, then Kinsey, while not to be despised, must be regretted. I incline toward the first of these viewpoints. But I will confess to a growing respect for the second. I would not gladly see sex become as uneventful as eating. My historical sense, however, is that we are still some way from such jadedness, and unquestionably the generation that came of age in the 1930s and 40s, to which the Kinsey volumes were addressed, suffered more from repression than from satiety. Thus Kinsey remains for me an attractive, even a heroic figure in our intellectual history.

3/William Masters
and Virginia Johnson

It seems supremely logical that after Kinsey the study of human sexuality should progress from interviewing to observing. Kinsey himself anticipated this step, but doubtless sensing that the public was unprepared for it, he made no mention in his writings of his observation or photographing of sexual acts. With William Masters and Virginia Johnson, however, the scrim of the interview is raised, and armed with a variety of mechanical devices to make our observations as accurate as possible, we find ourselves in the immediate presence of copulating and masturbating human beings.

In reality, of course, we do not observe human sexual behavior directly but only as it is interpreted by Masters and Johnson. Implicit in their apparently shocking and often ingenious empirical enterprise is a set of assumptions and prejudices no less distinct than those that informed the Kinsey studies. The most interesting differences between Kinsey and Masters and Johnson reflect not their different empirical procedures—interviewing in the one case, observing in the other—but their quite antithetical sexual values.

Masters and Johnson also differ from Kinsey in their explicit therapeutic intent. Kinsey liked to portray himself as a pure scientist whose sole concern was to establish the facts about human sexual behavior. He was, of course, a good deal more than a fact-finder, and in the *Female* volume he admitted that his research had been designed to shed helpful light on certain "problems" in sexual life. Nonetheless, despite the cathartic effect his interviews sometimes had on their subjects, he never descended to the level of individual cases. His therapeutic instincts functioned on a global plane: he wished to cure not particular patients but whole societies.

Masters and Johnson are clinicians first and scientists after. This fact is obscured in their first publication, which they describe as "an investigation of the anatomy and physiology of human sexual response."[1] But in *Human Sexual Inadequacy* the therapeutic impulse behind their work is fully revealed: "When the laboratory program for the investigation of human sexual functioning was designed in 1954, permission to constitute the program was granted upon a research premise which stated categorically that the greatest handicap to successful treatment of sexual inadequacy was a lack of reliable physiological information in the area of human sexual response."[2] The fact that Masters and Johnson's primary commitment is to therapy while Kinsey's was to research serves to explain why, although methodologically more radical, their thought is substantively more conservative than Kinsey's. The therapist tends to accept the established order and seeks to adjust his patient to it. The pure scientist, on the other hand, is free to imagine a better order. The contrast is illustrated on a grand scale in the career of Sigmund Freud, who wished to be physician to both the individual and humanity as a whole, and whose work accordingly is ripe with tensions between therapeutic conservatism and cultural radicalism.

Masters and Johnson pose certain difficulties for the intellectual historian not posed by Kinsey or Ellis. One of these stems from the incomplete state of their work. *Human Sexual Response* and *Human Sexual Inadequacy* contain references to several projects still in progress and reports yet to be issued. Obviously, they may take advantage of future publications to clarify and refine their opinions on some of the matters discussed here, or

1. *Human Sexual Response* (Boston, 1966), p. 3.
2. *Human Sexual Inadequacy* (Boston, 1970), p. 1.

even to change their minds altogether. I regret, therefore, that my discussion occasionally leaves the impression that their work is as finished as Ellis's or Kinsey's, particularly in view of the critical attitude I take toward many of their ideas.

Writing about contemporary intellectuals is a hazardous but hardly unusual undertaking. Much rarer is the task of assessing a body of literature that represents itself as the creation of more than one mind. The Kinsey Reports were authored by four men, but nobody doubted that Kinsey was in absolute command. Appropriately the names of Kinsey's three collaborators never entered the public consciousness. In contrast, Masters is unrecognizable without Johnson, and Johnson without Masters. Nevertheless, Masters is transparently the senior author, although, unlike Kinsey, he never refers to himself as such. He is older than his collaborator (by nine years); he is better educated (he is an M.D.; she has not completed her B.A.); he launched the sexual project on his own in 1954 (she joined him three years later); until recently he remained her superior at the Reproductive Biology Research Foundation (he as director, she as assistant director); and he is given top billing on the title pages of their publications, in violation of the rule that alphabetical order prevail when coauthors are truly coequal.

Given Masters and Johnson's explicit feminism (and the enthusiasm with which they have been embraced by feminist intellectuals), one might be tempted to make fun of a professional relationship that appears to conform to traditional notions about the proper order of authority between men and women engaged in a joint undertaking. I think, however, that the evidence deserves to be read otherwise. Since Masters clearly is the senior author, and since there is every reason to believe that his seniority is a result of circumstance rather than prejudice, the very fact that they have sought to disguise that seniority and allowed their work to become world-famous under both their names testifies to the depth of their feminist convictions. It is as if they wished to appear equals even though they are not such. Moreover, this egalitarian sexual ideal is reflected both in their therapeutic procedures, in which male and female cotherapists work together on a basis of absolute parity, and in the image of human sexual relations that they project in their writings. The ideal is a congenial one, and in my discussion of their thought I have in effect adopted it. Though I have sometimes wondered whether a particular idea originated with Masters or with Johnson, I have treated them as a single mind.

I

Human Sexual Response and *Human Sexual Inadequacy* are undoubtedly two of the worst written books in the English language. And although it might seem perverse to begin an analysis of Masters and Johnson with a discourse on their prose style, I hope to show that their inadequacies as writers are related to their inadequacies as sexual theorists. Ideas that receive vague or clumsy articulation often turn out to be vague or clumsy themselves.

If Ellis, Kinsey, and Masters and Johnson are representative figures in the history of modern sexology, there can be little doubt that the history of sexological style, like the history of style in general, has been a story of decline and fall. Ellis's prose is exactly what one would expect of a late-nineteenth-century English man of letters. Everything is well crafted and fluid, the metaphors bountiful but never mixed. There is, admittedly, little of the power or angularity of Freud's prose—by today's standards the writing is excessively lyrical—but it is always cogent and frequently eloquent.

Kinsey's prose was the product of an American scientific education, and placed alongside Ellis's it seems flat-footed. "Workmanlike" is the adjective that comes immediately to mind, although it is not without a distinctive (and to me enjoyable) flavor—an admixture of studied disinterest and heavy irony. Whether one likes the style or not, one must concede that it is unpretentious, grammatical, and unfailingly clear.

Masters and Johnson's prose, on the other hand, is a compound of unintelligibility, pomposity, and error. In fact, I confess that I found it difficult to concentrate on the substance of their remarks as I became increasingly, perhaps morbidly, preoccupied with unraveling their impossibly tangled syntax and translating their peculiar brand of sociologese into everyday English. A complete catalog of their crimes against the language would be inappropriate in this context, but a brief survey will convey some sense of the linguistic and intellectual world they inhabit.

Their most forgivable transgression is simply awkwardness. One could hardly take them to court for writing "it equally is obvious" instead of "it is equally obvious."[3] Nor is intelligibility seriously threatened when they select verbs and prepositions unsuited to their objects, although the examples are frequent and gross. There is also scant offense to sense, even if the language suffers grievously, in the hundreds of redundant or meaningless qualifiers that dot the text. In the same category (of harmless but homely) belongs the mismanagement of common rhetorical devices. "Decades of 'phallic fallacies,'" they write, "have done more to deter than to stimulate research interest in clitoral response to sexual stimulation,"[4] clearly unaware that their little flourish of deterring and stimulating implies a completely ludicrous alternative.

Most of their lapses are more consequential. Particularly damaging are their many errors of usage. For example, they think that "definitive" means "definite" (as in "a definitive color change that ranges from a cardinal-red to burgundy-wine color"), and that "define" is a synonym for "determine" (as in "the man has an opportunity to define the general level of her formal education").[5] They also think "reflect" means the same thing as "explain" or "tell" (therapists are forever "reflecting" things to their patients), and that "relative" and "relevant" are interchangeable. To be sure, if the reader is sufficiently resourceful, or if the mistake occurs often enough, it is usually possible to determine what they mean. But the burden of translation is tiresome, and there are still many words and phrases whose sense, in the particular context, remains mysterious. As an example, Masters and Johnson distinguish between the "functional" and "functioning" role of the vagina in impregnation. The distinction itself is fairly clear—"functional" refers to the vagina's role as a seminal receptacle, "functioning" to its influence on the motility and longevity of sperm. But one never learns why these particular terms have been chosen, and one's confusion is compounded when the terms reappear in a discussion of the penis, where "functional" now refers to the organ's role as a source of erotic pleasure, and "functioning" to its role in elimination and insemi-

3. *Response,* p. 140.
4. Ibid., p. 45.
5. Ibid., p. 231; *Inadequacy,* p. 152.

nation.[6] A similar uncertainty surrounds their use of such terms as "context," "baseline," "objective," and "concept," all of which show up repeatedly in the texts.

Their greatest offense against both sense and elegance, however, is consistently to prefer complex and pretentious expressions where simple ones would do. Thus they write "in the immediacy of the postorgasmic period" instead of "immediately after orgasm"; "to alter their verbal response patterns" instead of "to lie"; "since college withdrawal" instead of "since leaving college"; "interdigitate" instead of "combine";"vocalize" instead of "say"; "potentiator" instead of "cause"; "the sexual unit" instead of "the couple."[7] Indulged on a larger scale, this propensity can have truly hideous results, as witness the following not unrepresentative sentence: "In retrospect, had sufficient information been exchanged to relieve their intense anxieties and to enlist a return of interpersonal communication, there is every reason to believe that in view of their mutual level of sexual responsivity outside of marriage and the definitive residual of interpersonal concern present at the time of therapy, the innate levels of their mutual responsivity could have been concentrated in the marital bed."[8] This loses nothing in precision and gains enormously in readability if rendered, "Since they were successful with other partners yet still cared for each other, a frank confession would probably have resolved their problem." One is especially likely to encounter this kind of nonsense when Masters and Johnson try to generalize. Confronted with an abstraction, their prose goes almost madly opaque. On the other hand, their case histories and accounts of therapeutic procedure, while never graceful, can be relatively straightforward.

It is uninteresting, no doubt, to be told that Masters and Johnson are bad writers. They would probably plead guilty to the charge themselves, countering only that their actual work as researchers and therapists, not its written representation, is what truly concerns them. But the poor quality of the writing in *Human Sexual Response* and *Human Sexual Inadequacy* is not just a matter of style. Rather, it exactly reflects Masters and Johnson's single greatest failing as intellectuals: their chronic

6. *Response,* pp. 80–100, 188–89.
7. Ibid., pp. 62, 87, 135, 309; *Inadequacy,* pp. 28, 67, 267.
8. *Inadequacy,* p. 381.

inability to be precise. This is a particularly ironic failing in view of our tendency to think of them as the most scientific of sexologists, the researchers who have made the most detailed examination of what happens when human beings engage in sexual activity. They have measured penises (flaccid and erect), photographed vaginas during orgasm, and assessed the precise impact of sexual arousal on blood pressure, pulse rate, and ventilation. And, of course, they do provide a great deal of new and useful information about these and other matters, for which we are very much in their debt. But when they are obliged to place that information in an analytic framework—when, in other words, they are obliged to become sexual theorists—they are betrayed by the intellectual limitations so evident in their prose style. In a word, they become vague. Thus, insofar as science implies precision, Masters and Johnson must be judged the least scientific of the sexual thinkers dealt with in this book.

Their imprecision is dramatically illustrated in the conceptual device that they introduce at the beginning of *Human Sexual Response* and that serves as an organizing principle for the entire book, the theory of the "four phases" of human sexual response. In both men and women, they argue, the sexual "cycle" can be divided into four stages: the excitement phase, the plateau phase, the orgasmic phase, and the resolution phase.[9] This set of distinctions might be thought of as a refinement on Havelock Ellis's division of the sexual process into "tumescence" and "detumescence," the excitement and plateau phases representing subcategories of tumescence, the orgasmic and resolution phases subcategories of detumescence.

The distinction between orgasm and resolution is perfectly unobjectionable. It gives expression to a difference that has subjective reality—all persons with sexual experience know that orgasm is different from what follows it, though both could be called detumescence—and it also lends itself to objective physiological measurement. Particularly is this true for men, who normally experience what Masters and Johnson call a "refractory period" immediately after orgasm, during which any stimulation is not only unerotic but sometimes even painful. The only doubtful element in Masters and Johnson's exposition of this distinction

9. *Response*, p. 4.

is their assertion that the progression from orgasm to resolution involves an exact inversion of the earlier progression from excitement to plateau phase: "The human male and female resolve from the height of their orgasmic expression into the last or resolution phase of the sexual cycle. This involuntary period of tension loss develops as a reverse reaction pattern that returns the individual through plateau and excitement levels to an unstimulated state."[10] In this instance they have allowed themselves to be carried away by the symmetry of their conception, or perhaps by the notion that the sexual process is truly a "cycle." That process is obviously not symmetrical for men (otherwise one would have to posit a refractory period just before orgasm), and it is not demonstrably such for women, although their capacity for multiple orgasms makes the conception at least plausible.

The distinction between excitement and plateau phases is much more questionable. I wish to argue that, save in one narrow though significant area, it is an altogether groundless differentiation and a striking example of Masters and Johnson's intellectual ineptitude. At first glance the distinction seems quite reasonable. Most everyone would agree that there is a beginning stage of sexual arousal—from first stirrings to full erection or full vaginal lubrication—and that this stage is succeeded by a period, more or less prolonged, during which one is completely aroused but not yet orgasmic. It would appear unexceptionable to call the first of these stages the excitement phase and the second the plateau phase. But this common-sensical distinction is not at all what Masters and Johnson have in mind. On the contrary, they suggest that one can remain stuck in the excitement phase (as they think of it) long after achieving full erection or lubrication, and that in some instances one can progress to the plateau phase *without* full erection or lubrication.[11] Clearly, their distinction seeks to probe beneath the surface level of sexual experience.

Masters and Johnson's problem is not only where to draw the line between excitement and plateau phases, but how to justify drawing any line at all. One possibility would be to argue that the distinction is based on subjective experience—that plateau phase is perceived by the individual as quite different from ex-

10. Ibid., p. 6.
11. See, for example, *Inadequacy*, pp. 320, 322, 326.

citement phase, just as resolution is perceived as different from orgasm. There are occasional hints that Masters and Johnson subscribe to such a definition. For example, they characterize plateau phase as "that level of elevated sexual tension identified as thoroughly enjoyable," and in a reference to one female subject they speak of "five subjective plateau-phase experiences superimposed on maintained excitement tension levels."[12] A subjective (or psychological) definition of plateau phase is also implicit in their discussion of the preejaculatory fluid emitted by some males:

> As stated, it [the preejaculate] appears most frequently during voluntarily lengthened plateau-phase experiences. For example, in active coition a man may practice voluntary ejaculatory control at plateau-tension levels through several of his female partner's orgasmic cycles. Other similar situations tend to increase both frequency of occurrence and secretory volume of the preejaculatory mucoid material. They are automanipulative activity voluntarily maintained at plateau-phase tension levels for lengthy periods without ejaculatory release, and fellatio conducted in similar manner and with similar intent.[13]

The problem with defining plateau phase subjectively is that no definition would be precise enough to serve a useful scientific purpose. Even assuming that most persons could recognize "that level of elevated sexual tension identified as thoroughly enjoyable" (or, more crudely, "when it feels really good"), there would be little sense in trying to convert the feeling into an analytic category. Masters and Johnson seem aware of this liability, and accordingly, outside of a few remarks such as those I have quoted above, they attempt to distinguish between excitement and plateau phases in terms of objective physiological occurrences.

At this point one has to separate their discussion of men and women. A characteristic feature of their thought, as we shall see, is to stress the similarities between male and female sexual response. The four phases scheme is itself a significant element in this campaign: it suggests that men and women are sexually alike because the sexual process in both can be comprehended in

12. Ibid., p. 317; *Response*, p. 119.
13. *Response*, p. 211.

terms of the same four rubrics. I suspect, however, that the scheme was originally conceived to describe only the female's sexual cycle, and then later, and for ideological reasons, imposed upon the male. This suspicion is based on the discovery that the distinction between the excitement and plateau phases derives what little rationale it has from an occurrence that is unique to female sexuality. In other words, a case can be made, although only a slight one, for an identifiable plateau phase in the female's sexual cycle. In the male it is clearly nonexistent.

Masters and Johnson nevertheless employ the distinction between excitement and plateau phases in their discussion of nearly every aspect of male sexual response. A careful reading reveals that none of the phenomena they treat is truly "phase-specific"— that is, confined to a single phase and characteristic of that phase in its entirety. Instead, what one finds are a number of reactions that begin in the so-called excitement phase and carry over into the plateau phase. Or, alternatively, one finds reactions that occur toward the end of the plateau phase and that would more accurately be described as "preejaculatory." An example of the former is the response of the testes to sexual stimulation:

> As excitement-phase levels of tension develop, there is a specific elevation of both testes toward the perineum. . . . Actually, only partial elevation of the testes is accomplished during the excitement phase, unless there is to be a fulminating completion of the sexual response cycle. . . . As male sexual tensions rise through plateau-phase toward orgasmic-phase release, the specific reaction of testicular elevation progresses until the final preejaculatory positioning in tight apposition to the male perineum is attained.[14]

Clearly what is being described here, as their own language betrays, is not a two-stage process but a continuous progression, or, if you prefer a musical metaphor, a gradual crescendo. Moreover, the term "plateau" evokes a singularly inappropriate image for the intermediate moments of that progression, unless one fancies the notion of an inclined plateau. Nevertheless, Masters and Johnson write confidently that "the testes evidence specific reaction patterns during each of the four phases of the sexual response cycle."[15]

14. Ibid., pp. 206–07.
15. Ibid., p. 206.

An example of their effort to force what I have called a pre-ejaculatory phenomenon into their conceptual scheme is their treatment of the changes that occur in the penis just before orgasm:

> The penis that apparently has achieved full erection during excite-ment phase undergoes a minor involuntary vasocongestive increase in diameter as the orgasmic (ejaculatory) phase approaches. This additional plateau-phase tumescence is confined primarily to the corona glandis area of the glans penis. A color change also may develop in the glans penis late in the plateau phase of the sexual cycle.[16]

Once again, Masters and Johnson are betrayed by their own language. The expressions "late in the plateau phase" and "as the orgasmic (ejaculatory) phase approaches" reveal a conceptual apparatus on the verge of collapse. (In other contexts one finds such equally telltale formulations as "terminal plateau phase," "high plateau," "advanced plateau phase," and "full plateau phase.") The image of two orderly stages followed by orgasm is utterly foreign to what is obviously a sudden and short-lived occurrence, rather like the lightning before a summer storm.

As far as the male is concerned, then, the scheme of four phases proves altogether irrelevant. It merely creates the impres-sion of scientific precision where none exists. Ironically, Havelock Ellis's doctrine of tumescence and detumescence, though more general, turns out to be a more appropriate and far less preten-tious abstraction, since it allows for both those phenomena that are cumulative and those that are sudden and evanescent rather than imposing boxlike categories that correspond to neither.

Masters and Johnson apparently hope to deflect criticism of this sort by confessing, as they do on several occasions, that their scheme of four phases is an arbitrary construct, intended only to provide a "framework of reference" for their examination of the particulars of human sexual response.[17] This defense proves that they are well versed in the niceties of social science methodology, but it fails to speak to the issue at hand. The four-phases scheme is subject to criticism not because it is an abstraction, but be-

16. Ibid., p. 183.
17. Ibid., pp. 4, 7–8, 27, 223.

cause it is an unwieldy abstraction, one that obscures the reality it is meant to illuminate.

Most elements of the female's sexual response cycle are equally resistant to Masters and Johnson's categories. Like the elevation of the testicles in the male, some of those elements would appear to be essentially cumulative and show scant respect for the imagined border between excitement and plateau phases. Such, for example, is the development of what they call the "sex flush," a pink mottling that appears first on the abdomen and then, as arousal proceeds, spreads upward to the breasts and sometimes to more remote parts of the body as well.[18] Other elements of the female cycle fall into a preorgasmic pattern analogous to the changes that occur in the penis just before ejaculation. In this category belongs the rapid and deep breathing (or hyperventilation) that develops "late in the plateau phase," as well as the dramatic color changes of the labia minora "in the immediate preorgasmic phase of the sexual response cycle."[19]

Two sexual processes in women fit neither the progressive nor the preorgasmic patterns and appear to lend more credibility to the distinction between excitement and plateau phase. One of these is the production of vaginal lubrication, which, Masters and Johnson argue, reaches its peak soon after sexual stimulation begins (much like erection in the male) and actually decreases during the so-called plateau phase. A similar "reversal" occurs in the response of the clitoris, which in certain women becomes elongated in the early stages of sexual arousal (excitement phase), but retracts into its hood as stimulation progresses (plateau phase). I doubt, however, that Masters and Johnson fashioned their distinction to highlight these two processes. The reduction of vaginal lubrication is of little practical importance, and although the gradual withdrawal of the clitoris during the advanced stages of sexual excitement is a universal phenomenon, its elongation in the early stages occurs in but 10 percent of the population (or, more accurately, in but 10 percent of Masters and Johnson's sample).[20]

18. Ibid., pp. 30–32.
19. Ibid., pp. 34, 40–42, 231.
20. Ibid., pp. 50–51, 77.

Only one significant sexual process corresponds exactly with the notion of plateau phase, and that is the development of what Masters and Johnson term the "orgasmic platform":

> With the attainment of plateau-phase levels of sexual tension, a marked localized vasocongestive reaction develops in this specific area of the vagina. The entire outer third of the vagina, including the bulbus vestibuli, becomes grossly distended with venous blood. This vasocongestion is so marked that the central lumen of the outer third of the vaginal barrel is reduced by at least a third from the distention previously established during the excitement phase. Although this localized vasocongestion develops as an involuntary response, it is a sure indication that plateau-phase levels of sexual tension have been achieved.[21]

To an extent, the orgasmic platform, like the sex flush, is a progressive phenomenon. But as is not the case in their discussion of any other process associated with sexual arousal, Masters and Johnson never hedge about the timing of its appearance. It does not begin "either late in the excitement phase or early in the plateau phase." Rather, its onset veritably defines the onset of plateau phase, just as its convulsive collapse is for them the very definition of the female orgasm. I suspect that the term "plateau," which for the most part proves an extremely awkward metaphor for the middle stages of the sexual process, is unconsciously derived, in Masters and Johnson's private etymology, from the term "platform."

In short, their entire conceptual framework appears to have been devised to highlight a single phenomenon, the orgasmic platform. The reasons for this are not far to seek. Masters and Johnson hope to show that all female orgasms are alike, and in particular that the Freudian distinction between the clitoral and the vaginal orgasm is unjustified. This contention has become the most controversial feature of their thought and a major battleground for feminists and psychoanalysts. Masters and Johnson's tactic in this debate has been to assert that every female orgasm, whether the source of stimulation be superficial (clitoral) or deep (vaginal), involves the same empirically verifiable occurrence, namely the development of an orgasmic platform and its pleasurable resolution in contractions. Accordingly, like good

21. Ibid., pp. 75–76, 235.

logical positivists, they relegate the clitoral-vaginal distinction to the dustbin of metaphysics.[22]

Precisely, however, because the orgasmic platform is the centerpiece of their case against the Freudians, Masters and Johnson have allowed it, perhaps unwittingly, to dictate the conceptual scheme with which they seek to comprehend all other sexual processes as well. And although that scheme succeeds admirably in bringing the orgasmic platform to the focus of attention, it is largely meaningless as a general description of human sexual response. It thus contributes greatly to the sense of intellectual confusion and ungainliness that characterizes their work as a whole.

II

Human Sexual Response and *Human Sexual Inadequacy* are based on two separate research populations. The first book describes the reactions of 694 persons who volunteered as subjects in a laboratory study of human sexuality, while the second reports on 790 persons who came to Masters and Johnson for the treatment of sexual disorders.[23] Both groups differ in a number of significant ways from the population of the country as a whole. (The sample for *Human Sexual Inadequacy* is by definition unrepresentative, but like that for *Human Sexual Response,* it deviates from the national average in more than its sexual behavior.) To their credit, Masters and Johnson do not seek to hide the fact that their sample is unrandom. On the contrary, they draw attention to this liability repeatedly, and they are entirely persuasive in arguing that a degree of unrepresentativeness is unavoidable in a project of this sort. Nevertheless, the bias of their sample has serious implications for their findings.

The standard against which their work must be judged in this respect is the sample assembled for the Kinsey studies. Masters and Johnson's laboratory population is less than one twenty-fifth

22. Ibid., pp. 66–67.

23. Ibid., pp. 12–13; *Inadequacy,* p. 354. There was a limited (though unspecified) overlap between the two groups: "A number of family units, initially presenting clinical problems either of sexual inadequacy or conceptive inadequacy, subsequently became a part of the study-subject population" (*Response,* p. 11).

the size of Kinsey's sample. It is thus statistically inadequate for many of the finer distinctions that Kinsey was able to draw. More interesting than the sheer difference in size, however, are the differences in the social composition of the two populations, which account in part for the divergent conclusions at which Kinsey and Masters and Johnson arrive.

Masters and Johnson freely admit the social bias of their sample:

> The study-subject population as finally constituted for this investigation has been established from selected segments of a metropolitan community. More specifically, it has been developed primarily from and sustained by the academic community associated with a large university-hospital complex. The concentration of study subjects from upper socioeconomic and intellectual strata provided by this major source of supply has not been offset by a statistically significant number of lower-range family units obtained from outpatient clinic sources.[24]

Ironically, Masters and Johnson conducted their earliest laboratory investigations with prostitutes, who, had they been incorporated into the general research population, would have lent the sample greater social balance. But the information obtained from prostitutes was deemed unreliable because of the "pathology of the reproductive organs usually present in this population."[25] As study subjects, in other words, prostitutes were desirable sociologically but not sexually.

The reasons for the upper-class bias of the research population are perfectly understandable. The subjects of the investigation had to have considerable free time; they had to remain in the St. Louis area over a sustained period (the transiency of the prostitute population was another factor that made it less than ideal); they had to be articulate; and they had to have achieved a degree of sophistication that would permit their awareness of the project's scientific importance to overcome any natural reticence. Of course, the simple fact that the research population was recruited from an academic community guaranteed its essentially upper-middle-class composition.

Although they readily confess that their sample is socially unbalanced, Masters and Johnson fail to consider how that im-

24. Ibid., p. 11.
25. Ibid.

balance may have affected their findings. Here, unavoidably, one enters the realm of speculation. But from Kinsey we have learned that the sexual habits of the lower classes differ from those of their betters, or at least that such was the case in the 1940s and 1950s (and Masters and Johnson's subjects, observed during the decade after 1954, are not apt to have been all that unlike Kinsey's). Some of the differences, notably in the extent of homosexual activity, are irrelevant (Masters and Johnson's subjects are by definition heterosexual). But others are not. For instance, we know from Kinsey that masturbation is more common among the rich than among the poor. It is thus in a sense appropriate that masturbation should play such a prominent role in Masters and Johnson's laboratory experiments and therapeutic procedures. But we may well doubt that the masturbatory talents demonstrated by their subjects, and the degree of pleasure they derive from masturbation, are typical of the population as a whole. Because of the peculiar social composition of their sample, in other words, Masters and Johnson may have formed an exaggerated impression of the masturbatory capacities and inclinations of the human animal.

Another, and potentially more significant, effect of the underrepresentation of poor people in the sample relates to the role of foreplay in sexual life. If Kinsey is correct, foreplay is substantially curtailed in the sexual encounters of the poor; the lowerclass male tends to proceed directly to intromission and climax. Concern for the female's sexual satisfaction, manifesting itself above all in oral and manual stimulation of the female genitals, is a characteristic of the upper-class sexual life. Because of his solicitousness, moreover, the upper-class male is extremely vulnerable to such sexual disorders as premature ejaculation and impotence: the responsibility for gratifying his female partner imposes a dangerous psychological burden on him from which his lowerclass counterpart is relatively free. Masters and Johnson are aware of this fact and draw attention to it in *Human Sexual Inadequacy*.[26] What they do not consider is the possible effect of this class-based pattern of foreplay on their female subjects. It is

26. To be precise, they note that the lower-class male is less apt to *complain* of sexual disorder, although they are not confident that he is any more immune to it. See *Inadequacy*, p. 356.

not unreasonable to assume that these women, because of their social origins, had grown accustomed to a form of sexual stimulation that a Freudian would call "clitoral." That is, under normal circumstances they would experience prolonged stimulation of the external genitalia—the clitoris and labia—bringing them to high levels of excitement, perhaps even to orgasm, before intercourse was attempted. The clitoris—or, more generally, the external genitalia—would thus tend to become for them the center of sexual consciousness, as would not be the case among lower-class women who experienced little or no foreplay and who obtained whatever gratification they did from the relatively unceremonious penetration of the penis into the vagina.

I am suggesting, in effect, that there might be a clitoral bias in Masters and Johnson's sample, which would account for their failure to uncover examples of the so-called vaginal orgasm.[27] It may still be true that all female orgasms are alike, but one would feel more comfortable in accepting that conclusion had Masters and Johnson's sample contained a significant number of women from the lower classes, whose sexual experience was less likely to conform to the upper-class pattern of foreplay identified by Kinsey.

A second area of bias in the sample—and one to which, unlike the matter of social composition, Masters and Johnson draw little attention—relates to its age distribution. It is deficient at both ends of the spectrum. The relative underrepresentation of older persons comes as no surprise. Kinsey's sample had the same shortcoming, and if anything Masters and Johnson do a superior job in this respect. On the other hand, their sample is dramatically inferior to Kinsey's in its representation of young people. It contains no males, and only two females, under twenty-one.[28] The reasons for this are fairly obvious (although Masters and Johnson are silent on the matter): where Kinsey had merely to interrogate young persons about their sexual activities, Masters and Johnson, if they were to insist that all age groups be ade-

27. Irving Singer makes a similar criticism of Masters and Johnson in *The Goals of Human Sexuality* (New York, 1973). Singer's argument, however, is based not on the social composition of Masters and Johnson's sample but on the requirement that every subject be able to masturbate to climax. See especially p. 35.

28. *Response*, pp. 12–13.

quately represented, would have found themselves in the legally precarious position of asking underage individuals to perform sexual acts. Still, it is startling to realize that the sexual hero of the Kinsey studies, the adolescent male, does not even make an appearance in Masters and Johnson's study.

I suspect, moreover, that the absence of young people from the research population serves to accentuate certain tendencies in Masters and Johnson's thought. For instance, one gets the distinct impression from *Human Sexual Response* that women are sexually more vigorous than men. Women, we are told, enjoy an "infinite variety" of sexual response patterns, while men are limited to a single pattern.[29] We also learn that women are capable of multiple orgasms, while the unfortunate male is beset by his refractory period. Furthermore, although the number of males and females in the research population was roughly the same (312 men against 382 women), Masters and Johnson estimate that they have observed 7,500 female sexual response cycles to only 2,500 male cycles.[30] No explanation for this disparity is forthcoming (presumably it has something to do with the more complex and obscure nature of the female genitals and the corresponding need for a greater number of experiments to determine what occurs in the female genitals during sexual arousal), but the bare figures confirm the general impression of female sexual superiority. One wonders, however, whether that impression would survive had adolescents been adequately represented in the sample. If we can rely on Kinsey's findings, the teenage boy is a sexual dynamo, while his sister's sexual requirements are relatively modest.

Masters and Johnson's research population is unrepresentative in not only its social composition and age distribution, but also its sexual inclinations. Unlike the first two forms of selectivity, however, the sexual bias was intentionally imposed on the sample. All persons exhibiting "sociosexual aberrancy" or "grossly abnormal reproductive viscera" (neither of which deviations Masters and Johnson define precisely) were eliminated. On the positive side, each subject had to be orgasmic in heterosexual intercourse and to be able to masturbate to orgasm.[31]

29. Ibid., p. 4.
30. Ibid., p. 15.
31. Ibid., pp. 12, 32, 198.

The sexual standard demanded of the research population casts doubt on certain of Masters and Johnson's conclusions. For one thing, it again arouses the fear that the sample may have a masturbatory bias, since a truly random sample would contain a number of persons, particularly women, without "positive" masturbatory histories. It also leads one to suspect that the study subjects are in general a more libidinous lot than the population at large. One's suspicions are partially confirmed when one learns that among the most common motives for joining the project was the desire for sexual activity.[32] Masters and Johnson all but concede the point themselves: "Through the years of research exposure," they write, "the one factor in sexuality that consistently has been present among members of the study-subject population has been a basic interest in a desire for effectiveness of sexual performance. This one factor may represent the major area of difference between the research study subjects and general population."[33]

A potentially more damaging consideration than the general level of the sample's libido is the possibility that the typical subject might be some form of exhibitionist. At issue here is the influence of the laboratory atmosphere on study subjects, a matter that many critics, particularly popular ones, regard as the Achilles heel of Masters and Johnson's research. How, it is asked repeatedly, can individuals performing before an audience be expected to respond as they would in the privacy of their own bedrooms? Not surprisingly, Masters and Johnson have anticipated this objection. They answer it, first of all, simply by acknowledging that the problem exists and assuring us that they have given it grave consideration.[34] At the same time, they describe the procedures that were devised to neutralize the laboratory atmosphere and overcome the subjects' self-consciousness:

> The individuals considering active cooperation with the program . . . were exposed to the research quarters. All equipment was exhibited and its function explained to the uninitiated. Sexual activity first was encouraged in privacy in the research quarters and

32. Ibid., p. 305.
33. Ibid., p. 315.
34. Ibid., p. 9.

then continued with the investigative team present, until the study subjects were quite at ease in their artificial surroundings. No attempt was made to record reactions or introduce other members of the research personnel to the reacting unit, until the study subjects felt secure in their surroundings and confident of their ability to perform.[35]

Finally, Masters and Johnson note that their subjects reported no perceptible difference between their performance in the laboratory and at home, although some subjects felt that their sex lives had improved as a result of the laboratory exposure.[36]

This line of reasoning, although persuasive on its own terms, leaves out of account the possible selective influence of the laboratory atmosphere. One can accept their assurances that study subjects performed no differently in the laboratory than at home and still argue that only a certain type of person, namely an exhibitionistic one, would be inclined to volunteer for such a project. This objection appears to have occurred to Masters and Johnson, but the defense they offer is unconvincing: "Any assumption that definitive sexual stimulation accrues directly from exposure to research personnel or environment seems contradicted by the fact that overt exhibitionism has not been a factor in the laboratory. In fact, modesty, social control, and even an excessive regard for social mores has been the general response pattern."[37] However, it is precisely the person whose sexual inclinations do not encompass the most overt forms of exhibitionism who would find Masters and Johnson's laboratory the ideal setting for acting out his fantasies.

Even if they were to accept the imputation that their sample is sexually biased by reason of its masturbatory and exhibitionistic tendencies, Masters and Johnson would argue, I think, that the purported bias is in the end irrelevant to the kind of study they are conducting. Unlike Kinsey's, theirs is an analysis not of sexual "behavior" but of sexual "response." Such questions as how much a person masturbates or whether he is an exhibitionist are, they would contend, beside the point, since the physiological changes

35. Ibid., pp. 22–23.
36. Ibid., pp. 307, 311–12.
37. Ibid., p. 314.

that occur during sexual arousal—and these, of course, are the principal subject of Masters and Johnson's investigation—are largely unaffected by one's behavioral preferences.[38]

The argument has a certain validity. Much of the information that Masters and Johnson impart seems remote from any conceivable behavioral or attitudinal influences. It is difficult to imagine, for instance, how the orgasmic contractions of the vagina, which Masters and Johnson document to occur at 0.8 second intervals, could be seriously affected by the sexual inclinations or opinions of the woman experiencing the orgasm. Yet not all of Masters and Johnson's conclusions are so austerely physiological. Particularly is this the case in *Human Sexual Inadequacy*, in which the analysis of both the causes and cure of sexual disorders is characterized by rampant psychologizing. But even in *Human Sexual Response* some of their most distinctive ideas transcend the purely physiological realm (if any sexual response can be considered purely physiological) and thus make the behavioral and psychological peculiarities of their research population a legitimate matter of concern. Their emphasis on the similarity of male and female response, their belittling of the penis and the lore associated with it, their campaign against the vaginal orgasm, and their inclination to judge sexual experience from an essentially marital, even monogamous, perspective all exemplify tendencies that are subtly supported by the bias of their sample.

III

Havelock Ellis and Alfred Kinsey stood unambiguously on the sexual left. On nearly all important sexual issues they espoused positions that were more progressive, more typically modern, than those embodied in the prevailing sexual value system. Kinsey was perhaps more relentlessly modernist than his English forebear, but neither could be called conventional, let alone reactionary.

Masters and Johnson, by way of contrast, lack ideological con-

38. Their discussion of the influence of social mobility on sexual response seems to assume such a distinction between the physiological and behavioral realms. See *Response*, pp. 138–39.

sistency. They stand to the left of received opinion (and often of Kinsey and Ellis as well) on certain fundamental sexual questions, but on others they are on the right. Nor does any higher principle unify their disparate opinions into a single vision. Those opinions, for the most part, are not directly contradictory. But judged in historical perspective they are ideologically incoherent.

To be sure, the general tenor of Masters and Johnson's thought is what Wilhelm Reich would call "sex-positive." They are resolute foes of Victorianism. But anti-Victorianism can hardly be considered a distinctive ideological stance in the 1960s and 1970s. They are flogging a dead horse when they ostentatiously denounce ideas that Havelock Ellis challenged three-quarters of a century ago. Moreover, their anti-Victorian pronouncements cannot alter the profound conservatism of many of their own ideas.

That conservatism manifests itself in three broad areas of sexual inquiry. It is perhaps most apparent in their treatment of sex and marriage. They do not champion the cause of premarital chastity (although they reveal no aversion to it either). But to a greater extent than either Ellis or Kinsey, they conceive of sexual life in terms of enduring, heterosexual relationships of substantial affection. Nicely complementing this marital strain in their thought, and further distinguishing them from Kinsey (if not Ellis), is their interest in reproduction. In fact, they seem at times as much concerned with procreation as with pleasure. Finally, and perhaps most surprisingly, they betray an antimaterialistic bias and a weakness for upbeat psychologizing in the manner of the neo-Freudians. Here again they can be contrasted with Kinsey, who was at once too cynical and too humane to believe that "it's all in our heads."

On the other hand, Masters and Johnson take genuinely progressive or even radical positions on women, on the old, and on masturbation. They are, for example, the most consistently feminist of the thinkers examined in this book. They not only celebrate woman's sexual prowess, but assign her an authoritative role in the treatment of sexual disorders, both her own and those of her mate. They are equally enthusiastic about the sexual capacities of older persons, a relatively neglected topic in Kinsey's and Ellis's thought and one on which Masters and Johnson energetically challenge popular prejudices. And, finally, they complete the autoerotic revolution launched by Ellis and carried forward by Kinsey, stating the case for masturbation in its most extreme form.

The last of these topics is not actually a subject of investigation in *Human Sexual Response* or *Human Sexual Inadequacy*. But it figures prominently in both books, and the attitude Masters and Johnson adopt toward it is one of the most remarkable features of their thought. They advance beyond even Kinsey in arguing, first, that masturbation can serve useful therapeutic ends, and, second, that its rewards are in some respects superior to those of intercourse. In both cases, interestingly, their discussion is confined largely to women. And, although there is no necessary connection between the two, one senses that their apology for masturbation is intimately related to their feminism. By celebrating masturbation they have, at least theoretically, liberated women from their sexual dependency on men.

One of the therapeutic benefits of masturbation that they mention is the relief of menstrual pain. Forty-three of their subjects reported that masturbating during menstruation "increased the rate of flow, reduced pelvic cramping when present, and frequently relieved their menstrually associated backaches."[39] Masters and Johnson also prescribe masturbation for maintaining sexual fitness in old age. Thus they warn that postmenopausal women who do not masturbate regularly often "have difficulty in accommodating the penis during their rare exposures to coition."[40] The recommendation is admittedly veiled, but nonetheless unambiguous. An identical piece of advice for older men is implicit in the following: "The most important factor in the maintenance of effective sexuality for the aging male is consistency of active sexual expression. . . . It does not appear to matter what manner of sexual expression has been employed, as long as high levels of activity [are] maintained."[41]

Many of the procedures that Masters and Johnson advocate for the correction of sexual disorders, although not autoerotic in a strict sense, are recognizably akin to masturbation. Thus the wife of the impotent male is taught to manipulate him to erection, her

39. Ibid., p. 125.
40. Ibid., pp. 241, 246.
41. Ibid., pp. 262–63.

hand carefully guided by his own.[42] Husbands and wives of even sexually competent persons are also told to model their stimulation of the partner's genitals after the partner's own masturbatory technique. Spouses, in other words, are urged to ask one another about their respective masturbatory practices and adjust their lovemaking accordingly.[43] By thus emphasizing the heuristic function of autoerotism, Masters and Johnson effectively resolve the tension between the masturbatory and marital themes in their thought.

Even when patterned after the masturbatory model, however, intercourse turns out to be an inferior form of sexual release, at least for women. The female's coital orgasm, they report, is both less intense and less readily achieved than her masturbatory orgasm. A variety of evidence is presented to support this conclusion. For example, they show that the contractions of the rectal sphincter—"a significant indication of the intensity of orgasm"[44] —occur more frequently during a masturbatory than a coital orgasm. The female's cardiac rate is likewise higher during a masturbatory orgasm. Most important, women themselves report that their experience of orgasm is more intense when they masturbate. Masters and Johnson cautiously note that "more intense" does not necessarily mean "more satisfying." But as far as the brute physiological facts are concerned, masturbation is the winner.[45] Indeed, Masters and Johnson often write as if the superiority of masturbation were self-evident. Thus they speak, on one occasion, of the "psychic distractions of a coital partner," and, on another, of the fortunate penis that is "unencumbered by vaginal containment."[46] This presumption of masturbation's superiority is nowhere more strikingly illustrated than in the adverb that introduces their central statement on the subject. Its effect, though probably unconscious, is marvelously conclusive:

> Understandably, the maximum physiologic intensity of orgasmic response subjectively reported or objectively recorded has been achieved by self-regulated mechanical or automanipulative techniques. The next highest level of erotic intensity has resulted from

42. *Inadequacy,* p. 204.
43. *Response,* pp. 63, 66.
44. Ibid., p. 34.
45. Ibid., pp. 35, 53–55, 118, 313–14.
46. Ibid., pp. 65, 213.

partner manipulation, again with established or self-regulated methods, and the lowest intensity of target-organ response was achieved during coition.[47]

Masters and Johnson even pay masturbation the supreme medical compliment of translating its unsuccessful pursuit into a pathological condition: masturbatory orgasmic inadequacy. Characteristically, they mention the existence of this disorder only in women: "A woman with masturbatory orgasmic inadequacy has not achieved orgasmic release by partner or self-manipulation in either homosexual or heterosexual experience. She can and does reach orgasmic expression during coital connection."[48] This condition is clearly an authentic sexual disorder for Masters and Johnson. They discuss its etiology, and they report that they have treated eleven women who suffered from it, ten of whom they cured.[49] Unfortunately, they do not say whether the eleven sought professional help explicitly for masturbatory orgasmic inadequacy (they may have been in therapy for other problems or in their capacity as the wives of male patients). But the idea that a person might undergo treatment to learn how to masturbate is intriguing. It would be difficult to imagine a more complete turning of the tables on the nineteenth century.

In every respect, then, Masters and Johnson's work represents the most extravagant assertion of the modernist theory of masturbation. Pursued to its logical conclusion that theory envisions a radically atomistic sexual order, in which the individual would achieve the same autonomy in his sexual life as he has come to expect in his religious and political life. Sex, one might say, is the last and most intimate form of dependency, and Masters and Johnson would appear determined to liberate us from it. Thus it is not too farfetched to view them as the intellectual descendants of John Stuart Mill and Ralph Waldo Emerson. Self-abuse, they seem to be telling us, is the ultimate form of self-reliance.

They are, furthermore, not merely the theoreticians of this autoerotic revolution but its mechanics as well. The elaborate contraptions that they devised to observe and measure vaginal reac-

47. Ibid., p. 133.
48. *Inadequacy,* p. 240.
49. Ibid., pp. 248–49, 314.

tions during sexual arousal could well be prototypes of the kind of sexual appliance that will eventually join the toaster and the garbage disposal as standard equipment in every American home. In fact Masters and Johnson's description of one of these machines would not sound out of place in a commercial catalog:

> The equipment can be adjusted for physical variations of size, weight, and vaginal development. The rate and depth of penile thrust is initiated and controlled completely by the responding individual. As tension elevates, rapidity and depth of thrust are increased voluntarily, paralleling subjective demand. The equipment is powered electrically.[50]

It would seem safe to conclude that the reaction against the Victorian theory of masturbation is now complete. Indeed, the near future will probably bring a critical reexamination of the supposed benefits of autoerotism. It seems unlikely, for example, that the relationship between masturbation and intercourse can be quite so cozy as Kinsey and Masters and Johnson would have us believe. No doubt the two forms of sexual expression are in some respects mutually supportive, but so long as our sexual resources remain limited there must also be a certain tension between them. Some of Masters and Johnson's own findings strongly suggest that masturbation may have a deleterious influence on marital relations. Five of their male patients were unable to ejaculate intravaginally, even after coupling for as long as an hour. All five had masturbatory histories "reflecting some regularity of auto-manipulative or partner release."[51] One could hardly be regarded as an irresponsible sexual reactionary for suggesting that there might be a connection between the masturbatory practices of these men and their coital inadequacy. But Masters and Johnson do not even consider such a possibility. To do such would be to break with the modernist dogma of masturbation's innocence, to which they subscribe without qualification.

IV

In many ways the most radical, and attractive, feature of Masters and Johnson's thought is their treatment of the sexuality

50. *Response,* p. 21.
51. Ibid., p. 219.

of older persons. They devote a great deal of attention to this topic, and their discussion of it displays a sense of outrage similar to that to be detected in Kinsey's discussion of the young. They complain repeatedly that older persons have been unjustly neglected by sex researchers and that as a result many misconceptions about the old—in particular that they are, or ought to be, sexually inert—continue to enjoy wide currency. *Human Sexual Response* and *Human Sexual Inadequacy* set out determinedly to correct such misconceptions. Indeed, they represent the most authoritative statement of the sexual rights of the old to be found in the literature of twentieth-century sexology.

"Old" needs to be defined more precisely. In general, when Masters and Johnson speak of "geriatric sexual response" they refer to persons over fifty. Their research population included thirty-nine men and thirty-four women in this bracket. The vast majority of these subjects were between fifty-one and sixty, and the geriatric group also included a number of women in their forties who were either postmenopausal or married to older men.[52] To a considerable extent, therefore, Masters and Johnson's discussion of "geriatric" sexuality deals not with the old but with the middle-aged. Yet they make no such distinction, and their apologia is clearly intended to encompass even the truly ancient. They delight in recounting the lusty achievements of octogenarians, much as Kinsey loved to shock his readers with the erotic feats of adolescents.

One might well ask why the geriatric population became the object of Masters and Johnson's special attention. Kinsey's decision to concentrate on the young—if it was consciously made—probably reflected his judgment as to which segment of the population was the most abused sexually. He was also influenced by the fact that his research grew out of a sex education course for college undergraduates, who, in turn, were heavily represented in his sample. An analogous set of circumstances explains Masters and Johnson's interest in the old. The topic was relatively unexplored—thus much in need of demythologizing—when they began their project, and because of increased longevity the years after fifty were assuming ever greater significance in the human life cycle. Furthermore, as clinicians, Masters and Johnson were

52. Ibid., pp. 14–15, 18–19, 223, 248.

especcially apt to be sought out by older persons, who are not only more prone to sexual difficulties than the young[53] but in most instances better able to afford therapy. Thus for both biological and economic reasons the middle-aged and elderly figure prominently in Masters and Johnson's clientele, and hence in their thinking.

In arguing the case for geriatric sexuality, Masters and Johnson adopt a number of different attitudes. At their most optimistic they suggest that sex actually gets better in old age. They mention, for example, that women often experience an erotic renaissance in the postmenopausal years when they are relieved of the fear of pregnancy and the responsibilities associated with raising a family. Likewise they note that older men, because of their slowed reactions and somewhat muted sensitivities, are able to remain erect through prolonged coital encounters and thus make better lovers than their younger counterparts, many of whom suffer from premature ejaculation.[54]

For the most part, however, Masters and Johnson concede that sex in old age is not what it was in youth. But they argue that the differences are less marked than is generally imagined. Above all, they insist that the sexual functions of older persons are no more diminished than are their other bodily functions, and consequently that it makes about as much sense for the old to stop having sex as for them to stop eating, breathing, or defecating.[55]

When I first read Masters and Johnson's discussion of geriatric sexuality, I was struck by what seemed to be a discrepancy between their general assertions on the subject and their descriptions of specific physiological reactions. The generalizations, as noted, make brave claims for the integrity of geriatric sex. "Age," they write in a characteristic passage, "does not necessarily deplete the male's physiologic ability for or psychologic interest in sexual performance."[56] But the detailed accounts seem much less encouraging. Those of older men, for example, convey an overall impression of flaccidity and torpor, as in the following:

> The man over 50 years of age exhibits markedly reduced ejaculatory prowess, 6 to 12 [as against 12 to 24] inches being the

53. Ibid., p. 263.
54. Ibid., pp. 243–44, 251–52; *Inadequacy*, p. 326.
55. *Inadequacy*, p. 317.
56. *Response*, p. 301.

average distance that the seminal plasma can be expelled. If penile erection has been maintained for an extended period of time, the actual ejaculatory process may be one of seminal-fluid seepage from the external urethral meatus rather than the usual ejaculatory response with the seminal fluid under obvious pressure.[57]

The picture is less than alluring. The impression is further confirmed when one learns that in the aging male the sex flush no longer develops, turgidity of the nipples is less marked, contractions of the rectum decrease in frequency, erection occurs more slowly, the preorgasmic color changes in the penis fail to materialize, testicular elevation is reduced, and the refractory period prolonged. About the only thing the older male does rapidly is come down: after ejaculation he loses his erection in a matter of seconds.[58] Sex, it would seem, is but managed.

The aging female appears little better off. Masters and Johnson's detailed accounts leave the impression of a wizened and desiccated sexuality. The breasts no longer expand, the sex flush fails to appear, rectal contractions occur but rarely, the vasocongestive thickening of the labia is reduced, and the vagina, once well-corrugated and reddish purple but now "tissue-paper-thin" and a pale pink, becomes constricted and ungenerously lubricated, its orgasmic contractions reduced by half. Only clitoral response, it seems, remains unimpaired.[59]

Despite these evidences of decline I think that my first impression was inaccurate and that the discrepancy I detected between generalization and specific detail was largely imaginary. I was guilty of the kind of ageism that Masters and Johnson have explicitly set out to combat. In general, our culture is intolerant of the old, and we are particularly repulsed by the physical manifestations of aging. And since sex is in a sense the most physical of all human activities, we automatically conceive of its proper realization in terms of the intense and rapid reactions of the young. (Kinsey's work embodies this prejudice in its most perfect form.) Accordingly, the slower, more sustained response patterns typical of middle-aged and older persons impress us not as a legitimate variation but as a corruption of human sexuality. One

57. Ibid., p. 253.
58. Ibid., pp. 250–59.
59. Ibid., pp. 224–36.

can measure the depth of this prejudice by asking oneself why, in the passage cited two paragraphs back, the idea of semen "seeping" from the penis strikes us as so pathetic. It is pathetic, I would suggest, only because we have unconsciously accepted the youthful standards of our culture, which tell us that in matters of sex vigor and alacrity are preeminently desirable.

It is Masters and Johnson's great virtue to have brought to the study of geriatric sexuality a sense of relativism similar to that which the contemporary anthropologist brings to the study of primitive cultures. In effect, they argue that the sexual capacities of the old are not so much inferior to those of the young as simply different from them. Moreover, they demonstrate that the failure to appreciate this distinction is the main cause of the sexual difficulties experienced by older persons.

In the male those difficulties focus on erection. "The sexual myth most rampant in our culture today," they write, "is the concept that the aging process per se will in time discourage or deny erective security to the older-age-group male."[60] In reality, Masters and Johnson contend, the male who is otherwise healthy never loses the ability to achieve an erection. What he does lose is the ability to achieve it quickly, and he then persuades himself—or is persuaded by his mate—that his slower response is a sign of impending impotence. Naturally the prophecy is self-fulfilling.

All this could be avoided if older men simply accepted "the physiological appropriateness of their altered sexual response patterning."[61] Enlightenment, in other words, is the key to geriatric sexual success, and in particular enlightenment on the part of the older man's wife:

> The wife of the 50–70-year-old man . . . must understand the natural involutionary changes inherent in her husband's aging process. Once she appreciates the continuing male facility for sexual expression regardless of changed response pattern, she will be infinitely more comfortable about importuning her husband sexually. She will not worry about his delayed erection time when fully aware that it does not mean that he no longer finds her attractive. The less than fully erect penis sometimes present in the plateau phase

60. *Inadequacy,* pp. 325–26, 316.
61. Ibid., p. 320.

can be readily inserted by a perceptive woman with the sure knowledge after successful intromission that her husband's first few penile strokes will aid in full development of the erection.[62]

Masters and Johnson are perhaps overly sanguine here in thinking that a good dose of relativism will resolve the older man's doubts about his potency. I suspect that we are too much the victims of our own youth cult ever to regard the erective pattern of older man as simply different from and not inferior to that of the young. This is not entirely a matter of cultural prejudice either. For the older male the "other" pattern was once his own (here the anthropological analogy breaks down), and its passing is tinged with the same sense of loss that we feel about all that we once were.

After "erective security" the older male worries most about his "reduced ejaculatory demand." He finds, in other words, that he can't achieve orgasm with the frequency he once did. This becomes a problem because, as Kinsey discovered, the aging female does not experience a corresponding reduction. Masters and Johnson have found an ingenious solution to this dilemma. They propose that the older male be freed from the obligation to ejaculate every time he has intercourse:

> The message should reach both sexes that after members of the marital unit are somewhere in the early or middle fifties, demand for sexual release should be left to the individual partner. Then coital connection can be instituted regularly and individual male and female sexual interests satisfied. . . . If the male is encouraged to ejaculate on his own demand schedule and to have intercourse as it fits both sexual partners' interest levels, the average marital unit will be capable of functioning sexually well into the 80-year age group.[63]

A Catholic theologian might be inclined to call this mutual masturbation. And it does bear the mark of Masters and Johnson's autoerotic enthusiasms, or what I have called their sexual atomism. The context here is obviously interpersonal, indeed marital, but the actions themselves seem almost private.

Masters and Johnson view the sexual circumstances of older women in a slightly different light. The main roadblock for the

62. Ibid., p. 322; see also pp. 327–29.
63. Ibid., pp. 323–24; *Response*, p. 249.

female, they suggest, is the notion that the menopause marks the end of not just her reproductive but also her sexual capacity. This doctrine, as one might expect, is utter anathema to them: "We must in fact destroy the concept that women in the 50–70-year age group not only have no interest in but also have no facility for active sexual expression. Nothing could be further from the truth than the oft-expressed concept that aging women do not maintain a high level of sexual orientation."[64] This passage—and there are many others like it—leaves the unmistakable impression that the menopause is quite without sexual significance. Masters and Johnson clearly wish that such were the case. Unfortunately, it is not, and as honest, if reluctant, empiricists, they concede that the postmenopausal woman may suffer from "sex-steroid starvation," which has the effect of diminishing both her desire and her facility for sexual release.[65]

Sex-steroid starvation is readily treated with endocrine-replacement therapy. Masters and Johnson take note of this fact, but they are curiously unenthusiastic about such a chemical approach to the problem of sexual aging. This is but one example of their antimaterialistic bias. They tend to think that all sexual problems are fundamentally psychological. Thus, without much evidence, they imply that sex-steroid treatments would be unnecessary if older women would only maintain regular sexual outlets. As with the older male's erective inadequacy, in other words, her declining sexual interest or capacity simply reflects her mistaken notion that such a decline is both proper and inevitable. If she but thinks otherwise, and behaves accordingly, her sexuality will remain unimpaired.[66]

V

Feminists have welcomed Masters and Johnson as enthusiastically as homosexuals welcomed Kinsey. Their enthusiasm has not been misplaced. *Human Sexual Response* and, to a lesser extent, *Human Sexual Inadequacy* do more to advance the cause of

---

64. *Inadequacy*, p. 335; see also pp. 287, 337–40; *Response*, p. 245–47.
65. *Inadequacy*, pp. 340–41.
66. *Response*, pp. 227, 234, 236, 238, 240–42, 249, 262; *Inadequacy*, pp. 341–50.

women's sexual rights than anything else written in the last quarter century.

The female bias of Masters and Johnson's thought is evident even in the organization of the two books. *Human Sexual Response*, for example, devotes nearly three times as much attention to women as to men. The female version of each sexual experience is presented first, while the male's pattern is cast in the role of variation (this in exact contrast to Kinsey, who addressed himself to the male first and used the *Female* volume for comparative observations). Only in *Human Sexual Inadequacy* do Masters and Johnson allow the male to occupy the foreground, primarily because his sexual difficulties prove more numerous and recalcitrant than those of his mate. The two books could almost be retitled *Female Sexual Response* and *Male Sexual Inadequacy*.

The question of which sex is taken up first is no mere formality. One of the most significant indications of Masters and Johnson's feminism is their refusal to treat female sexuality simply as a reflection of male sexuality. They are very much interested in the similarities between the sexes. But they are equally anxious to expose the many mistaken notions about women that have arisen from the habit of thinking about their sexuality in terms of conceptions that pertain only to men.

The classic example of this tendency is the lore that has grown up around the clitoris. According to the modern foreplay ethic the clitoris must be stimulated before intercourse is attempted, because it is the focal point of female sexual sensitivity. Without contradicting the latter proposition,[67] Masters and Johnson demonstrate that the theory of clitoral stimulation rests on a false analogy between the clitoris and the penis. It presumes that the clitoris is in effect a miniature penis, which responds to sexual arousal in the same manner as the penis, and which, therefore, the conscientious lover must attend to as he would have his own penis attended to.

Masters and Johnson's critique of this "phallic fallacy" is among their most impressive achievements. It is, moreover, a critique that they alone could have undertaken, since it rests largely on direct observation of clitoral response. They show that

67. *Response*, pp. 56, 61, 63.

the clitoris, although the anatomical homologue of the penis, reacts to sexual stimulation in a manner quite different from the penis. It does not, for example, become erect during arousal but instead withdraws beneath its protective foreskin, its overall length reduced by at least half as orgasm approaches. Also unlike the penis, it responds most gratefully not to direct stimulation (which in any case is a practical impossibility as arousal progresses) but to generalized pressure in the mons area. These findings thoroughly undermine many supposedly sophisticated sexual techniques. In particular they establish that men are wasting their time when they try to "find" the clitoris or to position themselves so as to effect direct clitoral contact during intercourse.[68]

The primary evidence of Masters and Johnson's feminism, then, is their opposition to any concept or practice that would portray the sexuality of women as a pale replica of that of men. As in their discussion of sex in old age, they argue implicitly for a kind of sexual relativism. If, however, a direct comparison between male and female sexuality is to be undertaken, they leave little doubt that the female in their opinion is the superior sexual animal. Male sexuality they characterize as limited and one-dimensional—limited in that the refractory period prevents men from achieving the multiple orgasms enjoyed by women, and one-dimensional in that its expression invariably takes the same form of arousal, climax, and resolution. By way of contrast they not only describe the female's sexual capacity as greater than the male's, but even appear to accept Mary Jane Sherfey's contention that it is "infinite."[69] They also argue that, unlike the male, the female may express her sexuality in many different forms. Masters and Johnson don't seek to categorize all the variations of female response, but one of the most extraordinary of them, which they call "status orgasmus," illustrates their point quite nicely:

> This physiologic state of stress is created either by a series of rapidly recurrent orgasmic experiences between which no recordable plateau-phase intervals can be demonstrated, or by a single, long-continued orgasmic episode. Subjective report . . . suggests that

68. Ibid., pp. 45–65.
69. *Inadequacy*, p. 219.

the woman actually is ranging with extreme rapidity between suc-
cessive orgasmic peaks and a baseline of advanced plateau-phase
tension. Status orgasmus may last from 20 to more than 60 seconds.

Few men, I suspect, would believe that such a sexual experience
is within human possibility.[70]

Masters and Johnson's feminism is also evident in their generally patronizing discussion of the penis. Ostensibly this discussion is conducted to relieve men of any anxieties they might have
about the adequacy of their sexual equipment, since its main
point is that penile size is irrelevant to female gratification. By
implication, however, the argument goes much further: it suggests that not merely penile size but the penis itself is irrelevant
to a woman's pleasure.

The treatment of this issue is most revealing. It attests both to
Masters and Johnson's feminism and to their essentially democratic sexual sensibilities. Although, as noted, they ultimately
argue that the dimensions of a man's penis are erotically meaningless, they begin, somewhat contradictorily, by seeking to
create the impression that, when erect, all penises are about the
same size. Such, certainly, is the intent of the following:

> Of clinical interest is the fact that the greatest observed penile-size
> increase from flaccid to erect state occurred in a male study subject
> with average flaccid measurement of 7.5 cm. . . . This increase in
> size from flaccid to erect state was just over 9 cm. This penis more
> than doubled in length when reacting from flaccid to erect state.
> The smallest increase in size from flaccid to erect state was observed
> in one of the larger organs. This penis measured just under 11 cm.
> in its flaccid state, yet at full erection only 5.5 cm. had been added
> to the length of this organ. At full plateau-phase erection the two
> organs were measured at identical lengths on three separate oc-
> casions.[71]

Things aren't always so equitable, however. Much as they would
like to believe in penile democracy, Masters and Johnson must

70. *Response*, p. 131; see also pp. 4–6, 213–14, 314–15. By drawing
attention to the female's unique orgasmic capacities, Masters and Johnson
in effect take issue with Kinsey's contention that the most important differences between male and female sexuality are psychological, in particular
the argument that male sexuality differs from female sexuality only in its
greater dependence on mental stimuli. See *Response*, pp. 62, 127, 217; *Inadequacy*, pp. 156, 219–20, 298–99.
71. *Response*, p. 192.

admit that, despite its greater distensibility, the smaller flaccid penis usually remains smaller even when erect.[72]

Although they can't deny that some are bigger than others, they nevertheless declare that all penises are equal before the vagina. The vagina, one might say, is as impartial as the law. It recognizes no distinctions of length or breadth (the only exceptions being an insignificant number of extremely large or extremely small vaginas).[73] Thus they argue that no man should think himself the sexual superior of his fellow man. There may be sexual virtues, but they have nothing to do with natural endowment.

In support of this contention Masters and Johnson note that the vagina is "a potential rather than an actual space," which from a clinical point of view is "infinitely distensible."[74] What is noticeably absent from their discussion is any empirical evidence concerning how women themselves feel about large and small penises. It would have been a simple task for them to ask their female subjects whether the size of a man's penis influenced their pleasure in intercourse. They might even have conducted controlled experiments with their "electrically powered" equipment. Of course, they could always argue that any increment in gratification derived from a large penis was purely psychological. But the fact that they don't interrogate their subjects about the matter (or don't present the results of such an investigation if it was conducted) reflects the depth of their commitment to an egalitarian sexual standard. The idea that men might be naturally unequal is intolerable to them. Alexis de Tocqueville, one senses, would have recognized them as the quintessentially American sexologists.

Men, then, are to think neither well nor ill of themselves because of the size of their penises. In fact, as far as sexual matters are concerned, it hardly matters whether they have penises at all. Or such, it seems to me, is the upshot of Masters and Johnson's assault on the Freudian distinction between the clitoral and the vaginal orgasm. The distinction presumes that the vaginal orgasm is more profound than the clitoral orgasm, and that it can be achieved only through vaginal stimulation, normally as a

72. Ibid., p. 193.
73. Ibid., pp. 194–95.
74. Ibid., p. 71.

result of penile thrusting. Against this Masters and Johnson argue that in a given woman and under otherwise similar circumstances an orgasm that results from intercourse is indistinguishable from one that results from clitoral—or mons—stimulation. Both involve contractions of the vaginal platform, and both are described in identical fashion by the women who experience them. Masters and Johnson further suggest that both have essentially the same cause. On this issue they cannot speak conclusively, because the precise mechanism that triggers orgasm has not been identified. But they strongly imply that the orgasm resulting from intercourse is in reality a clitoral orgasm insofar as its proximate cause is not the penis's stimulation of the vagina but the indirect pressure exerted by the penis on the clitoris. It follows that the penis is no more apposite to a woman's sexual relief than a firm hand on the mons. That some women find intercourse psychologically satisfying and that it still makes reproductive sense are entirely different matters.[75]

Just as they oppose any conceptualization of female sexuality that would subordinate women to men, so they oppose any sexual practice that implies that a woman's need for or right to sexual expression is less compelling than a man's. An example of such a practice is the habit women have developed of pretending to have an orgasm in order to heighten their partners' sexual pleasure. In almost magisterial tones, Masters and Johnson announce that, as a result of their research, such dissembling is no longer necessary or even possible, since the objective evidence that a woman has climaxed—namely, contractions of the vaginal platform—cannot be simulated.[76] This is a curious, if charming, piece of reasoning. It presumes that the woman's sexual partner will have read or heard about Masters and Johnson's findings and also that he will remain sufficiently self-possessed during intercourse to notice whether or not there have been vaginal contractions. It is hard to imagine that a woman with a lover of such sophistication would be faking orgasms in the first place. Be that as it may, the ideological thrust of Masters and Johnson's argument is clear: sexual encounters must not be geared exclusively or even primarily to the gratification of the male. And since the

75. Ibid., pp. 56, 58–63, 66–67, 133–34.
76. Ibid., pp. 134, 138.

woman's right to orgasm is just as absolute as the man's, it follows that all men must learn ejaculatory control. It is no exaggeration to say that premature ejaculation for Masters and Johnson is just as serious a sexual inadequacy as impotence.[77]

Their insistence that men learn ejaculatory control represents the sole instance in their writings in which they dwell at any length on the sexual responsibilities of men. Indeed, it is a significant measure of their feminism that they spend most of their time arguing that men must relinquish what amounts to a monopoly on sexual responsibility. Women, they insist, must be allowed, in fact compelled, to accept an equal share of the burden. Put another way, Masters and Johnson break firmly and cleanly with the invidious assumptions of the foreplay ethic. They argue that women should participate not merely in the pleasure of sex, as Havelock Ellis urged, but in its management as well.[78]

This viewpoint is illustrated most dramatically in *Human Sexual Inadequacy*. If anything, Masters and Johnson assign women a greater responsibility than men in the treatment of sexual disorders. The female's authority is symbolized by the fact that in each therapeutic procedure, save that for orgasmic dysfunction, she is placed, quite literally, on top: the male is instructed to lie supine before or under his mate. The female is also put in charge of the couple's movements. If, for example, the object is to insert the penis into the vagina, this is accomplished by the woman lowering herself onto it. Likewise, if there is to be pelvic thrusting, she controls its tempo and duration.[79]

Masters and Johnson obviously hope to see this reversal of sexual authority carried beyond the therapeutic process. Thus they argue that "female superior coition," as it is significantly called, promises the most consistent and satisfying relief even for

---

77. *Inadequacy*, pp. 95, 101, 308. Their attitude toward premature ejaculation is just the opposite of Kinsey's, who, quite typically, championed the man's point of view: "Far from being abnormal, the human male who is quick in his sexual response is quite normal among the mammals, and usual in his own species. It is curious that the term 'impotence' should have ever been applied to such rapid response. It would be difficult to find another situation in which an individual who was quick and intense in his response was labeled anything but superior" (*Sexual Behavior in the Human Male*, p. 580).

78. *Inadequacy*, p. 87.

79. See for example, Ibid., pp. 106–110, 207–09.

those not threatened with sexual inadequacy. Above all it allows women a freedom of movement and a measure of control over the sexual process not possible in the missionary position.[80] If such a change in sexual manners is ever effected, it cannot, I think, fail to influence the general order of authority between men and women. Its effects will probably be revolutionary.

Masters and Johnson's feminism has its limits. They are unwilling to provide single female patients with a sexual partner for the two-week therapeutic program, although partners are provided for single men. They argue, rather weakly, that our cultural heritage prepares men to accept such surrogates, while women require more "meaningful" relationships.[81] They also back away from their categorical assertion of woman's right to sexual fulfillment, implying obliquely (and obscurely) that feminists ought not to press their case too hard:

> The ability to achieve orgasm in response to effective sexual stimulation was the only constant factor demonstrated by all active female participants. This observation might be considered to support the concept that sexual response to orgasm is the physiological prerogative of most women, but its achievement in our culture may be more dependent upon psychological acceptance of sexuality than overtly aggressive behavior.[82]

Such lapses are rare, however, and women have no better friends among the major sexual theorists of the century.

VI

Against the feminist and individualistic themes in Masters and Johnson's thought must be reckoned their commitment to traditional marriage, in which the sexual needs of the individual are subordinated to those of the relationship. On this issue they adopt a distinctly more conservative position than either Ellis or Kinsey. Their enthusiasm for marriage is reflected both in direct statements on the subject and in their elaborate and often

80. Ibid., pp. 110–11; *Response,* p. 59. Masters and Johnson actually give their warmest endorsement to a variation of the female superior position known as the "lateral coital position." See *Inadequacy,* pp. 310–13.

81. *Inadequacy,* pp. 155–56.

82. *Response,* p. 139.

strained attempts to demonstrate the complementary nature of male and female sexuality.

The marital perspective is particularly evident in *Human Sexual Inadequacy*. Masters and Johnson's clinical procedures assume that the object of therapy is not a single unattached individual but a couple. It is couples, they argue, that develop sexual disorders, and thus marriages, rather than husbands or wives, that must be treated.[83] One might say that from a therapeutic standpoint the individual does not exist for them. He or she is absorbed into the marriage. This therapeutic collectivism stands in marked contrast to the individualistic, even anarchic, attitude they adopt, particularly in *Human Sexual Response*, when discussing masturbation or female sexuality.

A further indication of the essentially marital cast of their thought is their aversion to all sexual relationships that violate the monogamous, heterosexual standard. Naturally they don't fulminate against irregular alliances in the manner of a Victorian cleric. Rather, they express their aversion by ignoring such relationships, or by discussing them solely from the standpoint of their marital significance. In other words, nonmarital relationships are cast in the role of dependent variable, to be judged good, bad, or indifferent according to whether they promote or frustrate marital success.

Premarital sex is dealt with by Masters and Johnson mainly through neglect. Although a significant portion of their patients are unmarried, most of these (including all the women) come to therapy accompanied by a partner with whom they have established a significant emotional relationship, usually of long standing. In other words, these "single" patients are married in every sense but the legal one, and Masters and Johnson treat their partners exactly as if they were legitimate spouses.[84]

There is, however, another kind of premarital sex, which, though often affectionate, does not necessarily imply a long-term alliance. This is the premarital sex experienced characteristically by the young, and it is also, I believe, the premarital sex that Kinsey had foremost in mind in his highly sympathetic treatment of the topic. Sexual experiences of this sort hardly exist in

83. *Inadequacy*, p. 3.
84. Ibid., pp. 154–55.

Masters and Johnson's universe. In fact, in their two volumes I came across only a single passage that even alludes to premarital sex in the "Kinseyan" sense. The passage is significant:

> During her formative years the female dissembles much of her developing functional sexuality in response to societal requirements for a "good girl" facade. Instead of being taught or allowed to value her sexual feelings in anticipation of appropriate and meaningful opportunity for expression, thereby developing a realistic sexual value system, she must attempt to repress or remove them from their natural context of environmental stimulation under the implication that they are bad, dirty, etc.[85]

On first reading this might appear to be a criticism of the repression of adolescent sexuality. But Masters and Johnson are not proposing (as, by implication, Kinsey did) that the adolescent girl be allowed to enjoy premarital intercourse. Rather, they argue that her sexual feelings are legitimate only "in anticipation of appropriate and meaningful opportunity for expression," that is, in anticipation of marriage or its practical equivalent. This hardly differs from the advice that adolescents get from Dear Abby.

One might contend that Masters and Johnson's willingness to supply male patients with partner surrogates contradicts the marital ethos I have attributed to their thought. In a strict sense, of course, it does, and, appropriately, they are somewhat uncomfortable with the policy and fret a good deal about its propriety (one imagines that the question would not have given Kinsey even a moment's pause).[86] At the same time, they seek to create the impression that the relationship between patient and surrogate is itself a kind of miniature marriage. "The specific function of the partner surrogate," they write, "is to approximate insofar as possible the role of a supportive, interested, cooperative wife. Her contributions are infinitely more valuable as a means of psychological support than as a measure of physiological initiation. . . ."[87] As in an ideal marriage, patient and surrogate are carefully matched as to age, personality, social background, and

85. Ibid., pp. 215–16.
86. Ibid., pp. 147–48.
87. Ibid., p. 150.

education. Their first meeting, like a first date, is devoted to establishing personal rapport ("Usually the couple go to dinner and spend a casual evening in order to develop communication and comfort in each other's company"), and throughout the period of treatment the emphasis is on psychological compatibility rather than mere mechanical facility. The relationship even has an authentic marital outcome: of the thirty-two men who overcame their sexual dysfunctions with the aid of partner surrogates, twenty-four subsequently made "on-going, successful" marriages.[88]

The notion that sex is properly a marital activity also informs Masters and Johnson's references to infidelity. To a certain extent their antipathy to extramarital sex simply reflects their feminism: they dislike the fact that sexual variety has traditionally been the exclusive prerogative of men. But even if sexual adventure were available to men and women on an equal basis, one senses that they still would have little use for it. It is for them a confession of marital failure, never an innocent departure from sexual routine. In fact, it is worse than a confession of failure. It is itself a significant contributor to sexual inadequacy. By way of example they cite the case of the older male who begins to doubt his potency and thinks that a younger companion will provide just the added stimulus he needs. This plan backfires when the new partner makes increased sexual demands on the aging philanderer, thus transforming a "passing concern for performance" into an established disability.[89] Similarly, the unfaithful wife "can only double her levels of frustration, if she realizes comparatively through successful sexual experience with other men the inadequacies of her own husband's sexual performance."[90] The same line of reasoning leads them to reject sexual relationships between patient and therapist, such as were advocated by Wilhelm Reich.[91]

The argument that extramarital activity may compound one's sexual difficulties is not in itself evidence of a marital bias. The tendentious element in Masters and Johnson is their apparent

88. Ibid., pp. 152–54.
89. *Response*, p. 270.
90. *Inadequacy*, p. 97.
91. Ibid., pp. 390–91.

unwillingness to consider extramarital sex from any other standpoint. They never ask (as did Ellis and Kinsey) whether sexual variety might not in fact be good for one's marriage, or, more significantly, whether, although bad for one's marriage, it might not be good for one's life.

A marital bias is also evident in their remarks about homosexuality. They have yet to express their full views on this topic (it is to be the subject of a forthcoming publication), but their occasional references to it in *Human Sexual Response* and *Human Sexual Inadequacy* already betray an attitude strikingly different from that of the Kinsey studies. Kinsey tended to view homosexual experience, like masturbation or premarital sex, as a practice ground for later (usually heterosexual) activities. His general assumption was the more of it one had the better. Masters and Johnson, by way of contrast, discuss homosexuality from only one perspective: as a factor in the etiology of sexual inadequacy. In other words, they view it, as they do extramarital sex, primarily as an impediment to successful marital relations. Significantly, the homosexual experiences to which they attribute such unfortunate influence often involve the seduction of a young person by an older homosexual, and there is a general tendency in their writings to identify homosexuality with pederasty.[92]

When "homosexual" clients—that is, clients whose sexual difficulties Masters and Johnson trace to homosexual urges—present themselves for therapy, they are never advised to abandon marriage and embrace a homosexual way of life. Yet their motives for seeking therapy, like their motives for marrying in the first place, are usually the most sordid: "Men moving into secondary impotence subsequent to failed bisexual functioning are primarily interested in maintaining some semblance of heterosexual connection to protect their professional situation, their social position, and their financial commitments. For this reason, they visit the Foundation as a member of a distressed marital unit."[93] Incredible as it might seem, Masters and Johnson mount the same heroic campaign to restore the heterosexual functions of these patients as they do for those whose sexual inadequacies are totally unrelated to homosexuality. A marriage, in their opinion,

92. See for example, ibid., pp. 181, 244–47, 379–80.
93. Ibid., p. 183; also p. 181.

is almost always worth saving no matter how slender its sexual or emotional capital. It is for them the *summum bonum,* even when it makes its participants miserable.

The marital atmosphere of Masters and Johnson's thought is reinforced by their attempt to establish parallels between male and female sexual response. Admittedly the argument that male and female responses are essentially alike is not in itself an argument for marriage. But it does suggest that men and women are well suited to each other sexually, and, consequently, that marriage is based on solid biological premises. This impression differs markedly from that left by the Kinsey Reports, which stressed the disjunction between male and female sexuality, particularly in the matter of sexual aging, and thus implied that from a sexual standpoint marriage was a risky business. In fact, Kinsey often seemed to suggest that marriage succeeded, when it did, not because of but in spite of the sexual obligations it entailed.

The doctrine of male-female sexual similarity is one of the most prominent leitmotifs of Masters and Johnson's work. It is enunciated in the introductory chapter of *Human Sexual Response:*

> Obviously, there are reactions to sexual tension that are confined by normal anatomic variance to a single sex. . . . However, again and again attention will be drawn to direct parallels in human sexual response that exist to a degree never previously appreciated. Attempts to answer the challenge inherent in the question, "What do men and women do in response to effective sexual stimulation?", have emphasized the *similarities, not the differences,* in the anatomy and physiology of human sexual response.[94]

This general proposition is supported by three kinds of evidence: examples of responses that are identical in the two sexes, examples of responses that are analogous in the two sexes, and examples of responses that are complementary in the two sexes. The last category actually involves a different set of assumptions from the first two. It is not really an argument for similarity at all but rather for significant and useful differences between the sexes. Nonetheless, it serves the same marital end.

The discussion of identical responses is unremarkable. Most of these phenomena are evident even to the nonexpert, although

94 *Response,* p. 8; also pp. 273, 284–85.

Masters and Johnson sometimes succeed in defining them more precisely. Among such shared responses are the heavy breathing, the increased pulse rate, the heightened blood pressure, and the general muscular tension (or myotonia) that accompany sexual excitement. Masters and Johnson also establish that both sexes may develop the vasocongestive reaction known as the sex flush, though it is more frequent and more extensive in women, and they further note that nipple erection, a universal reaction among females, develops in more than half the male population. Anal contractions would be another example of sexual response common to both sexes.[95]

The argument for the complementary nature of male and female sexuality is equally straightforward and familiar. Primarily it consists of Masters and Johnson's drawing attention to various ways in which vaginas appear to have been made for penises and, to a lesser extent, penises for vaginas. Thus they note that the formation of the orgasmic platform and the engorged labia minora "provide supportive containment for the penile shaft," while the expansion of the vaginal barrel indicates an "involuntary preparation for penile penetration."[96] Their opposition to the vaginal orgasm makes them reluctant to stress the equally obvious fact that an erect penis is ideally suited to fill an aroused vagina. But they do suggest that "cul-de-sac distention" may be as relevant to the female's pleasure as "vaginal engulfment" is to the male's.[97] In short, male and female genitals are shown to fit one another nicely.

The argument from analogy is much more problematic, but at the same time more revealing because it finds Masters and Johnson straining to make their point. As one might expect, the argument is directed primarily to genital responses. It is, moreover, an argument that must be managed with some delicacy. There is a fine line between celebrating marriage by drawing attention to parallels in the sexual responses of men and women and reinforcing male chauvinism by portraying female sexuality as a mere copy of male sexuality. If the analogy is improperly drawn, as, for example, in the case of the clitoris and the penis, the effect

95. Ibid., pp. 171–72, 276–78.
96. Ibid., pp. 42, 68.
97. Ibid., p. 60.

can be profoundly reactionary, as Masters and Johnson themselves are quick to demonstrate.

Human Sexual Response takes note of more than half a dozen significant parallels in male and female response. The first, and in some ways the most important, is that between erection and vaginal lubrication. It would be easy enough to argue that these two processes are complementary in that erection makes vaginal penetration possible while lubrication makes it easy and enjoyable. But Masters and Johnson forgo this more obvious line of reasoning in favor of asserting that erection is "the neurophysiologic parallel" to lubrication.[98] What they mean by this, however, is less than entirely clear.

The analogy appears to rest on two considerations. First, erection and lubrication are the earliest manifestations of sexual arousal, and their similar timing perhaps suggests that they are neurologically parallel. Second, both reactions, we are told, are "primarily . . . vasocongestive in character."[99] Now, erection is obviously a vasocongestive reaction, and I presume that Masters and Johnson are correct when they attribute vaginal lubrication to vasocongestion as well. But the common vasocongestive nature of these processes hardly makes them analogous. Nearly all sexual responses involve vasocongestion. In fact, in terms of this criterion one might as well compare erection to blushing (as Freud does). The analogy, in short, is too abstract, and it fails to encompass the most distinctive feature of each process: the dramatic expansion of an organ in the one instance and the excretion of a fluid in the other.

Nevertheless, Masters and Johnson return to this analogy over and over again. They even invest it with therapeutic significance for their patients suffering from impotence. The recommended treatment for this disorder involves convincing the patient that erection is a natural occurrence, which is frustrated only when he tries to will himself erect. As a means of getting this message across, Masters and Johnson advise therapists to draw explicit attention to the parallel between erection and vaginal lubrication. When he learns that erection is "the same" as lubrication, so the reasoning goes, the impotent male will realize that, like lubrica-

98. Ibid., p. 181; also *Inadequacy*, pp. 275, 336.
99. *Response*, p. 279.

tion, erection simply "happens," if only he relaxes and permits it to.[100] This is not the first (nor, I'm sure, the last) successful therapeutic procedure based on a highly questionable empirical assumption.

Having equated erection with lubrication, Masters and Johnson proceed to draw a further analogy between the reactions of the scrotum and those of the major labia:

> There is a second vasocongestive response to excitement-phase levels of sexual tension that is identical for both sexes. It is demonstrated in the male by thickening of the scrotal integument, with resultant flattening, constriction, and elevation of the scrotal sac. In the nulliparous female the major labia elevate and flatten against the perineum; in the multipara the labia separate from the midline and thicken from venous congestion.[101]

Although there is some stretching here (it is hard to imagine what one could mean by the "flattening" of the scrotal sac), this is among the more persuasive of Masters and Johnson's parallels. The tissues in question are homologous, and the transformations they undergo occur at roughly the same point in the sexual cycle. Also reasonable, though imperfect, is the equation of the pre-orgasmic color changes of the minor labia (known as the "sex skin") with the darkening of the coronal area of the penis just before ejaculation. Each of these reactions, obviously, involves the issue of color (another manifestation of vasocongestion), and each occurs at the same moment in the course of arousal. However, the preorgasmic discoloration of the corona occurs in only 20 percent of the male population, while the sex skin is a nearly universal accompaniment of female orgasm.[102]

Against these not implausible examples of male-female sexual affinity must be set those of Masters and Johnson's parallels that lack any empirical or logical basis. Such, for example, is that between testicular elevation and engorgement and vaginal expansion:

> As the excitement phase progresses toward plateau, the male responds to increasing sexual tension by moderate elevation of the

100. *Inadequacy*, pp. 198–99.
101. *Response*, pp. 279–80.
102. Ibid., pp. 183–84, 281.

testes. Simultaneously the testes undergo a deep vasocongestive size increase. Correspondingly, the female expands the inner two-thirds of the vagina, adding 2-3 cm. to the length of the vaginal barrel, and develops a two- to threefold increase in vaginal width at the transcervical diameter.[103]

It is unclear from this passage whether vaginal expansion is to be considered the analogue both of elevation and engorgement or just of the latter. Elevation and expansion have only one thing in common: movement. But even the comparison between engorgement and expansion has little to recommend it. The testes and the vagina are not homologous organs, and the processes in question appear to have entirely unrelated causes and implications. In effect, there are no grounds for linking these phenomena other than the desire to impose an artificial symmetry on male and female response patterns.

Equally unpersuasive is Masters and Johnson's effort to find an event in the male's response cycle that might be said to correspond to the development of the vaginal platform in the female. They ultimately settle on the increase in penile circumference just before orgasm:

> If sexual tension is elevated to plateau-phase levels, the male reflects these higher tension levels with further vasocongestive response. Although the penis may have appeared fully erect, an obvious increase in penile circumference at the coronal ridge develops before ejaculation.
> The female's physiologic response to plateau-phase levels of sexual tension also provides further evidence of deep pelvic vasocongestion with the development of an orgasmic platform in the outer third of the vagina.[104]

The trouble with this analogy is that it equates occurrences of radically different magnitude and import. The increase in penile circumference, as Masters and Johnson admit, is "minor" and "confined primarily to the corona glandis."[105] Moreover, it appears to have no particular erotic significance. By way of contrast, the development of the vaginal platform is a major event ("The entire outer third of the vagina," they write, "becomes

103. Ibid., p. 280.
104. Ibid.
105. Ibid., p. 183.

grossly distended with venous blood"),[106] and a *sine qua non* of the female orgasm.

There is also little to be said for the parallel that Masters and Johnson draw between the preejaculatory emission experienced by some males and the mucoid emission from the Bartholin's glands in the female. Both, obviously, are emissions. But neither has been identified as to purpose or erotic significance, and even the source of the male emission is not absolutely certain (nor does it appear to have been given a scientific name).[107] In other words, this, like the previous two analogies, is extremely tenuous, and I think it reasonable to view all three as evidence of an ulterior, namely marital, motive on Masters and Johnson's part.

I have reserved until last Masters and Johnson's discussion of the parallels between the male and the female orgasm. In a sense it is ironic that they should seek to draw this analogy at all, since their most widely publicized findings concern precisely the differences between the orgasmic experiences of men and women. Here one has simply to recall their many allusions to the female's greater and more varied orgasmic capacity, particularly her ability to achieve multiple orgasms. Characteristically, however, this feminist side of their thought is balanced by an effort to rationalize heterosexual relations, and ultimately marriage, by arguing that male and female orgasm exhibit a number of similarities.

The most important of those similarities relate to the rhythm and perception of orgasm. For both men and women, they report, orgasm is preceded by a feeling of "orgasmic inevitability" or "orgasmic onset," which occurs two to four seconds before the penile or vaginal contractions that mark the beginning of orgasm proper. They identify this sense of inevitability in the female with an initial spasm of the orgasmic platform, which, they speculate, "may parallel the contractions of the prostate and, questionably, contractions of the seminal vesicles before onset of regularly recurrent expulsive contractions of the penis."[108] Even more significant for Masters and Johnson's marital theme is the identical timing of the orgasmic contractions themselves. In both the penis and the vagina they occur at precisely the same 0.8 second intervals. This is a truly remarkable finding, which, as one would

106. Ibid., p. 76.
107. Ibid., pp. 42–44, 210–11, 281.
108. Ibid., p. 133; also p. 118.

expect, Masters and Johnson draw attention to on more than one occasion.[109] Somewhat surprisingly, however, they refrain from commenting on its erotic or reproductive significance. One would think that the discovery of an affinity of such unusual mathematical exactness would inspire extensive editorializing. But their silence makes perfect sense. The similar timing of penile and vaginal contractions is of little practical significance, since the occasions on which intercourse results in exactly simultaneous orgasms are extremely rare. And even when orgasms are simultaneous it is not at all clear what erotic advantage is gained from synchronized contractions. The true significance of Masters and Johnson's finding is not practical but symbolic. It suggests that at the supreme sexual moment men and women are in perfect harmony. They march to the same drummer.

Given the marital orientation of Masters and Johnson's thought, it should come as no surprise to find that saving marriages is the ultimate objective of their therapeutic program. They entertain a most urgent sense of their calling in this regard. "A conservative estimate," they write, "would indicate half the marriages as either presently sexually dysfunctional or imminently so in the future."[110] The traditional authorities—marriage counselors, psychiatrists, clergymen—have proven helpless in the face of this national sexual disaster. Thus the "only hope," Masters and Johnson argue, lies in the creation of "a major postgraduate training program to develop seminar leaders for therapy training centers throughout the country."[111] In other words, they envision sex-treatment clinics like their own springing up in every village and town, which would make sexual therapy as readily accessible as dental. This is a remarkable (which is not to say unrealistic) prospect, and an appropriate reflection of their commitment to the marital order. Their own marriage in 1971 adds a neat personal footnote to that commitment.

VII

In traditional sexual thought sex was justified primarily, sometimes exclusively, because it was necessary to the propagation of

109. Ibid., pp. 129, 184–85, 282–83.
110. *Inadequacy*, p. 369.
111. Ibid.; *Response*, p. vi.

the species. Since one of the premises of the modern tradition in
sexual thought has been that sex is a valuable end in itself, modern theorists, by way of reaction, have generally inclined to belittle the reproductive perspective on sexuality. One sees this
tendency already in Freud, who made a great deal of the need to
distinguish sexual from reproductive categories.[112] But the tendency found its ideal spokesman in Kinsey. The only question
Kinsey asked his subjects about reproduction was whether the
fear of becoming pregnant (or getting somebody pregnant) had
served to inhibit their sexual activities. Appropriately, the Kinsey
Reports contained a grand total of five references to the subject
of pregnancy, all trivial save for the following passage on its role
in women's dreams:

> Something between 1 and 3 percent of the females had dreamed
> that they were pregnant or that they were giving birth to a child.
> It is notable that these were reported as "sex dreams." For nine out
> of every ten of the females who had had such dreams, the dreams
> had not led to orgasm. Such dreams need further consideration,
> because the connection between the reproductive function and
> erotic arousal is probably not as well established as biologists and
> psychologists ordinarily assume. By association, many males and
> apparently some females may become erotically aroused when they
> contemplate any reproductive or excretory function, probably be-
> cause it depends at least in part on genital anatomy, and this may
> explain why some females consider dreams of pregnancy as sexual.
> It is more likely they consider their pregnancy dreams as sexual
> simply because they know, intellectually, that there is a relation-
> ship between sexual behavior and reproduction.[113]

The passage nicely illustrates Kinsey's aversion to the reproductive perspective on sexuality. In his own mind, evidently, sex and
pregnancy were related only "intellectually," and not intrinsically.
He was also disinclined to find erotic significance in the other
biological processes associated with reproduction, such as menstruation, nursing, or the menopause. It was as if he had reacted
so violently against the Victorian identification of sex and repro-

112. See, for example, *Introductory Lectures on Psychoanalysis, The
Standard Edition of the Complete Psychological Works of Sigmund Freud*
(London, 1963), Volume XVI, pp. 303–04, 311, 320, 324.
113. Kinsey, *Sexual Behavior in the Human Female*, p. 213.

duction that he simply could not conceive of reproduction as a sexual subject.

With Masters and Johnson the tide has unquestionably turned. They restore reproduction to an honored place on the roster of sexual "topics." This is not to suggest that they are neo-Victorians. Much of their thought is inspired by the same modernist impulse that one finds in more undiluted form in Kinsey. Their insistence on the fundamentally clitoral nature of female sexuality, for example, has distinctly antireproductive connotations (it implies that intercourse is extraneous to a woman's gratification), as, more generally, does their celebration of autoerotism. Equally modern is their enthusiasm for geriatric sexuality, which in the case of women obviously involves a separation of sexual and reproductive functions. They are also generally hostile to any suggestion that reproductive functions ought to inhibit sexual life. Thus they attack the notion that women should avoid intercourse or masturbation while menstruating, and they are particularly critical of obstetricians who categorically forbid intercourse during the six weeks before and after childbirth (the main disadvantage of which, they note disapprovingly, is that it causes restless husbands to be unfaithful). In all these matters, Masters and Johnson are in step with modernist orthodoxy.[114]

Nevertheless, they retreat from the extreme position occupied by Kinsey. Perhaps the most important evidence of that retreat is their simple willingness to discuss the reproductive significance of various sexual processes. Where Kinsey treated sex solely from the perspective of individual pleasure, Masters and Johnson also consider its relevance to the survival of the race. They even acknowledge that the interests of the individual and those of the race—or, to put it another way, the claims of pleasure and of procreation—are not always compatible, and on occasion they appear to commit the ultimate modernist sin of siding with the race against the individual. That is, they advise their clients that under certain circumstances pleasure must be sacrificed in the interest of propagating the species.

Their most important findings about sexual response and reproduction concern, not surprisingly, the reactions of the vagina.

114. *Response*, pp. 124–25, 148–50, 163–68.

Put very simply, they show that sexual arousal leads to the creation within the vagina of a "pool" in which seminal fluid may collect. This pooling effect helps retain sperm within the vagina after intercourse, thus facilitating conception.[115]

The discovery of a vaginal pool seems to suggest a natural harmony between erotic and reproductive interests. Unfortunately, the matter is not so simple. For one thing, the pooling effect presumes that the female is on her back during intercourse, and, as noted, Masters and Johnson argue that this position is not the most satisfactory from a purely erotic standpoint. By implication, therefore, pleasure must be circumscribed if conception is one's primary goal. Masters and Johnson also report that a woman can contribute to seminal pooling (and thus to the chances of conception) by avoiding orgasm during intercourse, since the unrelieved orgasmic platform then serves as a kind of stopper in the vagina:

> From an anatomic point of view, there is probably a greater chance of conception if the parous female achieves only plateau-phase levels of response during her sexual encounter, as opposed to enjoying an orgasmic experience. If only plateau-phase levels of tension are experienced, the orgasmic-platform vasocongestion will be dissipated at a much slower rate than that expected in a post-orgasmic sequence and consequently the physiologic aid in seminal-pool containment will be of longer duration.[116]

Particularly in the "knee-chest" position, they urge, "orgasmic-phase responses should be avoided for the female partner attempting to conceive."[117] This is a most unmodern piece of advice. It also prompts one to speculate whether there may not be an evolutionary tendency to frigidity. If a woman's failure to achieve orgasm contributes to impregnation, then by Darwinian logic the frigid ought to be the more fecund.

Masters and Johnson don't limit their concern to the influence of sexual response on reproduction. They are also interested in the influence of reproductive functions on sexuality. In general, they find that influence to be considerable, both for the woman

115. Ibid., pp. 80–88.
116. Ibid., pp. 84–85.
117. Ibid., p. 86.

who is pregnant and for the woman who has already borne children.

The sexual responses of multiparous and nulliparous women, they show, exhibit a number of significant differences, most of them to the advantage of the woman with children. For example, the sex skin of the labia minora becomes more vivid after a woman has had children, and Masters and Johnson comment that "generally, the more brilliant and definitive the color change, the more intense the individual's response to the particular means of sexual stimulation."[118] Similarly, the secretion of mucus from the Bartholin's glands and the expansion of the uterus during sexual arousal both increase after a woman has borne children.[119] Although no explicit conclusion is drawn, one gets the unmistakable impression that childbearing has a beneficial influence on female sexuality.

Masters and Johnson are less reticent about the influence of pregnancy itself on female response. With the exception of the first trimester, during which nausea and fatigue seem to undermine sexual interest, pregnancy, they argue, increases a woman's desire for sex and the pleasure she takes in it as well. Their research subjects enjoyed "fulminating orgasmic experiences" and sometimes had multiple orgasms for the first time while pregnant. This association of pregnancy with intensified sexual response also carries over into the period after childbirth, during which, it was found, women who nursed their children experienced "significantly higher" levels of sexual tension than they had before becoming pregnant.[120]

Masters and Johnson even suggest that pregnancy is itself a kind of sexual experience, or at least that it is in many ways analogous to one. For instance, they explicitly compare the reactions of the breasts during pregnancy to their reactions during sexual arousal:

Hundreds of observations of nonpregnant women have established the fact that nulliparous breasts undergo a transitory 20–25 percent increase in size in response to plateau-phase levels of sexual tension.

118. Ibid., pp. 41–42.
119. Ibid., pp. 43–44, 120.
120. Ibid., pp. 137, 145, 149, 156–62.

The same relative size increase usually develops in the nulliparous breast as a normal physiologic change by the end of the first trimester of pregnancy.[121]

Similarly, pregnancy, like sexual arousal, causes the labia minora to become engorged, and it appears to be accompanied by a constant "low grade production" of vaginal lubrication, "even when the individual is not exposed consciously to sexual stimuli."[122] Masters and Johnson also suggest that the act of birth itself is in some respects similar to sexual climax: "Twelve women, all of whom have delivered babies on at least one occasion without anesthesia or analgesia, reported that during the second stage of labor they experienced a grossly intensified version of the sensations identified with the first stage of subjective progression through orgasm."[123] One is inevitably reminded of the Freudian identification of the child with the penis. This seemingly extravagant psychoanalytic conception suddenly takes on an aura of plausibility when one learns that the child's passage through the vagina results in an experience not unlike orgasm.

The net effect of Masters and Johnson's discussion of pregnancy and sexual response is to bring reproduction back within the sexual realm. This fits perfectly with the overall marital tenor of their thought. One senses that they hope to see our sexual future dominated not merely by marriage but by the nuclear family as well. In short, they are sexual conservatives.

VIII

By far the most perplexing feature of Masters and Johnson's thought is its mixture of materialistic and (for want of a better term) psychological perspectives on human sexuality. In the popular mind, I am certain, their work is identified with a dispassionate scientific approach to sex—with measuring physiological

121. Ibid., p. 143.
122. Ibid., pp. 146–47.
123. Ibid., p. 136. Elsewhere Masters and Johnson surmise that orgasm and the initiation of labor may have the same efficient cause: "Just as the trigger mechanism which stimulates the regularity of expulsive uterine contractions sending a woman into labor is still unknown, so is the mechanism that triggers orgasmic release from sex-tension increment. Probably they are inseparably entwined—to identify one may be to know the other (*Inadequacy,* p. 297).

reactions and prescribing fancy "techniques" for overcoming sexual infirmities. And, of course, there is a good deal of hard-nosed physiology and, as it were, mechanics in Masters and Johnson. At the same time, however, their thought has a soft psychological underbelly. In fact, they sometimes leave the impression that the physical side of sex is a mere accident and that in its essence human sexuality is a thing of the spirit.

Their propensity for psychologizing doesn't fully come into its own until *Human Sexual Inadequacy*. *Human Sexual Response*, for the most part, is confined to a description and analysis of sexual physiology. Moreover, Masters and Johnson don't seek to hide the book's essential materialism. "If problems in the complex field of human sexual behavior are to be attacked successfully," they write in the Preface, "psychologic theory and sociologic concept must at times find support in physiologic fact."[124] Conscious perhaps of the criticism Kinsey received for neglecting the affective realm, they more than once affirm that psychological matters are extremely important in sexual life. But by and large these affirmations lack conviction. In its essential features *Human Sexual Response* remains an account of how the body reacts to sexual stimulation, and in terms of sheer empirical ingenuity and industry it is a remarkable accomplishment.

Ironically the book's basic materialism is most evident in those sections treating what Masters and Johnson call the "psychology" of orgasm. Having completed their detailed account of the physiological aspects of sexual arousal (including, as noted, the precise timing of the orgasmic contractions of the penis and the vaginal platform), they turn their attention to the "subjective" side of the same process. If, however, the reader anticipates here some discussion of the ecstasy, the sense of transcendence, and the loss of self that accompany orgasm, or of the psychological "meaning" of sexual experience, he will be sorely disappointed. The "psychology" of orgasm turns out to be nothing more than the individual's conscious perception of the physiological changes that Masters and Johnson have observed and measured. In other words, it is body psychology, the mental representation of physical occurrences. Their account of the "psychology" of female orgasm runs as follows:

124. *Response*, p. vi; see also pp. vi–vii, 4, 203.

Orgasm has its onset with a sensation of suspension or stoppage. Lasting only an instant, the sensation is accompanied or followed immediately by an isolated thrust of intense sensual awareness, clitorally oriented, but radiated upward into the pelvis. . . . The sensation of intense clitoral-pelvic awareness has been described by a number of women as occurring concomitantly with a sense of bearing down or expelling. Often a feeling of receptive opening was expressed. . . .

As a second stage of subjective progression through orgasm, a sensation of "suffusion of warmth," specifically pervading the pelvic area first and then spreading progressively throughout the body, was described by most every woman with orgasmic experience.

Finally, as the third stage of subjective progression, a feeling of involuntary contraction with a specific focus in the vagina or lower pelvis was mentioned consistently.[125]

The male's "subjective" experience is also described as a sequence of body perceptions. In this instance Masters and Johnson's account is even more literal (there is nothing so metaphorical as "a sensation of suspension" or "a suffusion of warmth"), and it is also surprisingly inadequate purely as a description of what orgasm feels like:

In the human male a sensation of ejaculatory inevitability develops for an instant immediately prior to, and then parallels in timing sequence, the first stage of the ejaculatory process (accessory-organ contractions). This subjective experience has been described by many males as the sensation of "feeling the ejaculation coming." From onset of this specific sensation, there is a brief interval (2 to 3 seconds) during which the male feels the ejaculation coming and no longer can constrain, delay, or in any way control the process. This subjective experience of inevitability develops as seminal plasma is collecting in the prostatic urethra but before the actual emission of seminal fluid begins. The two- to threefold distention of the urethral bulb developing in the terminal portions of the plateau phase also may contribute proprioceptively to the sensation of ejaculatory inevitability.

During the second stage of the ejaculatory process (propulsion of seminal-fluid content from prostatic urethra to the urethral meatus), the male subjectively progresses through two phases: First, a contractile sensation is stimulated by regularly recurring contractions of the sphincter urethrae. Second, a specific appreciation of fluid

125. Ibid., pp. 135–36; see also p. 127.

volume develops as the seminal plasma is expelled under pressure along the lengthened and distended penile urethra.[126]

This seems a satisfactory rendering of the preface and conclusion of male orgasm, but it hardly does justice to the main event—that "brief interval" of two to three seconds between the sense of inevitability and the perception of contractions. My point, however, is not that the description is inaccurate but that it assumes an extremely narrow, and fundamentally materialistic, conception of psychology. Even when it addresses itself to supposedly psychological questions, *Human Sexual Response* never strays far from the realm of "physiologic fact."

In general, Masters and Johnson's tough-minded, materialistic examination of human sexual response can be said to serve progressive ends. But their materialism can also become reactionary, especially when it results in transforming sex into labor. Much of *Human Sexual Response*, like Freud's writings on sexuality, is dominated by economic and industrial metaphors, which have the effect of making what should be the most playful of human activities seem altogether grueling. A particularly blatant example is provided by their account of an experiment conducted to measure the extent of pelvic vasocongestion during sexual arousal:

> One individual underwent repeated pelvic examinations during a six-and-a-half-hour working period and for six hours of observation thereafter. During the working period multiple coital exposures maintained the woman at excitement-phase levels of response. There were five subjective plateau-phase experiences superimposed on maintained excitement tension levels, but orgasmic relief was not experienced.
>
> Toward the end of the working period the uterus was increased two to three times the unstimulated size; the broad ligaments thickened with venous congestion; the walls of the vaginal barrel were edematous and grossly engorged; and the major and minor labia were swollen two to three times normal size. Pelvic examinations and coital activity became increasingly painful toward the end of the six-and-a-half-hour period.
>
> During the six-hour observation period gross venous engorgement of the external and internal genitalia persisted—so much so, in fact, that the woman was irritable, emotionally disturbed, and

126. Ibid., p. 215.

could not sleep. She complained of pelvic fullness, pressure, cramping, moments of true pain, and a persistent, severe low backache.[127]

This sounds more like an account of child labor in nineteenth-century Manchester than an experience of erotic excitement. Sex here has become torturous and alienated, much of it, appropriately, carried out in the presence of, or aided by, machines.

Obviously the passage I have cited describes an experiment and hardly represents Masters and Johnson's notion of the ideal sexual experience. Nevertheless, it accurately reflects their tendency, if not to identify sex with work, at least to describe it in imagery borrowed from the world of work. "After the routine plateau-phase checks," they write, "the study subjects returned to sexual activity,"[128] just as if they were returning from a coffee break. "To help develop a level of sexual interest for the marital unit which is realistic to their life style, vacations from any form of specific sexual activity are declared for at least two 24-hour periods during the two weeks, in a system of timely checks and balances."[129] Again one thinks of business rather than recreation, particularly when, in the next sentence, one learns that such twenty-four-hour vacations assure "maximum return" from the therapeutic program. In their defense, it should be noted that Masters and Johnson are not insensitive to the dangers of confusing sex with labor. They report brilliantly on the role of the "performance principle" in the development of impotence, specifically linking the American male's fear of failure in bed to his fear of failure at work ("he simply cannot 'get the job done' ").[130] Here they write as if they were disciples of Herbert Marcuse. But for the most part their descriptions of sexual response are only too businesslike. As Marcuse himself might complain, they rob sex of its subversiveness when they imprison it in a language that mirrors the established organization of society.

It is perhaps not wholly unfair to mention in this context that Masters and Johnson have themselves become sexual entrepreneurs. That is, they operate a sex therapy business, and a two-

127. Ibid., p. 119.
128. Ibid., p. 121.
129. *Inadequacy*, p. 18.
130. Ibid., pp. 164–66, 175.

week stint at their St. Louis clinic can be an extremely expensive proposition.[131] Their motives in this enterprise are transparently humane and never less than disinterested. But because of the nature of their work they are drawn into the economic system in a fashion unknown to either Kinsey or Ellis (among major sexual theorists one would have to go back to Freud to find a comparable situation), and it is thus not surprising that the values of that system should have insinuated themselves into their thought.

Materialism lacks the critical distance of idealism, and thus it is always at least potentially reactionary. This is no less true for Masters and Johnson than it was for the Darwinist social theorists of the late nineteenth century. But materialism can also be liberating. In particular it can pull the philosophical rug out from under repressive values and convictions. The metaphysical materialism of the most radical of the eighteenth-century *philosophes* had this critical impact on Christian religious dogma, as did Marx's historical materialism on the philosophical doctrines of German idealism.

To a remarkable extent, the materialism implicit in Masters and Johnson's treatment of human sexuality has a similar liberating effect. It achieves that effect by forcing us to confront the physical fact of our sexuality without apology or euphemism. Sex can with difficulty be banished to the realm of abstraction, there to become the object of disapproval or ridicule, when it is shown to be a matter of bits and pieces, of particular organs and particular responses. High-mindedness and decorum, the usual masks of repression, are overwhelmed by the sheer weight of physiological detail.

The liberating impact of Masters and Johnson's materialism is most directly evident in those parts of *Human Sexual Inadequacy* that treat the "mechanics" of sexual therapy. Their clinical instructions are unrelentingly, almost painfully, specific. Here, by way of example, is their account of the procedure (called the "squeeze technique") that they recommend for premature ejaculation:

131. Masters and Johnson's policy is to offer 25 percent of their patients free care and another 25 percent adjusted rates (*Inadequacy*, p. 356). The full fee for the two-week treatment was $2,500 in 1970.

The female partner's thumb is placed on the frenulum, located on the inferior (ventral) surface of the circumcised penis, and the first and second fingers are placed on the superior (dorsal) surface of the penis in a position immediately adjacent to one another on either side of the coronal ridge. Pressure is applied by squeezing the thumb and first two fingers together for an elapsed time of 3 to 4 seconds. . . .

Rather strong pressure is indicated in order to achieve the required results with the squeeze technique. As the man responds to sufficient pressure applied in the manner described, *he will immediately lose his urge to ejaculate.* He may also lose 10 to 30 percent of his full erection. The wife should allow an interval of 15 to 30 seconds after releasing the applied pressure to the coronal ridge area of the penis and then return to active penile stimulation. Again when full erection is achieved the squeeze technique is reinstituted. Alternating between periods of specifically applied pressure and reconstitution of sexually stimulative techniques, a period of 15 to 20 minutes of sex play may be experienced without a male ejaculatory episode, something unknown to the marital unit in prior sexual performance. . . .

The next step in progression of ejaculatory control involves nondemanding intromission. The male is encouraged to lie flat on his back and the female to mount in the superior position, her knees placed approximately at his nipple line and parallel to his trunk. . . .

After bringing her husband to full erection and employing the squeeze technique two or three times for his control and orientation, the wife then should mount in this specifically described superior position. Once mounted, she should concentrate on retaining the penis intravaginally in a motionless manner, providing no further stimulation for her husband by thrusting pelvically. . . .

When the husband's level of sexual excitation threatens to escape his still shaky control, he should immediately communicate this increased sexual tension to his wife. She then can elevate from the penile shaft, apply the squeeze technique in the previously practiced manner for 3 or 4 seconds, and reinsert the penis. . . .

In subsequent days, with some degree of performance reliability established for penile containment in the female-superior position, the husband is encouraged to provide just sufficient pelvic thrusting to maintain his erection. . . .

As her partner's control increases, female pelvic thrusting can be encouraged, initially in a slow, nondemanding manner, but soon with full freedom of expression.[132]

132. Ibid., pp. 103–10.

This is certainly unlovely. But when one considers the mental and, in the case of the wife, physical agony caused by premature ejaculation, and the spectacular success Masters and Johnson have enjoyed with this method of therapy (they failed in only 4 of 186 cases),[133] one's aesthetic reservations seem not merely supercilious but downright cruel. It is Masters and Johnson's glory that they despise the delicacy and sense of propriety that have stood between Western man and his sexuality. Their "mechanistic materialism," like that of the *philosophes,* is in reality proof of their humanism.

One senses, nonetheless, that they are themselves embarrassed by the materialistic strain in their thought. They recognize their duty to report the facts unadorned, but they long for the respectability that comes from clothing human sexuality in the decorous language of psychology. Hence their compulsive, one is tempted to say guilt-ridden, tendency to psychologize. Some of this psychologizing is perfectly unobjectionable, and their treatment of human sexuality would be imbalanced, to say the least, if the affective realm were totally neglected. But all too often they rush to offer psychological explanations or solutions without giving sufficient attention to the relevant physiological realities. Even more damaging, the particular brand of psychology they espouse is disarmingly simpleminded. It remains at all times on the surface of things and is relentlessly uncritical.

Their discussion of the causes of frigidity (which they call "orgasmic dysfunction") offers a convenient illustration. They begin their analysis with the unexceptionable proposition that women are victims of the double standard: to a greater extent than men they are taught to repress their sexual feelings. From this they leap to the highly dubious conclusion that repression, in the form of historical, and largely psychological, experiences, is the most important factor in the development of frigidity.[134] The conclusion would be legitimate if one could show that frigid women were more severely victimized by the double standard than are other women. But Masters and Johnson don't even attempt to establish that such is the case. Evidently they are so certain that frigidity is caused by ideas—that it is a psychological

133. Ibid., p. 113.
134. Ibid., pp. 214–18, 222–26.

rather than physiological disorder—that they see no need to test the proposition scientifically. They also ignore Kinsey's argument that the double standard is grounded in the female's distinctive pattern of sexual aging. Of course, Kinsey may be wrong and Masters and Johnson right on this question. But the significant matter is that Masters and Johnson move directly to the psychological level of explanation without testing, let alone exhausting, the possible physiological explanations for frigidity.

The same tendency is apparent in the more specific etiologies that they assign to frigidity. They distinguish between two forms of the disorder, which they call primary and situational orgasmic dysfunction. The first refers to women who have always been frigid, the second to those that have become so. Not surprisingly, the situationally dysfunctional provide the best argument for a psychological etiology. The classic example is that of the wife who breaks off relations with her husband after learning that he has been unfaithful, later relents and returns to the marital bed, only to discover that she can no longer achieve an orgasm.[135] Whatever interpretation one chooses to place on this sequence of events, it cannot fail to be a psychological interpretation. The woman's problem is clearly in her head, not in her genitals.

Most of Masters and Johnson's cases, however, are far less clear-cut. For example, there is the frigidity that they attribute to extreme male dominaton:

> Every social decision was made by Mr. F during the courtship. The same pattern of total control continued into marriage. He insisted on making all the decisions and was consistently concerned with his own demands, paying little attention to his wife's interests. A constant friction developed, as is so frequently the case with marital partners whose backgrounds are diametrically opposed.
>
> Mrs. F had not been orgasmic before marriage. In marriage she was orgasmic on several occasions with manipulation but not during coition. As the personal friction between the marital partners increased, she found herself less and less responsive during active coital connection.[136]

This etiology has a nice feminist ring about it: it identifies frigidity with patriarchy. Unfortunately, it is not at all evident that this

---

135. Ibid., pp. 242–43.
136. Ibid., p. 243.

woman's problem is mental rather than physical. Many wives resent their husband's domination yet remain orgasmic, and this particular patient's failure to achieve a single coital orgasm makes the assumption of a physical disability not unreasonable. At the very least one would have to give such a possibility serious consideration. But Masters and Johnson place the entire blame on the wife's inability to "identify" with her authoritarian mate.

Finally there are the cases of situational orgasmic dysfunction that Masters and Johnson attribute to the influence of homosexual experiences—women who have enjoyed orgasm with other women but who find that they are frigid in heterosexual relations. These might appear to represent obvious examples of psychological conditioning. But, in fact, that is the case only if one assumes that homosexuality itself is a psychological condition. Officially, Masters and Johnson take a neutral stand on this issue (although one suspects them of being pure environmentalists). They include homosexuality in the category of "environmental factors," but, they write, "in no sense does this placement connote professional opinion that homophile orientation is considered purely environmental in origin."[137] Yet if homosexuality is in any sense organic, one cannot logically treat specific homosexual experiences as the source of a woman's heterosexual frigidity. Granted her frigidity probably has nothing to do with her genitals (and in this sense it is not physiological), its causes nevertheless lie well beyond the realm of "experience." Put another way, she is not frigid because of what's in her head. Rather what's in her head and her frigidity are both reflections of a congenital predisposition. Once again Masters and Johnson are guilty of irresponsible psychologizing, although their position would at least be consistent (if not necessarily correct) had they espoused a purely psychogenic theory of homosexuality.

As one might imagine, the psychological etiologies that they invent for their patients suffering from primary orgasmic dysfunction are even more questionable. These include an overprotected childhood, disappointment in marriage (that is, settling for less than one's first choice), and, somewhat banally, an impotent husband[138]—all plausible enough but hardly unique to

137. Ibid., pp. 169, 244.
138. Ibid., pp. 233–39.

the frigid. They make perhaps the best case for the etiological significance of religious indoctrination, which they show is present in the backgrounds of a suspiciously high percentage of nonorgasmic women (to be specific, in 41 of their 193 cases of primary orgasmic dysfunction).[139] This hypothesis is in keeping with Kinsey's findings about the influence of religion on female sexual behavior, although there is a characteristic difference in emphasis between Kinsey's and Masters and Johnson's treatment of the issue. Where Masters and Johnson attribute frigidity directly to religious ideas, Kinsey puts the blame on the believer's lack of sexual practice. Their implied solutions to the problem also differ accordingly: for Masters and Johnson it is sufficient that repressive attitudes be replaced by permissive ones; for Kinsey there must be a transformation in behavior, starting, if possible, during the formative years of adolescence. Put another way, Kinsey views sexual behavior as considerably less malleable than do Masters and Johnson.

After rehearsing all the supposed psychological causes of orgasmic dysfunction, Masters and Johnson concede, with reluctance, that some of their cases don't conform to any of the above patterns and thus appear to imply the existence of a purely physiological frigidity: "There seems to be a clinical entity of low sexual tension which by history does not represent specific trauma to a sexual or any other value system." But, they hasten to add, if such an entity in fact exists, "it is rare in occurrence and in professional identification."[140] In short, they cannot tolerate the idea that the body itself might be the source of the problem.

A similar pattern emerges in Masters and Johnson's treatment of all sexual disorders: they steadfastly ignore physiological considerations and leap to psychological conclusions on the skimpiest evidence.[141] Their motives for doing so are easy enough to comprehend: they posit psychological etiologies because they intend to advocate psychological cures. This is undoubtedly the single most surprising feature of their thought. Despite their concern for the specifics of sexual physiology and their admirable

139. Ibid., pp. 229–33.
140. Ibid., p. 247.
141. See, for example, ibid., pp. 93–95 (premature ejaculation), 117–26 (ejaculatory incompetence, or the inability to ejaculate), 137–45, 159–83 (impotence), 252–56 (vaginismus), and 275–77 (dyspareunia).

readiness to tell patients exactly what to do with which parts of their bodies, Masters and Johnson are at bottom psychotherapists. They address their attention, above all else, to the way people think and feel.

The components of their psychotherapy are almost embarrassingly simple. Its first precept is enlightenment. Indeed, they are as certain as any eighteenth-century *philosophe* that the main obstacles to sexual health are ignorance and superstition. From this it follows that patients have but to learn the facts about human sexual response—and about their own circumstances in particular—and most of their fears and the disabilities those fears have given rise to will evaporate. Masters and Johnson express this conviction by means of a characteristically obscure and confusing metaphor, that of the "professional mirror":

> By holding up the mirror of professional objectivity to reflect marital-unit sexual attitudes and practices, and by recalling constantly that the marital *relationship* is the focus of therapy, information necessary for marital-partner comprehension of the sexually dysfunctional status can be exchanged rapidly and with security. . . . When the partners in the sexually inadequate relationship can see themselves as they have permitted the cotherapists to see them, when they can have their rationales for sexual failure and their prejudices, misconceptions, and misunderstandings of natural sexual functioning exposed with nonjudgmental objectivity and explained in understandable terms with subjective comfort, a firm basis for mutual security in sexual expression is established.[142]

In essence the "mirror of professional objectivity" is nothing more (or less) than the truth. It is a body of knowledge, presented in authoritative but nonthreatening fashion, which allows the patient to compare his misconceptions and self-delusions with reality and thereby to correct them. The road to recovery lies by way of enlightenment and self-knowledge.

Yet by itself enlightenment, or the dissolution of errors, is not entirely sufficient. The patient must also be persuaded that, in a manner of speaking, he has nothing to fear but fear itself. Over and over again Masters and Johnson urge their patients to banish anxiety from the sexual universe and accept sexual functioning as a natural process that can be frustrated only by negative and

142. Ibid., p. 62; also pp. 10, 21, 53, 83, 88–89, 199–200, 352.

fearful attitudes. In a sense this therapeutic tack is just the opposite of enlightenment. Here not knowledge but artlessness and
unselfconsciousness become the preeminent sexual virtues.[143]

The last essential element of Masters and Johnson's therapeutic
program is communication. Like psychoanalysis, theirs is fundamentally a "talking cure," only talking has now become "vocalization." They argue that sexually inadequate marriages result not
merely from ignorance and fear, but also from the inability of
husbands and wives to speak to one another. Therapy, therefore,
must aim to break through this communications barrier. To their
own credit, Masters and Johnson do not limit "vocalization" to
one's grander, and presumably more presentable, sexual emotions. Rather, husbands and wives must tell each other, and in no
uncertain terms, exactly what feels good and what doesn't. Ultimately, however, the communication that heals is a communication of the spirit. Sexual well-being is restored when alienated
husbands and wives face their difficulties honestly, acknowledge
their mutual responsibility, and thus reestablish a sense of communion.[144]

It would be difficult to exaggerate the importance of these
psychological elements in Masters and Johnson's therapeutic
plan. Far from being mere window dressing for the mechanical
tricks (such as the squeeze technique) advocated in *Human
Sexual Inadequacy*, they are in fact the very heart of Masters and
Johnson's teaching. The struggle for sexual happiness, in their
opinion, is essentially a struggle of the mind.

Moreover, they take a highly sanguine view of the struggle's
ultimate outcome. Only rarely do they admit that a marriage
might be so ravaged by sexual or other antagonisms as to be
beyond repair. Their relationship to earlier sexual thinkers is thus
analogous to that of the neo-Freudians to classical psychoanalysis. They share with the neo-Freudians an aversion to any
"merely" biological conception of human sexuality, as well as
their optimistic estimation of the therapeutic prospect. Such
idealism and therapeutic cheerfulness stand in marked contrast
to the sober materialism of Kinsey's or Freud's analysis of the
human sexual condition.

143. Ibid., pp. 10–14, 65–66, 196–98, 202.
144. Ibid., pp. 14–15, 27, 32, 105–06.

Masters and Johnson, in short, are not what they seem. Or at least, they are not what they seem to the public at large. Much of their laboratory research is obviously inspired by the modernist impulse to demystify sex. But their clinical work can only be described as neo-Romantic. Combined with their marital and familial enthusiasms it leaves the impression of a style of sexual thinking that is surprisingly unmodern, sometimes even reactionary. It would be rash to compare them to the Victorians, but after Kinsey they unquestionably represent a step back toward a more traditional conception of human sexuality.

IX

Anyone who has read the detailed accounts of genital reactions in *Human Sexual Response* or the unfailingly explicit therapeutic instructions in *Human Sexual Inadequacy* will be inclined to think that sexual thought has now reached its natural limits and that there is nothing more to say. Yet the same feelings were probably entertained following the publication of the Kinsey Reports in 1948 and 1953—although in retrospect Masters and Johnson seem so obviously to be the next step. We can be confident, therefore, that sexual thought still has a future, and it might be useful to speculate about the possible form sexual thinking will assume in the years to come.

Masters and Johnson are still very much with us, and they have themselves a stake in the future of sexual thought. Yet their two major scientific publications have clearly defined the general framework within which any further contribution from them will be made, and one senses that they will be satisfied to elaborate the basic ideas they have already formulated. Certainly their recent *The Pleasure Bond*,[145] which provides a popular account of their thought, breaks no new theoretical ground. It merely makes more explicit the monogamous refrain already discernible in their earlier writings.

The most important sexual topic yet to be addressed in systematic fashion is that of the causes of human sexual response. Masters and Johnson themselves write that the "fundamentals of human sexual behavior cannot be established until two questions

145. (Boston, 1975).

188 / The Modernization of Sex

are answered: What physical reactions develop as the human male and female respond to effective sexual stimulation? Why do men and women behave as they do when responding to effective sexual stimulation?"[146] Their own research, however, rarely moves beyond the level of description. In fact, they freely admit in the introductory chapter of *Human Sexual Response* that "the question of why men and women respond as they do to effective sexual stimulation is not answered in this text."[147] It is precisely because their research stops short of true causal knowledge that they get bogged down in amateur psychologizing: they have to invent psychological explanations because the physiology of sex is still largely a mystery to them. There is, of course, no guarantee that a proper understanding of the physiological causes of sexual response will be forthcoming. But one thing is certain: we will know the role played by psychological factors in sexual arousal only when its neurophysiology has been unambiguously established.

Yet even when the physical record is complete, sexual thought will still stand in need of a more sophisticated psychology than it has employed up to now. One would never know from reading Masters and Johnson that the study of the human mind had progressed beyond the optimistic consciousness psychology of the nineteenth century. One hopes, therefore, that the coming years will witness a fusion of the latter's physiological findings with a more worthy body of psychological theory. That theory need not necessarily be Freudian, but it certainly must be more probing and nuanced than the confection of enlightenment, self-confidence, and communication served up by Masters and Johnson.

Among the substantive issues with which sexual theorists concern themselves, two in particular seem sure to command special attention in the years ahead. The first is homosexuality, which, three-quarters of a century after Havelock Ellis's *Sexual Inversion,* is still as much a riddle as ever. We are, for example, no closer now than we were then to understanding its causes, and even its prevalence remains uncertain. The general primitiveness of our knowledge, along with the Gay Liberation movement and

146. *Response,* pp. 3–4.
147. Ibid., p. 8.

the current bisexual chic, practically guarantee that the subject will figure prominently in the sexual theorizing of the future. My guess is that the most important breakthroughs will come at the somatic level. Seventy-five years of psychoanalysis have done little to clarify the matter (and in many instances a good deal to exacerbate the homosexual's miseries), and a return to Ellis's hypothesis of a congenital predisposition seems in order.

The second issue almost certain to dominate sexual thought is the tension between monogamy and variety. This is a perennial issue, made even more compelling by the distinctive form that sexual adventure has assumed in the last decade. In his own day Havelock Ellis spoke intelligently on this subject, but the sole departure from monogamy he felt prepared to endorse was of rather grand and romantic dimensions. In effect Ellis sanctioned an "affair," as that notion came to be understood and, in a sense, tolerated in the first half of the century. The new pattern is altogether different. Increasingly, sexual adventure is taking the form of casual and usually brief extramarital alliances that are not only known to, but approved by, the other partner. This is in many ways the most distinctive feature of our contemporary sexual culture, and yet our thinking about it remains muddled and embarrassingly propagandistic. What seems to be called for is a theorist of stature who will contemplate the phenomenon sympathetically, but without giving way to uncritical effusings.

The immediate future will, I think, see a period of retrenchment in sexual thought. Masters and Johnson's work is itself already a part of this process, insofar as it is a defense of marriage and the family. Yet an even more conservative mood seems to be descending upon us, and some of Masters and Johnson's own teachings, particularly those with feminist overtones, are now coming under attack from the sexual right. In the recent publications of Irving Singer and Seymour Fisher, for example, the vaginal orgasm appears to be staging a comeback, and along with it a more traditional conception of the sexual order as a whole.[148]

The vaginal orgasm stands for sexual aristocracy, as well as for a hierarchical notion of the relation between the sexes. It assumes the existence of a privileged realm of ecstatic sexual experience,

148. Singer, *Goals of Human Sexuality*, pp. 66–104; Seymour Fisher, *The Female Orgasm* (New York, 1973), pp. 409–17.

qualitatively different from the humdrum of clitoral excitation. It is a world in which large penises make a difference and masturbation can't hold a candle to intercourse. Masters and Johnson, of course, deny the very existence of such a realm, since it deeply offends their egalitarian sensibilities. *Human Sexual Response* and *Human Sexual Inadequacy,* one might say, are the *Consumer Reports* of sexology, arguing the virtues of a low-priced compact against the wasteful luxury of a Cadillac or a Lincoln.

In the late 1960s Masters and Johnson seemed to carry the day, as the radical mood of the country and the neo-feminist movement in particular welcomed their critique of sexual chauvinism and privilege. But as we move further into the conservative 70s one anticipates that sexual aristocrats will seek to recoup their losses. I doubt, however, that the old order will ever fully recover from the democratic blow that Masters and Johnson have dealt it. Sexual democracy has established itself as the reigning assumption, and those who cling to the traditional values will find themselves in the role of challengers. This "democratic revolution" is undoubtedly Masters and Johnson's most significant contribution to sexual thought, and, for all their conservative impulses, it alone should earn them a secure place in the history of the modernization of sex.

Epilogue /
Sexual Modernism
and Romanticism

I began by defining sexual modernism as a reaction against Victorianism. The major sexual theorists of our century have repudiated both the specific doctrines and the underlying assumptions of Victorian sexual thought, and that repudiation has grown more emphatic as the century has progressed. One sees this most clearly in the evolution of modern attitudes toward masturbation: as one moves from Ellis to Kinsey to Masters and Johnson, the absurdities of the Victorian prohibition are denounced with increasing vehemence, and the virtues of masturbation asserted with ever greater abandon. The history of modern ideas about female sexuality, about sexual deviation, and about the role of sexual experimentation within marriage exhibits a similar pattern.

The definition of sexual modernism as anti-Victorianism is thus useful and accurate, but it is also, I fear, relatively superficial. In particular it creates the impression that modernism can be equated simply with permissivism, and it thereby obscures the underlying tensions of the modern sexual tradition. Those tensions become intelligible only when we understand modernism in terms of its dialectical relation to the sexual values of European Romanticism. At a deeper level, the history of sexual opinions in the twentieth century represents an inconclusive revolt against the sexual ideology fashioned by certain German and English thinkers in the early years of the nineteenth century.

The European Romantics did not of course subscribe to a unified body of sexual doctrine. But one can, I think, construct an ideal type of Romantic sexual theory on the basis of certain key texts that explicitly address themselves to sexual questions. A brief examination of that theory should serve to place sexual modernism in proper historical perspective.

Romantic sexual theory, like modern sexual theory, affirmed the essential worth of erotic experience. This was most vividly evidenced in the poetry of the Romantics, in which the pleasures of the senses, and often explicitly sexual pleasure, were recurrent themes. Keats's poem "The Eve of St. Agnes," for example, has been called "a hymn in honor of the senses," its extraordinarily voluptuous narrative culminating in the "solution sweet" of sexual union.[1] Similarly, much of Novalis's poetry employed a unifying conceit in which the afterlife was portrayed in expressly erotic terms. The dead were happy, Novalis asserted, because they enjoyed eternal sexual delight:

> We alone hear the whispered prayers of sweet desire, . . . look for ever into blissful eyes, taste for ever mouth and kiss. All that we touch turns into balsamic fruits, into soft and lovely breasts, ripe food for our desires.
> In this voluptuous passion we have revelled ever since the glaring light of earthly life was extinguished.[2]

On a less exalted level, erotic pleasure was celebrated in perhaps the single most important statement of Romantic sexual theory, Friedrich Schlegel's *Lucinda,* a collection of letters, conversations, and philosophical reflections treating the experiences of two young lovers.[3]

The Romantics thus set themselves against the repressive and

1. Harold Bloom, *The Visionary Company* (Garden City, New York, 1961), p. 398; John Keats, "The Eve of St. Agnes," XXXVI, *The Poetical Works of John Keats,* H. W. Garrod, ed. (London, 1956), p. 205.

2. Novalis (Friedrich von Hardenberg), *Heinrich von Ofterdingen,* cited and translated by George Brandes, *Main Currents in Nineteenth Century Literature,* Vol. II (London, 1905), p. 196n; cf. Bruce Haywood, *Novalis: The Veil of Imagery* (The Hague, 1959), *passim.*

3. Friedrich Schlegel, *Lucinda,* Bernard Thomas, tr., in *The German Classics,* Vol. IV (Albany, n.d.). See, especially, pp. 125–26.

sublimating values of traditional Christianity. Shelley, for instance, called the ideal of chastity "a monkish and evangelical superstition," and he criticized the political economist Thomas Malthus for seeking to deprive the poor of "the soothing, elevating, and harmonious gentleness of . . . sexual intercourse."[4] In much the same spirit Friedrich Schlegel complained of the abbreviated treatment of sex in most novels: "Every complete novel must be obscene," he wrote; "it must present the absolute in voluptuousness and sensuality."[5]

The Romantics' affirmation of sexuality was not unqualified. On the contrary, it was attended by a most important condition: sex was of value for them only within an intense psychological relationship. The physical union was entirely illegitimate if the lovers were not joined by emotional and intellectual ties as well. Thus Schlegel denounced "mere sensuality without love," just as he took issue with the opposite extreme of a deeroticized spirituality.[6] In a similar vein, Keats expressly organized "The Eve of St. Agnes" so as to contrast the physical and spiritual union of the lovers with, on the one hand, the asceticism of a beadsman saying his rosary, who introduces the poem, and, on the other, the gross physicality of a group of courtiers who revel and carouse in the castle where the lovers meet.[7] Even Shelley, who represented the right wing of the Romantic movement in sexual matters (no one was a fiercer critic of prostitution), subscribed to this doctrine of physical and emotional union. "The act," he wrote,

> ought always to be the link and type of the highest emotions of our nature, . . . [and] the person selected as the subject of this gratification should be as perfect and beautiful as possible, both in body and in mind, so that all sympathies may be harmoniously blended, and the moments of abandonment be prepared by the entire consent of all the conscious portions of our being.[8]

4. Percy Bysshe Shelley, "Notes on *Queen Mab*," *The Complete Poetical Works of Percy Bysshe Shelley*, Thomas Hutchinson, ed. (New York, 1933), p. 808; "A Philosophical View of Reform," *Shelley's Prose*, David Lee Clark, ed. (Albuquerque, 1954), p. 247.

5. Cited by Paul Kluckhohn, *Die Auffassung der Liebe in der Literatur des 18. Jahrhunderts und in der Romantik* (Halle, 1931), p. 363n.

6. Schlegel, *Lucinda*, pp. 146–49, 157.

7. Bloom, *Visionary Company*, pp. 396–403.

8. Shelley, "A Discourse on the Manners of the Ancient Greeks Relative to the Subject of Love," *Shelley's Prose*, p. 222.

The Romanitics, in sum, argued for a liberation of sexuality, but they were anything but libertines. They stood in direct opposition to an eighteenth-century thinker like the Marquis de Sade, who insisted that physical and spiritual passion need have little to do with one another. Sade was the arch anti-Romantic when, in the novel *Juliette*, he asked, "Can't you go to bed with a woman without loving her, and can't you love her without going to bed with her?"[9]

Modern sexual thought, I would argue, begins from the same premise as Romantic sexual thought, but it moves in the direction of Sade. Its movement, however, is not unilinear but dialectical. In the writings of Ellis, Kinsey, and Masters and Johnson the Romantic ideal of physical and spiritual union is reaffirmed, criticized, and ultimately transformed.

Havelock Ellis is the most unambiguously Romantic of the great modernists. He transcends the Romantics in the explicitness and breadth of his sexual interests (hence his modernity), but at the heart of his sexual writings stands the same union of physical and emotional energies that one finds in Keats and Schlegel. Even his sympathetic discussion of the need for sexual variety (a need to which the Romantics were not insensitive) remains loyal to an essentially Romantic conception of human sexual relations: a proper affair, in his opinion, was a matter of the heart, not merely of the flesh.

Alfred Kinsey, by way of contrast, represents most perfectly the anti-Romantic impulse in sexual modernism. He is not so unqualified a sexual materialist as was the Marquis de Sade, but he sought above all else to separate human sexual experience from its elaborate emotional associations. Those associations, he believed, placed unnecessary restrictions on the expression of an innocent physical need. Only when repressed did sexual urges threaten emotional stability, and thus a rational society, he implied, would seek to promote not only a positive but an essentially casual attitude toward sexuality. The notion that sex was permissible only when persons truly loved one another was to him no less absurd than the belief that masturbation caused insanity.

9. Marquis de Sade, *Juliette*, cited and translated by Geoffrey Gorer, *The Life and Ideas of the Marquis de Sade* (New York, 1962), p. 189.

If only for the sake of intellectual neatness, one would like to argue that Masters and Johnson have achieved a synthesis of Ellis and Kinsey, of the Romantic and the Modern. Unfortunately, this is simply not the case. Indeed, such a synthesis may be by definition impossible. What is most striking in their work is precisely the incongruous and often jarring coexistence of both Romantic and anti-Romantic points of view. On the one hand there is the clinical, some would say heartless, subjection of human sexual behavior to laboratory scrutiny and manipulation, and on the other hand there is the repeated insistence on the need for communication in sexual relationships and the implicit critique of all sexual encounters devoid of serious emotional content. It would seem that they belong neither to the party of Keats nor to that of Sade.

The almost schizoid character of Masters and Johnson's thought exactly reflects the unresolved tensions of the modern sexual tradition as a whole. As moderns, we remain permanently divided between a Romantic past, whose repressions we would gladly rid ourselves of, and a deromanticized future, whose emotional emptiness we fear even while we anticipate its greater freedom. It is precisely in this antithesis of Romantic and anti-Romantic impulses that the distinctly modern element in sexual modernism is to be located.

Index